In the
Ballpark

In the **Ballpark**

THE WORKING LIVES
OF BASEBALL PEOPLE

**George Gmelch and
J. J. Weiner**

SMITHSONIAN INSTITUTION PRESS • Washington and London

Copy Editor: Jenelle Walthour
Production Editors: Jack Kirshbaum and Robert A. Poarch
Designer: Kathleen Sims

Library of Congress Cataloging-in-Publication Data
Gmelch, George.
    In the ballpark : the working lives of baseball people / George
Gmelch and J. J. Weiner.
        p.   cm.
    Includes bibliographical references (p.) and index.
    ISBN 1-56098-876-2 (alk. paper)
    1. Baseball—Interviews   2. Baseball fields.   3. Baseball.
  I. Weiner, J. J. II. Title.
  GV863.A1G62   1998
  796.356′092′273—dc21   97-28388

British Cataloguing-in-Publication Data available

A paperback reissue (ISBN 1-56098-446-5) of the original cloth edition

Manufactured in the United States of America
05 04 03 02 01 00 99 5 4 3 2 1

⊗ The Paper used in this publication meets the minimum requirements of the American National Standard for Information Sciences—Permanence of Paper for Printed Library Materials ANSI Z398.48-1984.

For permission to reproduce illustrations appearing in this book, please correspond directly with the owners of the works, as listed in the individual captions. (The authors own the rights to the illustrations that do not list a source.) The Smithsonian Institution Press does not retain reproduction rights for these illustrations individually or maintain a file of addresses for photo sources.

Contents

Preface

In the Ballpark: The Working Lives of Baseball People is a behind-the-scenes look at the world of professional baseball as seen through the lives of twenty-one individuals who work in the game. The subjects of this book range from owner to beer vendor, and are drawn from every level of the sport, from the major leagues to rookie ball. When baseball fans think and talk about baseball, however, they usually refer to the players, sometimes to a manager who has been hired or fired, and occasionally to an outrageous owner. Little attention is paid to the people backstage, the large supporting cast that is needed to produce the game we see on the field. In this book's narratives, these people describe their work in baseball and the all-encompassing role the game plays in their lives.

Baseball organizations today would scarcely be recognizable to the founders of the game. A century ago professional baseball clubs were run by a few dozen full-time employees besides the players and coaches, many of whom were veritable jacks-of-all-trades, with a variety of additional responsibilities. Today major league clubs are complex organizations with a highly specialized division of labor and a distinct corporate culture. The list of the departments found in most clubs says much about the scope of the organizations' work: ticketing, travel, clubhouse, public relations, finance, marketing and sales, train-ing, minor leagues, scouting, and stadium operations. In the scouting department alone, each club has at least twenty-five full-time scouts based in North America as well as several international scouts, who work in the Caribbean and travel as far afield as Australia and Asia. Each major league club has its own minor league "farm system" with six ball clubs, ranging from Rookie League through Triple A. Each of these clubs has twenty or more players, a manager, a pitching coach, and a hitting instructor, all of whom are looked after by a trainer, a clubhouse attendant, and others. Though operating on a much smaller scale than its big-league parent, each minor league club also has its own work force that includes sales people, ticket sellers, ushers, ven-dors, groundskeepers, and scoreboard operators.

In the Ballpark is divided into four sections—Stands, Field, Press Box, and Front Office—that reflect the way baseball people think about and categorize the different work environments within the ball-park. Since each setting is distinctive, with its own norms and shared understandings and its own perspective on the business of baseball, each section is introduced by a description of the physical setting, its ambience, and the nature of the work that is performed there.

The occupations represented in the book vary widely in the degree to which they involve workers in the business. The seasonal "game day" staff—ticket takers, ushers, and vendors—who only work the eighty-one home games have a different engagement in baseball from that of the full-time baseball professionals—owners, general man-agers, coaches, scouts, players, trainers. For them, baseball is more than an occupation: it is a lifestyle. For this reason their interviews are longer, describing how their lives outside the ballpark are shaped by their involvement in the game.

The interviews reveal much about the people who work in profes-sional baseball. For example, baseball is dominated by men. In the dozens of ballparks and baseball organizations in which we conducted interviews, we found no women among the general managers, man-agers, coaches, players, mascots, groundskeepers, clubhouse atten-dants, trainers, or broadcasters. Although women do work in the front office (usually from one-fourth to one-third of the staff), most are in secretarial or clerical positions. Only in concessions and the kitchen—among game day staff—do women begin to approximate men in num-ber. But even here the bosses or "directors" are men.

Another characteristic of baseball people revealed by the narratives is that most of them had a serious interest in baseball during childhood. Over half aspired to play professional baseball; others were devoted fans. Most, upon realizing that they did not have the ability to play competitively, looked for alternative careers in baseball. As an eleven-year-old, Rob Evans turned his ambition from playing to broadcasting. Paul Zwaska, after a trip to Wrigley Field where he had admired the setting as much as the game, began to think about becoming a groundskeeper. By his sophomore year in high school, Mark Letendre knew he wanted to become an athletic trainer. Today they are not just employees of baseball organizations but also perpetually loyal fans of the game.

Baseball people share a feeling of being part of a select group. This is evident in the tendency of some to refer to themselves as belonging to the "baseball fraternity" or "baseball family." This shared identity is strengthened by the long hours they spend together at the ballpark, often working in close cooperation with each other. Those who travel with the team share meals, recreation, and hotel rooms, which contributes to their identity as "baseball people." Being in a high-profile profession in which many others would like to work adds to their sense of specialness. The owner of a minor league ball club described working in baseball as being part of a closed society:

Either you're in it, or you're out of it, and those who aren't part of it won't get much respect from those that are in it. . . . Baseball people are nice to you if you're inside baseball, but they ignore you if you're not.

The interviews reveal the considerable sacrifices baseball people must make to stay in the game—long hours, holidays spent at the ballpark, stunted family life, and, for many, low wages. Yet most baseball people genuinely like their jobs. Some could make more money and work fewer hours outside baseball, but they choose to remain. Some have left baseball jobs only to return a few years later. The interviews say much about what produces this level of job satisfaction. The case for players and managers is easy to understand. For them, quite simply, there is no other type of work that offers the same camaraderie, level of competition, or limelight. Players and managers are known to a wide public and are heroes to some. Also, the pay is not bad. The reasons for satisfaction with baseball are more subtle but no less certain for those who broadcast baseball, write about it, or scout young talent. Baseball, no less than it is for players and managers, is often their passion—the focus of their lives. Some actually feel "blessed" to be in baseball; for many, it is fulfillment of childhood ambition.

There is also status. Baseball workers earn a certain cachet by being part of an institution that is still widely regarded as the national pastime and by being associated with ball players for whom there is much public fascination. They are reminded of this each time they meet a new acquaintance and are asked what kind of work they do. Jim Goodwin was the president of a Florida bank before he bought the Jacksonville Suns, a Double A franchise:

When you get on an airplane—you know how people ask you what you do. When I used to say I'm a banker, I didn't get much of a response. But now I say, "I own a minor league baseball team," and you should see people's eyes light up.

Not just ownership or management positions elicit such interest. Secretaries, groundskeepers, ushers, and others also bask in baseball's glow. Linda Reiner, a secretary to the New York Yankees' director of media relations, described the reaction of people when they learned where she works:

They're usually amazed. They usually say, "You work for the Yankees! That sounds so exciting." Then, one of the first questions they ask is if I know the players. I say, "No, I work on the office level of the stadium, but my boss does. He travels with the team." I might tell them that I know a lot of people in the TV end, the announcers, and press guys. . . . They think it's neat that you work at Yankee Stadium, no matter what you do there, even if you are just stuffing envelopes.

The public's esteem for baseball jobs increases from the low minors to the big leagues. The public usually perceives minor league employees to be on a track working toward the big leagues, no matter how successful or content they may be with their present positions. As one minor league club official put it: "Americans think that making the big leagues, like winning football's Superbowl, must always be the ultimate goal. Nothing short of that is seen as real success. But either way, if you're in baseball, they're impressed."

The narratives in this book also explain aspects of the ballpark environment that fans have observed countless times but usually never given much thought. Why, for example, are there different mowing patterns in the infield versus the outfield grass? What tactics do vendors use to sell beer? How do public-address announcers speed up the game? How do umpires quell disputes? In sum, *In the Ballpark* ultimately presents an insider's view of life and work in the world of professional baseball.

ABOUT THE RESEARCH

The idea for this book emerged in 1991 when I (George Gmelch) was traveling with a minor league team, the Birmingham Barons, while beginning an ethnographic study of baseball players. After interviewing players and coaches during the long pregame practice, I would sit in the stands or press box with various baseball people to watch the game. The conversation often turned to their work, and it didn't take long to discover that the lives of these "other" baseball people was interesting in its own right, though much less understood. The following season J. J. Weiner, then a student of mine, worked as an intern with the Barons. He was to assist with my study of players but instead began a series of interviews with baseball people in the Southern League. We decided to collaborate, and the following year (1993), we each went back on the road visiting a number of ballparks. *In the Ballpark* is based on the tape-recorded interviews we conducted from 1993 to 1996. We collected other data through participant observation in the clubhouse, dugout, and press box, and on road trips. We draw upon these data in our introductions and conclusions to the narratives. Because the research spanned a period of four years, we were able to update information from the earliest interviewees and thus follow up on changes in their careers. This information appears in epilogues.

In our search for good interviewees, we asked just about anyone, especially media directors, secretaries, and coaches, for recommendations. Some subjects, accustomed to players and managers being the focus of attention, were puzzled about why we would want to interview them. But usually it wasn't difficult to convince them that their baseball lives were worth telling.

In choosing the narratives for this book, we first wanted at least one person to represent each of the primary occupations in baseball. Second, we wanted the interviewees to be somewhat evenly divided between the major and minor leagues. Thirteen of the subjects are in the big leagues and eight are in the minor leagues. We also wanted to include women. However, with two exceptions, all of the interviewees are men. That more women are not included reflects both their small number in baseball and their concentration in a few areas of the game.

Our approach in editing the interview transcripts was to ensure that the narratives were faithful to the subject's story while making them topically and chronologically coherent to readers. This usually involved pulling together broken pieces of narrative and organizing the stories so that they progressed in accordance with the chronology of the individual's life. Invariably, the transcripts were condensed to enhance clarity, to avoid repetition, and to eliminate material unrelated to the book's themes. However, we have tried to preserve the style of the interviewees' speech. While all the interviewees were given the opportunity to revise and delete embarrassing detail, only minor changes were requested. For example, two individuals asked that we remove or disguise the names of an individual and ball club that they had criticized.

We each brought different backgrounds and experiences to the research that undoubtedly influenced the kinds of questions we asked. I am an anthropologist who was a professional baseball player during the 1960s (Detroit Tigers, minor leagues), while J. J. Weiner, an anthropology student, worked in and studied the front office of a minor league baseball team—the Birmingham Barons—and knew best the "business side" of baseball. Both of us had a prior interest in the anthropology of work. Conducting the interviews for this book has fundamentally altered our own perspective on baseball. Now when at the ballpark, we find ourselves paying as much attention to the workers off the playing field and their routines as to the game itself.

Acknowledgments

We began work on this book in 1992, and many people helped out. Marty Kuehnert, Tony Franklin, Bill Hardekopf, and Rodney Dalton of the Birmingham Barons got us started. Many media directors—among them Rob Butcher, Dick Bresciani, Richard Cerrone, Kevin Kalal, and Jim Trdinich—gave us access. Stephen Crandall, Jason Getz, Andrea Modica, Darren Mrak, Michael Ponzini, the San Francisco Giants, and the Pittsburgh Pirates kindly provided photographs.

We especially thank our friends and colleagues who offered ideas, read drafts of chapters, or provided critiques of the entire manuscript: Margaret Dalton, Mike DeLucca, Jeffrey Gmelch, George Gmelch Sr., Dan Gordon, Bill Kirwin, Lee Lowenfish, Mary McKay, Meredith Melzer, Michael Lynch, Sally O'Leary, Betsy Phelps, Naomi Quinn, Erin Rosenberg, Bill Tierney, Walter Weiner, Jill Weiner, and Bob Wheelock. At Smithsonian Institution Press, our acquisitions editor, Mark Hirsch, gave us wise counsel; and Robert Lockhart and Jenelle Walthour also contributed. The Dana Foundation and Union College provided support for several summers of research. Special thanks also to Mary McKay, Janet McQuade, and Kerry Cassidy for their editorial advice and resilient transcribing. Our greatest debt is to the people of *In the Ballpark* for opening up their lives and telling us their stories.

In the
Ballpark

THE STANDS

The workday in the stands starts long before the sun comes up. Cleaners armed with backpack leaf blowers move through each row, blowing trash from the night before into the aisles. They work from the top of the stands down, the trash pile growing on the way, until finally it is put into bags and taken away. Every seat is wiped down, the concourse is scoured with pressure hoses, and the toilets are scrubbed and sanitized.

Once cleaned, the stands sit silent, except for an occasional worker eating lunch or jogging on the concourse. Cavernous, the empty stands generate echoes; you feel as if you could talk to someone clear across the ballpark. The stands slowly come alive again after the gates open two hours before game time. The players are already on the field taking batting practice as the first fans trickle in. Despite the rock 'n' roll music blaring from the sound system, the crack of the bat from the batting cage can be heard distinctly everywhere in the stadium. "Pregame" is a time when fans are allowed to move close to the field, to seek autographs, and to get a good view of the players. As the stands fill up, the bold, uniform bands of brightly colored seats, each section in a different color, disappear beneath the throng of spectators.

The stands are the workplace of ushers, security personnel, food vendors, and mascots. Known as "game day staff," they only work when the team is playing at home. Ushers and security personnel maintain order among the spectators, whether by helping people find their seats or by keeping drunks off the field. City police are also present to deter would-be lawbreakers and to make arrests when necessary. Vendors, with their rhythmic refrains—like "Ice-cold beer here"—and their quick pace provide ambiance and the convenience of food and beverages without leaving your seat. Mascots, who mock everyone from umpires to fans, entertain.

Stand workers, like field personnel, are uniformed to make their roles clear to the public. Ushers and security personnel are attired in

Vendors boxing popcorn at Heritage Park in Albany, New York. (Photo by Darren Mrak)

blazers and matching slacks, while vendors usually wear vests and caps with a large button announcing their product and its price. Mascots wear costumes with exaggerated features—oversized heads, large midsections, and big feet.

The stands in major league stadiums sit on multiple decks of concrete and are divided into bleachers, grandstand, loge, and box seats, with the price of the seats in each section determined by their proximity to and view of the action. While most fans sit in the open air, an affluent few (often corporate executives and their clients and friends) sit in air-conditioned sky boxes, furnished with couches, wet bars, and television sets. Beneath the stands are the wide concourses where one can find souvenir shops, fast-food outlets, and toilets. Television sets hang from the concourse walls to ensure that no one misses the action while buying a pennant or a hot dog and beer.

The stands in minor league ballparks, of course, are smaller; rarely do they have an upper deck. Instead of seats that wrap entirely around the field, as in major league parks, they have picnic areas for groups and play areas for children along the foul lines. With virtually every seat close to the action, minor league parks have an intimacy not found in the big leagues.

But the stands, whether in the major or minor leagues, are always more than a collection of seats. There is activity in the stands that contributes to a fan's experience and enjoyment of being at a ballpark—mascots; vendors hawking hot dogs, beer, and peanuts; Diamond Vision; chants; human waves; and the jeers and taunts of spectators. The crowd, moreover, produces noise of its own, a murmur periodically interrupted by cheers for good plays by the home team and groans of disappointment for setbacks. There are Americans who can't bear to sit through an inning of televised baseball but relish spending hours in the bleachers or grandstand.

What sets the workers of the stands apart from other baseball employees is their face-to-face interaction with the fans. As evident in the following narratives, after the players it is the vendors, ushers, and mascots who have the most impact on the fan's experience at the ballpark.

Jerry Collier

BEER VENDOR, ORIOLE PARK AT CAMDEN YARDS

During the day, Jerry Collier works as a bond trader at a major bank in downtown Baltimore; on weeknights and on weekends, when the Orioles are in town, he is a beer vendor at Camden Yards. He is also an adjunct professor of finance and accounting at a local college. With blond hair and a 6 foot 7 inch frame, Collier, age thirty, looks like a professional beach volleyball player.

꩜

I really started to get into baseball in 1979. That was the year of Orioles Magic. They were about ten games out of first place in June, and they turned it around, kicked butt, and wound up winning the championship. Everybody in town caught the fever. After that the stadium was always sold out, and that was when I became a big fan.

When I was in the Boy Scouts, some guys who were troop leaders were paying their way through college by vending beer. Back then they were making five or six thousand dollars during the course of the summer—which back in the mid-seventies was a lot of money. So I knew that [the money] was out there, and I would see those guys doing their thing when I would go to the games as a kid.

I got into beer vending purely by coincidence. It was 1984 and I had the chance to move to the Caribbean for a summer to be a scuba-diving instructor. I was between jobs when I saw an ad in the paper and went down to the stadium. All you had to do was take a simple math test, to make sure you were not an absolute idiot, and you got the job. I thought, "This is a cool part-time job while I'm waiting to go to the Caribbean." I made about ten bucks my first game. Back then minimum wage was about three bucks an hour, so I wasn't even making minimum wage. The next game, I made fifty bucks, which was the equivalent of about fifteen dollars an hour. I was supposed to move to the Caribbean, but all of sudden I had this job. I was in college and that was huge money. That was a week's pay in one night.

I started to ask around and discovered that some of the vendors who had been there for years were making ten, eleven thousand dollars a year. This was my second year of college and I said to myself, "This is a good deal: I can hang around here and if I work hard, I can make some pretty nice bucks. Plus, I was a big baseball fan." That's how I started. That was the beginning of '84 and I'm still plugging along.

The way it works is they have a list of about 110 vendors. When I started it was about 190 names long because they were selling a lot more beer. But, because of alcohol awareness, they've cut back some; so there are fewer beer sellers. You start out number 110 on the list of 110 names. You go to work that night, and the guy with the number 1 gets his product first and goes out into the stadium, number 2 gets his product next, and so on. If you're number 110, you're left selling whatever is left. That means when it's 30 degrees outside you're selling ice cream and when it's 90 degrees you're selling hot coffee. It ain't easy to make money with a terrible product.

There's no hourly wage. You work on straight commission. It's 15 percent up to a certain amount—for Budweiser beer it's fifteen cases. Once you sell fifteen cases of Bud, every sale that you make for that whole game skips up to 17 percent. Seventy-eight dollars a case times 17 percent is $13.26. Multiply that by fifteen cases and you're making at least $200 a game.

You can sell anywhere in the ballpark you want. But your seniority determines which commissary you get your product at. Camden Yards has six commissaries around the stadium, and they're not all equal. If your commissary is in the upper deck in the outfield, for you to come down and sell in my territory, you've got to get your beer and walk down through the whole stadium to where I am. It would take you twenty minutes to run back up to get another case and run down again. It's just not feasible. So you sell in an area near to where you pick up your beer.

Where the competition comes in is trying to get to the choice areas. The box seats in the lower deck hold half the people in the stadium. They're also the people who have the most disposable income. It's mostly corporate types who hang out there because they have the $3,000 to buy two box seats for the season.

I sell Budweiser from third base in. I have a natural monopoly because I'm the only Budweiser seller down there. I'm there every day. That's a competitive advantage I have over everybody else. If you're not at the top of the list and you can't always get the same spot, people don't really get to know who you are. You're just another face in the crowd. But, if you've been serving the same five sections for ten years, you know the names of people's children, where they work, and what ticket plan they're on.

Now it sounds like easy money, but you have to remember that you get there by selling hot coffee when it's 90 degrees outside. It takes a long time to get to the top and once you're there, it's purely competitive. The only way to make that kind of money is to go out there and consistently beat everybody else. If you don't, they'll take your job.

On opening day 1985, they told me I could serve Ronald Reagan a hot dog, but I couldn't sell beer until the second inning because I had to go through some Secret Service clearance. There's no way I could serve the President a hot dog and not sell beer for an hour-and-a-half. That's thirteen cases I'm behind the rest of the troops! No way. Some hot dog vendor sold Reagan a hot dog. Oh well.

You can see the environment I'm in. Financial services is hugely competitive. You've got to be a tenacious animal to make money as a bond trader, and it's the same way here in the ballpark. It's just something that some people excel at, and others don't. The top six vendors consistently make more money than everybody else. I was always very aggressive. The level of Type A personality that I have from working at the stadium—that continuous pressure: "Pass the money, I've got to go as fast as I possibly can"—has carried over and pushed me to where I am now as a bond trader. I work in the bank like a nut. I work tremendous hours. Everything I do is with a passion and that is purely a function of my vending job. What it did was it took a personality trait of mine and amplified it to the nth degree.

Both my jobs give instant gratification. You make a trade that makes money and you see it right away. Same thing with vending. You make a sale, and you feel good about it. It's fast paced and there's a lot of pressure. At the stadium it doesn't seem like pressure, but let's say I sell seventeen cases and the competition sells twenty-one. In a sense, I had a good day, but it wasn't a good day because I got beat. If that happened too often, they'd give my job to somebody else. I'd lose $200 a game times 81 games; that's about $16,000. To think that I might lose that is a hell of an incentive to work hard. So there is pressure.

You don't need to know someone to get into vending, but it helps. If someone referred you, then you are more likely to stay on. Opening day, you have 150 vendors. Of those 150, 100 are returning from last year, 10 are referrals, and 40 just answered ads in the paper. The 10 who are coming in with the referral have a big-brother figure to watch over them. They tell them where to work, how to work and how the system works and help them to get acclimated. The 40 who walk in— no one ever tells them anything because we have absolutely no incentive to keep them here. They are potentially your competition. So, they'll walk around and make three dollars after three hours of work and say, "This is bogus." And they walk. The attrition rate is astronomical in the first ten games of the season. Everybody quits.

Then we're down to the 100 old vendors and the 10 new referred vendors who knew what they were getting into beforehand. I would take the people who have been working here over three months and put them in almost any job, and I know they would succeed. They're the hardest workers in the world. They show it every day, because if they don't work hard, they don't get paid.

When Curt Schilling was with the Orioles, I ran into him in a pub one night. He came up to me and said, "My man, you're the hardest working person I've ever seen in my life." I said, "What are you talking about?" He said, "I've got a view that's not good for watching the game. I sit in the bull pen all game and we have nothing to do. So we just pick out certain people, and we watch you all the time. We make bets on how fast you can get from one section to another and on how many beers you'll pour." And he said, "You must work 100 miles per hour. You should be on the team." Sometimes you don't think that people notice.

Most people think a guy that's a beer vendor is the scum of the earth. I have a master's degree in finance. I advise corporations on how to manage huge amounts of risk. There's a guy down there that has a master's degree in biology, there are three engineers, we have medical students, dental students, and Johns Hopkins University students and graduates working here. They got the job when they were in school. They were making ten to fifteen thousand dollars a year. They got out of school and said, "Why should I give up making that kind of money?"

One of the things that's happened over the years is that most regulars [in the stands] know what I do now. In fact, I got my job at the bank because of what I do at the stadium. I was interviewing with one of the senior people in the bank and he kept looking at me. He saw ARA Services on my résumé and said, "Oh, ARA, that's a good company." And then it just hit him—ARA—the beer man! The interview totally changed from "Where are you going to be in five years?" to "How much money do you make out there?" And, "You work harder than anybody I've ever seen. If you work as hard here as you do there, you can start tomorrow." People admire it.

A TYPICAL NIGHT AT THE BALLPARK

I get to the stadium at 6:15, dead tired because I just worked nine hours. I have to be out of the suit and tie that I wear to the bank and into the ballpark uniform that they give you by 6:30. The uniform we have is black vinyl pants, a green top, a green smock, and a Camden Yards hat that they make you wear religiously. When you're 6 foot 7 inches the uniform doesn't fit, and they always give me a hard time because I modify it. I run around with my pant leg pulled up so I don't look like a buffoon. Quarter of seven they call the roster starting with the number 1 guy—you pick your product and your location and by ten of seven, you're out in the stadium working.

I'll go over there and I'll be dead tired. It's seven o'clock and I'm dragging myself around the stadium. Once the sales start to pick up, you get into a zone. You get an adrenaline rush and you can't turn it off. The game starts at 7:30. My adrenaline high will kick in at about 7:45. I could go home and take three tranquilizers and I would be up until two o'clock in the morning just from running around and being with people. You're working fast, plus you're working smart. It's like trading securities all day where big sums of money are flying by and there's no time for mistakes.

Weather is also a big factor in how much money you make. At the beginning of the year, when it's really cool and damp at game time, people don't drink, so it hurts sales. We go from that to 100-degree days in the summer. It cools off at night and it's comfortable, so people drink tons and tons of beer. At a Sunday day game, if it's 100 degrees, beer just doesn't fly. You can sell all day, but people drink two beers, get a headache, and don't want to drink anymore.

What I do—and this is part of the sales strategy—is carry three or four cases of beer at a time when I leave my commissary. It takes me about eight minutes to sell a case of beer when I'm rolling. I take three cases of beer and I start in section 56 and work my way to 54, 52, and then 50. A half hour has passed by the time I get back to 56. Most people who are drinking at a moderate rate drink a beer in about twenty minutes. That's a way for me to control the types that are guzzling. That puts people on a schedule where they can't get obliterated. The guy has had about ten minutes of conversation before I'm back and he's ready for another.

By the end of the sixth inning, top of the seventh, you start shouting, "Last call," because we stop beer sales after the end of the seventh. That's another forty-five minutes for the guy to sober up. If you leave the stadium with no more than two beers in your body, you're safe.

To speed things up, especially with two-beer sales, you open both cans of beer. You put one between your fingers in one hand, hold two cups and punch a hole in the back of the can to let air in so it will pour faster. Then you pour two beers at time for speed. Even though you're torpedoing it, it still takes six seconds for the beer to pour out of there.

One guy here has created a can opener that is hooked up to a nickel cadmium battery that he has in his belt pack. The battery powers a mechanical can opener that decapitates two tops of a beer can in half a second. What it does is spin the two cans side by side, the lid lifts up, a magnet grabs the can so it won't spill, and he turns them upside down and just floods the beer out of the can. It's like pouring a cup into a cup instead of it coming out of a small hole from the can into the cup. It's just like the electric can opener in your kitchen, but it's ten times as fast and it can do two at a time.

He's doing a two-second pour and I'm doing a six-second pour. It's a competitive advantage. He's even been on *Good Morning America,* but he cannot interact with individuals as well I can. His productivity has gone up, but he hasn't been able to crack the top four—and that's where the big money is.

The point I'm trying to make is that even vending beer requires people skills; it's salesmanship. Plus, I'm 6 foot 7 inches—being tall, being visible helps out a lot too. One of the things that makes me different from everybody else is trivia. At the beginning of the game, I go down to the front of the field, in front of the thousands of people in my sections and say, "Here's a trivia question—the first one to get it right gets three free beers." Immediately they've keyed into my face and my voice.

Another thing that I do relates to my relationship to people in the business community: I see lots and lots of faces that I know. The Orioles are supported by the business community; lots of companies own those box seats. I also know many of these people from having worked over here for years. So if I see somebody that I know, I'll run that person a tab. I call it the frequent-flyer program. In the vending community, most everything you do is pay as you go. You buy two beers, you give me a few bucks. What I'll do is come out and say, "That's okay. You just drink all night and I'll give you a cash receipt at the end of the night. If you're with a business and you want to write this off, here's a cash receipt." Four guys sit down and drink four beers each over the course of the game. I've carried sixty-five or seventy dollars for them. They don't treat that casually. I'm doing them a service, so they remain loyal throughout the game.

For instance, there's a man who runs a restaurant where we eat lunch at sometimes; he has season tickets in my section. He gave his seats to some business contacts. The restaurant guy called me up and asked me to put them on my frequent-flyer program. I go up to them before the game and say, "Are you a friend of this guy? Yeah? He's got all your beers covered. You don't have to spend any money the whole game. I'm going to be here every twenty minutes to check on you to make sure you guys are good to go." These guys feel like they're king of the world. They're at the baseball game, they've got their own waiter, plus they have credit and somebody else is picking up the tab. I'll go over and talk to my man next week, he'll pay me the money that he owes me. And that's what makes the world go 'round.

You've got to lift weights all winter for this job. It's physically demanding. They put the cases in plastic racks so they stack easily and don't fall all over the place. Because a lot of vendors are afraid that somebody might rip them off, they physically carry two or three cases of beer up at a time. That is brutal to the body.

What I'll do is say to the customers that sit in the top row, "You guys mind if I put these beers here today? I'll give you a few free beers." So they watch my beers. I take a case off the top and leave two cases at the top of the step. I take two cans out from the top case, and put the cups in that space upside down to make a cup dispenser. Then I run up and down the steps with one case. It saves tons of energy and wear and tear on your body.

To start, I run all the way down to the field, turn around, and start selling on the way up. You don't sell on the way down because people see you better when you're coming up. You're visible the whole way.

Being loud is important. A lot of people have a lot of different sayings. My nickname used to be the Terminator because, one, I would aggressively take people's business from them and two, I say things as if I'm a very efficient robot: "Budweiser. Cold Bud. Budweiser. Budweiser. Bud." That's it, totally monotone. I save my voice as much as I can. Then when I get a sale and it's more intimate, I can talk to the person and become more friendly. When you're walking around, who cares what you say as long as they know what you have? I haven't found a need to be creative.

You have to card everybody under thirty. It's another advantage I have because in the lower deck most of the people who buy those seats are older. They definitely look like they're over thirty. In the cheaper seats, where you might get a lot of college students, you have to card more people and it slows you down. You've got to be cognizant of what you're doing. To work as a vendor now, you have to take a course every three years called "TIPS: Techniques in Intervention Procedures by Servers of Alcohol." It's a training program on how to judge when people are drunk and how to card people.

You don't have time to watch much of the game. You catch a little Diamond Vision when there's a replay, but you're just so into the fact that you've got to make your sales, that you don't really see much. To be honest, I get more of a kick out of selling beer than watching the game. I'm a big Orioles fan and I watch them all the time when they're out of town, but when you're there, you go from being a watcher of the game to being a part of the game. For most people, going to a ball game is more than just watching eighteen guys run around on the field. It's the whole aura of being in a baseball stadium, of having a beer vendor and somebody flipping peanuts at you, and ushers that have been there forever, and all that. It's a scene. It's the people at the stadium who make a good time happen.

No one has ever come up to me and said, "Hey, it's my bond trader! What a great guy!" But they do when they recognize me as the beer vendor. Some people come up and hug me, "Hey, this is my main man!" My wife and I can't go into a Baltimore restaurant without somebody saying, "Hey, it's the beer man! Hey, how you doing? Tell me a trivia story. Tell me a good joke." They don't even know what my name is. But they were at a baseball game and I told them some jokes or they won a trivia beer from me, the Orioles won, and they left walking on air. The game is part of it, and everyone else is part of it.

I've been doing it for ten years. How many people have any job for ten years? It's like my *Field of Dreams*. It gets into your blood. Let me put it into perspective: In 1989 I got out of graduate school and got a job in New York working on Wall Street for a major firm. At the end of the summer, I had a chance to come back to the Orioles and have my old position back. It was sad to not be part of something that I felt such a strong connection to. I asked myself, "Do I want to work on Wall Street or go back home, get a similar type of job there, and be able to work at the stadium?" You can see which one won out.

⚓

EPILOGUE

Automation and corporate expansion have recently posed a threat to Collier's work. There are now three of the battery-powered can openers in the ballpark. The man who invented the device lets his two brothers use it, but no one else. The way Jerry describes it, "They're piloting a spacecraft and I'm still flying a bi-wing plane." On top of that, ARA Services has expanded beer sales in the stadium. Draft beer has always been sold at the concession stands, but it is now being sold at portable stations throughout the park. The new competition has cut into profits, although Jerry retains his number 2 position among the 110 vendors. "The glory days of vending and good money," says Collier, "may be passing."

Tom Burgoyne

MASCOT, PHILADELPHIA PHILLIES

In the mid-1970s the Philadelphia Phillies' marketing department decided that the team needed a mascot. For a costume design they went to Harrison and Erikson, the company that designed the Seasame Street *characters, and soon the Phillie Phanatic was born.*

The Phillies made no real introduction of the Phanatic to the fans. They thought that mascots do best when they are not presented with a great deal of fanfare. The Phanatic was just there—fans didn't know if he was there for one day, one inning, or ten minutes, and whether they'd ever see him again.

Dave Reymond was the principal performer, but there has always been a backup Phillie Phanatic, primarily to make appearances in the community and on the road. Six years ago, when the backup took a job with the Orlando Magic, the Phillies needed a replacement. They placed an ad in the paper that said nothing more than "mascots wanted." At the time Tom Burgoyne, a recent graduate of Drexel University, was selling business forms and computer supplies. He had been a mascot in high school—The Hawk at St. Joseph's Prep in Philadelphia. Unhappy in his job, Burgoyne answered the ad and after auditioning with thirteen other people, he was hired.

Today he makes two hundred appearances a year as the Phillie Phanatic at Veterans Stadium, minor league parks, basketball and hockey games, business openings, and charity functions.

⚛

Baseball was always a dream job of mine. I liked to write. I thought it would be great if I could be a sportswriter and follow the team. In my eighth grade yearbook it asked where are you going to be ten years from now, and I wrote "a sportscaster for the Phillies." I'm pretty close. It's kind of living out a dream.

When I auditioned and had to wear the costume, I wasn't sure I wanted the job. The costume weighs 35 pounds, and I was gasping for air. Unlike the Chicken, the Phanatic is 6 feet 8 inches tall and has an 86–90 inch waist and an unknown shoe size. It definitely took a while to get used to. But otherwise the costume's design is awesome. Sometimes the Phanatic can be standing there and just give somebody a look and it's hilarious. I give it some life, but the costume itself really carries a lot of the show. Despite the weight, the design allows for good mobility; a lot of mascots have big heads and can't get around. The Phanatic is built for acrobatics and carrying on and dancing and things like that. Because he can't speak he must be able to perform.

The Phanatic act is family-oriented—nothing rude or crude. We try to get away with a few things, but there is a fine line between being funny and being offensive. Comedy comes from surprising people; you set up an image and then destroy it by doing something that nobody expects. We try to make everything spontaneous or try to make it look like it's spontaneous. If you try to set it up and it's elaborate, it's doomed to fail. Our gags are simple things—something like going through somebody's cooler and picking up a coke and shaking it and throwing it back in gets huge laughs.

⚛

On the night I watched the Phanatic perform at a game in Hickory, North Carolina, he danced on the dugout and called up a chorus line of attractive young women from the stands. Although he planted them directly in front of the dugout, he made it look like the Phanatic was surprised to see that they were there.

⚛

Tom Burgoyne as the Phillie Phanatic. (Photo by Al Tielemans; courtesy of the Philadelphia Phillies)

What makes the Phanatic work so well is the slowness of the game. The Phanatic spends time in the stands with people just goofing around. You don't want to miss a dunk in basketball or a goal in hockey. Those sports are more time-oriented—you have two minutes during a time-out, you go out and you have to have something set up. Baseball is a lot easier.

I'm amazed at what the character can get away with. One time the *Today Show* was broadcasting from the lawn in front of Independence Hall. I went down there in my van just to check it out and I put the outfit on. There was a lot of commotion—cameras, trucks, and lights with the Philadelphia Pops playing for the crowd during the commercials. Their conductor, Peter Nero, loves the Phanatic; I had been on-stage at the Academy of Music with him. I pushed him out of the way and I grabbed the baton and started conducting. Now there's a stir in the crowd, and Bryant Gumbel is looking over. I'm excited, and the Phanatic is waving and people are loving it. The Phanatic gets into the director's chair as they were about to shoot. We had about three spontaneous minutes with Bryant Gumbel. He was asking me questions and I was nodding my head. He asked me about the Cardinals and I shot him the tongue, bowed, and kissed his feet, the whole nine yards. When it was done and they broke for a commercial, I went over to the crowd and threw my fists in the air and it was like, "Yeah I did it! I just got on national television." The mayor was on before and he only got about one minute; we got three, so it was pretty comical.

At the ballpark just before the game I go out on the field for about twenty minutes. Mostly I'm on the bike doing crazy stuff.

⚾

He demonically rides a four-wheel ATV. It gets lots of laughs, and other baseball mascots have copied it.

⚾

I go back out again in the third inning. I am out the whole inning running through the stands. That's where the Phanatic is different from any of the other mascots. We cruise around the stands and we have fun with the fans. We have a number of different routines: shining bald heads, eating fans' popcorn, spilling popcorn, goosing vendors, stealing ice cream and passing them out, and things like that. In the fifth inning we do a dance on the dugout. In the seventh inning we're back on the dugout for another dance, and we give the opposing pitcher a whammy and do a few other gags.

The majority of the time we get a positive response. Eighty percent of the people on the field love the Phanatic to the point where they're ready to get into the act. There's another percentage that would rather not be bothered, and a few like Tommy Lasorda who do not like to be bothered at all. There are purists in every game, but we're pretty well tolerated. Most of the players get into it. When we get out and do our pregame show in Philadelphia, it's really directed toward the visiting team because they're the ones that haven't seen it as much, and they get into it. A problem with all mascots is that they can be distracting to the players who need to concentrate to perform well. Good mascots try to be sensitive to the players.

The Phanatic is part of the overall fan experience. The Phillies have a strong marketing philosophy, and it starts when you're out trying to find a parking spot and extends to the guy who gives you a hot dog. We have other characters we call Funsters that go through the stands and sing "Happy Birthday" to people and throw confetti and that type of stuff. There's the scoreboard, and the Fanvision runs videos. There's a lot of competition out there for the entertainment dollar, so you have to be upbeat and have lots of things going.

The people in the front office are very supportive and they give me ideas. When Vince Coleman hit Doc Gooden with a golf club in the dugout, they said I should include a golf club in my act when Gooden comes to town. I mix with the front office people some, but since I'm on the road so much, I'm more of a gypsy.

When you work for a baseball team you're always going to have wild hours. I have to make appearances on Friday nights and I'm traveling a lot, but once you get the costume on you're ready to roll.

My favorite part of my job is making people laugh. That's the bottom line. When I go to hospitals to visit sick kids, that's probably the most rewarding. Last night in Martinsville [Virginia] there was a kid with leukemia who threw out the first pitch. He had a Phanatic T-shirt and hat on. He'd written the Phanatic a letter, so a visit really pumps him up.

Every team should have a mascot, both from a marketing and a community relations standpoint. It's real tough to get the players out and do things today because their time is so limited and most of them are out of town during the off-season. Teams need to be involved in charity walks and business openings and things like that. The Phanatic is really a goodwill ambassador for the team. And if it's done right, a mascot at a ballgame can be very entertaining.

When I'm old enough to retire from this, I'd like to get more into the front-office end. The skills that it takes to be the Phanatic do translate into other areas. If you're upbeat and energized—and the Phanatic is all of that—you can go wherever you want to. You live every day with a happy-go-lucky attitude, and that's what the Phanatic is all about. He's a ten-year-old kid, he's a little bit mischievous, and he doesn't have a care in the world. Everyone is so uptight in the real world. I think everyone should try to be a little bit more like the Phanatic.

EPILOGUE

Shortly after this interview, Tom became the number one Phanatic after Dave Reymond retired. Another anonymous ad for mascots was placed in the Philadelphia newspapers, and a new backup was chosen from a field of forty.

Walter Banks

USHER, ATLANTA BRAVES

Walter Banks began working as an usher for four dollars a game at Atlanta's Fulton County Stadium in 1965. Newly built, the stadium was then the home of the Atlanta Crackers; the Braves did not arrive from Milwaukee until the following year. Soon after the Braves' arrival, Walter was promoted to section 105, the "VIP section," and later to owner Ted Turner's dugout-level box, where he has worked ever since.

⚾

When I was a child, we didn't have a TV set. My dad used to listen to the Atlanta Crackers on the radio. They were in the Double A Southern Association. A lot of times my mom would tell me to go to bed, and I would get the radio and put it in the bed with me and turn it down very low. Back then I thought the Atlanta Crackers were the greatest. Anything that had Atlanta on it made me feel proud. In those days, Atlanta only had Stone Mountain, the zoo and the state capitol for attractions. Any time a new building went up downtown, I got excited. I wanted our town to be popular like New York or San Francisco.

Chambers of commerce have commercials for their cities, but when a city has a team in the World Series, all the money in the world couldn't buy that kind of advertising. When you have major league baseball on the eleven o'clock news, your city's name is all over the country. A person may not have known anything about Atlanta before the Braves arrived, but they know us now.

I wanted to work in baseball when I first heard that the Braves were coming to Atlanta. I've always had a big enthusiasm for sports. The Braves kept saying that they were going to come even though they had another year in Milwaukee. When they built this stadium, Atlanta didn't have a football or a baseball team. Charlie Finley told the city that if you build a stadium, you'll get a team. We thought that maybe Charlie Finley was going to move his team here.

I was present at the ground-breaking ceremony on April 15, 1964. The house where I grew up was located where the infield is now. I was hired before the team arrived, and I got to know the people who worked in the office, which was located in trailers in the parking lot while the stadium was being built. Dick Cecil and Jack Carlings hired me. Jack moved over to the Coca-Cola Company, but Dick Cecil is still around. Even now, after all these years, when I see him in the ballpark, I thank him for hiring me.

The usher's job is to direct people to their seats. We look at their tickets and we point out their seats to them, or we tell them how to get there. Between innings we go down to the railing and face back up at the crowd to make sure everything is okay, but also to let them know that we are there. Even when I worked in a grocery store when I was in high school, I was taught that you never turn your back on the customer. So I am always facing the fans. It's not a strict rule like in the military—no, it's just the proper thing to do.

I answer a lot of questions, like where the restrooms are, and how to get back to the expressway. I get a lot of requests too. The most common one is fans ask me to take a foul ball down to the dugout for autographs. Fans also make excuses to get down to the dugout. Sometimes they will tell you that a player left tickets for them and they want to go down and thank the player. None of that surprises me.

Some folks come down to my section before the game looking for autographs and to be nearer to the field, to see it up close. Once 6:40 rolls around, fans without a ticket in that section must return to their seats. It's our responsibility to make sure they do. But human behavior is human behavior. There are always some fans who don't like being told to return to their seats. Usually you can control people when it's

Walter Banks, usher at Atlanta
Braves game.

done in a friendly manner. If you have some cattle going down the road, you have some cowboys on each side. When the cowboys give the cows a nudge, they move in the direction the cowboys want them to go. That's the way most people are. We're the cowboys when it comes to clearing out the dugout level.

After the game starts, you get other folks moving down from the upper deck or somewhere trying to get a better seat, to get closer to the action. A lot of times they give themselves away. When they approach my aisle, they often pause, just looking around, so when I see that, 99 percent of the time I know they don't belong down here. It's their body English, their behavior that gives them away. You have to get them out. Usually they go when you ask them to, but there are always some that don't want to budge. They tell you, "Man, I am just visiting for awhile." If they are still there when I come back, I may have to call the usher captain on the radio. We are ushers, not policemen, so we don't put our hands on anybody. When you get them out, some might just move over a couple of sections and try again. Some of them just keep trying until they succeed and aren't chased out.

Rain delays make your job harder because people like to get up and walk around, and they will drift down into your section. Some people get more rowdy after a rain delay because they have been on the concourse drinking beer. About the only real problem you get is guys drinking too much. I watch them. And if they get too loud or start yelling cuss words, then I speak to them, "Sir, there are children around. We'd appreciate it if you would watch your language." That kind of thing. But never put your hands on them. If they don't tame down, I call the usher captain or have security handle it.

⚰

Spectators arrested for disorderly behavior or trespassing onto the field, usually young males, are taken to the police precinct within the stadium. They may be issued a citation. Most major league ballparks also have a holding pen where serious offenders are detained.

⚰

Funny, you got to monitor yourself when a person starts getting out of line. If you feel yourself getting out of hand, getting angry, it is time to start backing off. You don't want to be drawn into any type of confrontation. If you can control yourself, usually you can control others. It's just like a car—if you stay the speed limit and stay in your lane, well, that car is not going to get out of control; it's not going to crash. It's the same thing with people. You learn a lot about human behavior doing this job. Yes, it's a great teacher of human behavior.

A big plus to being an usher is meeting all the different people you would never meet anywhere else—people from all parts. Working in the VIP box I meet anybody that is a somebody: President Carter, Governor Askew of Florida, Mayor Riley of Charlotte, . . . And you know, they are all such down-to-earth people. But Ted Turner and Jane Fonda are my favorites. They even had me out to their ranch in Montana.

I try real hard to extend myself in any way that I can. I don't care what the score is. If someone asks, "Walter, the next time you get a chance, will you get me a hot dog?" I'll go get it then. I can see a ball game anytime. I've seen close to three thousand ball games. My specialty is treating the fans special. If someone is sitting in the VIP box, there is a reason. Somebody invited them. Once they're here, it's up to me to make sure they are treated like VIPs. You try not to overdo it because you get to be a nuisance and you worry the people. But every few innings I'll ask if they need anything. Along with my co-worker, Lisa Colbert, I'm also responsible for the sections around the VIP box.

I try to have a little treat for the folks who tell me it's their first Braves game. I give them a stat sheet, because it has the date on it, or a book of matches. As long as it's a Braves item, they are pleased. If I see a youngster who's real mannerly and polite, I'll go over to his parents and let them know that they have done a fine job raising him. That's also part of our job. We put the fan first. After the game, I try to position myself so that when the people are leaving I can tell them to have a nice day and thanks for coming. If the Braves won, I say something about the game—like if they're wearing an unusual outfit, I tell them it gave the team luck. Something like that. The Braves believe in good customer service. If the fans don't come to the stadium, you're going to have slow business and folks are going to be out of work.

Getting to know the fans is like a ripple effect. One person will say, "Do you know Walter?" Then another person will do the same. And all of sudden I have a lot people asking for me when they come to the park. Some folks come up and say, "Do you remember me? I'm from Miami and I came here to watch the Braves and you made me feel welcome." Once you make a fan feel welcome, they will return to the park and look you up—especially fans from out of town.

Even if Atlanta only had a minor league team, I would still be here because I like people and I like baseball. I am an usher for football (Atlanta Falcons) at the Georgia Dome and a ticket taker for Georgia Tech basketball games. And I like that too, but it ain't like baseball. Baseball crowds are better. At football you have more adults, less children, less families. And you have more drinking. They often get filled up with alcohol before they get to the game—especially being that all their games are on Sundays. In baseball you get a chance to talk to people because many get there so early. And with over eighty games over the season, you get to know some of them. Some folks give you their business cards and keep in touch. Some say, "If you're ever in my part of the country, please stop by." The thing about that, you can tell when they really mean it. There are many season-ticket holders in my section. And do you know that no two personalities are alike? At football you only got a handful of games, so you don't get to know folks so well. Also there is a lot more to baseball—more statistics, more trivia, more history.

Not all ushers agree. Some who work both football and baseball say that people coming to baseball games are more likely to need assistance. Most football spectators, they say, are season ticket holders and know the location of their seats.

Sometimes the hours can really wear you down—especially during those ten-game home stands and rain delays. But once you're here at the park, your energy is recharged. I forget about the long day. What you see now is me. I don't rehearse anything. No matter how tired I am or how bad I feel, once I'm here, I forget the pain. I don't ever get bored of it. Being in the stands is like going to school. If you're not there, you feel like you've missed something.

I've seen a lot of changes in my thirty years here. When I started out, Atlanta only had 300,000 people and it was just a big town. Now it has four million and it's an international city. Atlanta is the place to be. There were times here when you couldn't give a ticket away. The smallest crowd we ever had was 737 fans on September 8, 1975. Today, everybody wants to come out because the Braves are a winning team. Some people from out of town are not really Braves fans at all; they're here because of all the hoopla about Atlanta. When things change, you've got to adjust. It's like if you throw a frog into boiling water, he will hop out; but if you put him in the water before you turn up the heat, he will stay in there and get cooked. Having done this for thirty years, I've been educated, I've learned a lot about human behavior, and I've adjusted to the changes. If you took me straight from when I started ushering in '65 and dropped me down today, it would be tough. But then, people are still people. If you smile, they will smile back at you. If you are courteous, they are courteous back at you—well, most of them.

Hep Cronin

SCOUT, ATLANTA BRAVES

Every major league organization has upwards of twenty-five full-time scouts whose job is to find the nation's best baseball talent. While some scout players who are already in the professional ranks, most look for prospects among amateur players, "free agents" who have not yet signed a professional contract. The typical scout watches hundreds of high school, college, American Legion, Connie Mack, and semiprofessional games every season. His job is to locate, to identify, to observe, to evaluate, and to report to his organization all players in his geographical area, or "territory," who have the potential to play in the major leagues.

At the ballpark we often see scouts sitting behind home plate—the best vantage of the pitcher and batter—aiming radar guns at the pitcher as he enters his windup and recording the digital readout of the pitch's velocity in a notebook. An embroidered logo on a knit shirt or cap, or a sticker on the radar gun's black Samsonite case often reveals which major league organization they represent.

Hep Cronin, age fifty-two, is a territorial scout for the Atlanta Braves. After playing college baseball at the University of Cincinnati, Hep taught biology and typing and coached at high schools in Ken-

tucky and Ohio while scouting part-time for the Braves. In 1982 he
quit teaching and became a full-time scout.

⚈

Scouting is a very different life from teaching high school. When I taught, I always had a six o'clock wake-up because my first class was at 7:30. It was the same thing day in and day out. Whereas now, if I want to wake up at nine o'clock, I'll wake up at nine o'clock. If I want to have breakfast here, I will have it here; or if I want to have it up the road, I will have it there. It's my decision. In scouting you have a certain independence and freedom that you don't have in most lines of work. When I leave Birmingham, it's my decision whether I stop in Knoxville or go on to Youngstown.

I have a territory of two-and-a-half states, and it's basically my baby, my responsibility. Whoever the Braves take [draft] or don't take for these two-and-a-half states is totally on my shoulders, and I will live and die with it. In other avenues of life, you don't get that. In most avenues of life, everything is a joint decision by forty people, and then sometimes they don't even make decisions.

In scouting, I still have a few months off every year. When you teach, you have June, July, and August free. Now I have November, December, and January free. Those are good months to have off because I don't have to wake up early, I don't have to fight the weather. I can go south if I want to because there is nothing tying me to home.

But the rest of the year, once the kids start playing in February, scouts spend much of their time on the road. If you scout in some kind of order, you can save a lot of wear. There are some guys who don't organize themselves and don't take into account the weather. They waste their time by traveling way more than they have to. In February I go down to Texas and help Ray Corbett and Ralph Garn, our scouts down there. When I leave Texas in late February, I go to the bottom of Tennessee, right across the Arkansas border to the Memphis area, so I can see Memphis State University, Christian Brothers College, and a couple of other colleges play. Then I'll work Tennessee for the next three weeks or so before I start working my way back up north; I'll see University of Kentucky, Eastern Kentucky, and Western Kentucky. Once I hit Cincinnati, my hometown, it's mid-April and I won't have to stay overnight in hotels anymore. My territory only includes half of

Ohio plus Tennessee and Kentucky, and I can scout most of Ohio without having to stay away overnight.

You spend a lot of the fall and early spring gathering leads and names and doing a lot of phone work. Once the school season starts, it's just trying to see as many games and prospects as you can. I try to be sure that at every game I watch there is at least one potential prospect on the field, rather than just seeing games and hoping that I'll discover somebody. If I am at a four o'clock game watching two Cincinnati high school teams play and I know in my mind that there is no one on the field I am interested in, then I'll get up and leave. Some of the older scouts hate it when the younger guys leave. But you can't worry about them. If there is six o'clock game somewhere else, there may be a guy over there you'll like. There's no point sitting for another five or six innings just because no one else is leaving.

But when you leave, you try not to embarrass the kids you came to watch or the coach who recommended them to you. You try to sneak out if you can. You go down to the right-field fence, watch three outs, and then slide out into the parking lot so that everybody doesn't see you walk away. If somebody says something, you try to be kind and diplomatic about it. You say you have another game at six o'clock but that you're coming back to see these guys another time. You don't want to walk on them, especially when a coach thinks he has a player [prospect]. It looks bad: the coach called you to come see his guy play, and you only saw him bat once and you're gone. So you have to be diplomatic.

The traveling is easier when you are scouting pro teams because then you can settle down in one place for four or five days for a home stand. Then you can get some continuity in your life. Traveling gets lonely at times. The Texas trip is the hardest for me because I don't know the scouts down there except for our own guys. In your own territory you usually stay in motels where there are other scouts. You know everybody and you eat dinner with them. But everybody has different hobbies, different ways of passing the time. Some guys carry golf clubs. There are four of them playing today. I wish I were a golfer. But my ball doesn't go straight, so I gave it up. A lot of guys go to the mall and do some shopping for their families.

The three weeks in Texas are the only time I'm really kind of alone, and it does get boring. You can only see so many movies. So you catch yourself sleeping in for as long as you can, trying not to get up too early so that the day goes by a little faster. And you hate it when it rains because you can't work and you've got nothing to do. In Texas I once got rained out four straight days. I was ready to go crazy. I was walking around the Galleria Mall doing everything I could think of just trying to keep busy. Have you ever tried sitting in a motel room for four days straight?

How early in the draft your organization is picking can influence where you spend a lot of your time and which players you are going to zero in on. If there is a kid in your territory everybody else is looking at, but your club doesn't have an early pick, then why waste your time there? He'll be taken [in the draft] before your club gets a pick. So you move down to a lower level and try to find some guys your club would have a chance for.

❧

Hep Cronin also is also responsible for nine minor league teams in the Southern League and the Florida State League. He must watch each of his teams play five times. He tries to plan his trips according to when his teams are playing one another. At the time of this interview, he was in Birmingham to watch the Barons play the Huntsville Stars in a four-game series. Both teams are in his territory.

❧

After the June amateur draft, I scout my assigned minor league teams. During the summer, we also hold tryout camps. Each scout runs his own camp—Roy Clark in the Carolinas, Rob English in Georgia, Steve Givens in Florida, and so on. Usually you put an advertisement in the newspaper and arrange to use a local college field or park. You want to get the best facility you can and in the best location. Usually sixty to eighty kids turn out. My sons, Dan and Mick, who played on a national championship team, and a friend, Bubba Nienaber, help me out.

As the kids come in, you get them to fill out information cards—all the usual background stuff plus their age, weight, school, graduation year, summer team, and so on. This way, if a kid catches your eye, you don't have to run around asking a hundred questions. You've already got some background on him. At 9 A.M. I group them by position—infielders, outfielders, pitchers, and catchers—and talk to them, explain what we're going to do. Then we put them through the paces. Basically you try to see if they can do the five necessary things—hit, hit with power, field, throw, and run. You clock them in the 60-yard dash. After you've made sure they're good and loose, you send them to their positions and have them throw. After you've graded their arm and their speed, you hit them some balls and grade their fielding. These three things you can do pretty quickly. The next two—hit and hit with power—are more difficult. If there aren't too many guys, I try to let everybody hit. But sometimes, if you get ninety guys, you just can't do it. You'd be there forever. So you eliminate the pitchers and the kids who were so slow in the 60-yard dash that they will never be prospects. You try to stay there until you get a good evaluation of everybody, until you get a good feel for them.

I might run six or seven camps and find just one guy. Tryout camps are for two things. One, to find that diamond in the rough, the guy who has fallen through the cracks—like a college senior who was missed. We can send him out to Idaho Falls [the rookie Pioneer League] and maybe get lucky. About five years ago I took a college senior at the University of Cincinnati named Judd Johnson. He was an undrafted player, and we found him seven or ten days after the draft at a tryout camp. Judd is in Triple A right now and he's three and one. He pitched good and won at every level; he has a chance to maybe pitch in the big leagues. One of our scouts, Roy Clark, signed a kid, Terrel Wade, out of a tryout camp. He's throwing 95 miles per hour now at Double A and probably will pitch in the big leagues. It's always a long shot, and probably 99 out of a 100 aren't going to get to Triple A. But you never know.

The camps are also good for spotting some talented younger players you'll want to follow over the next couple years. Here in Cincinnati I might spot two or three sophomores and maybe six or seven juniors I'll want to follow.

⚉

The scout's task requires more than just accurately assessing a player's skills. Rather, the scout must project into the future how each prospect will develop. Major league clubs care little that a teenager can hit .400 in high school. They want to know what kind of hitter he will be in five or six years and against pitchers who throw 85 miles per hour, have an assortment of pitches, and consistently aim for the corners of the plate. The standard that scouts use in assessing talent is called the OFP, or Overall Future Potential, rating. To arrive at an OFP rating,

*the scout scores the player on each of the five different talents (run-
ning, fielding, throwing, hitting, and hitting with power) using a scale
from 20 to 80, with 20 being poor, 50 being the major league average,
and 80 being the maximum possible points. The scout then averages
the points for the different categories to produce the OFP.*

Good scouting is being able to visualize how a boy is going to develop.
That's projection. That's what scouting is all about: being able to look
at the body, the ability, and the attitude of a player today and project
how good he is going to be in the future as he gets bigger and older.
Take two pitchers who are pretty similar in their velocity today. I may
look at one and say this guy is going to throw 93 to 94 [miles per
hour] in four years, while the other guy is still going to be doing 89 to
90. Why? Because of his delivery or because of his growth potential,
which you may be able to judge by looking at the parents. If his father
is six-four and the other guy's is five-nine, that tells you something. So
while these two guys may be throwing the same velocity today, they
have different potentials. But it's still mostly a crapshoot. Hopefully,
enough of the time you're going to be right.

In position players, what you look for depends on the position. In
first and third basemen you're looking more for hitting and hitting
with power; in the middle infield you're looking for the speed; and in
the outfield you're looking for speed, arm, and hitting. Scouts talk a
lot about speed and arm, but when you come down to it, he who hits,
plays. You can draft all the track runners you want, but if they don't
hit, they're not going to play. If you can't swing the bat, it's going to be
tough, real tough. If you check, you'll find that every good hitter in the
big leagues was a doggone good hitter in high school and amateur
ball. I mean a doggone good one.

In a pitcher, you're looking at his velocity, his breaking stuff, his
control, his confidence, and his command. Only the velocity can you
measure accurately, with a radar gun. You and I might see the same
kid and come up with very different evaluations. You might like him,
and I might think he's a dog. In five years we'll find out who is right. I
think scouts who were pitchers themselves are more confident and do
a better job in scouting pitchers than scouts who were hitters, and vice
versa. But the toughest to scout of any is a hitter. There are just so
many factors at work, and you have the added difficulty of assessing

Scouts clocking pitches on
Jugs radar guns at a Double
A Eastern League game.
(Photo by Darren Mrak)

how the kid will do in pro ball where he won't have the benefit of using an aluminum bat. There are kids who hit great with aluminum
bats in college or high school but never make the adjustment to wood.

You grade the kid on each variable—hitting, fielding, and so on—
based on the future, not the present. You might put down a 40 for his
present arm but project his future arm to be a 50 because he is going
to get bigger and stronger. The present grades don't mean anything.
The future is what everyone cares about. After you do that for all five
talents, you come up with his OFP rating. The kids who get drafted in
the first round usually have OFP numbers of around 60 to 65; second
and third rounders probably 55 to 59; and the guys in the bottom end
of the draft are probably in the 45 to 49 range. Before the draft, you
rank the kids in your area in the order of their OFP. When I turned in
my draft list this year, I had 21 guys on it, from OFP 45 to 65.

The older the player is, the easier it is to project how he will develop. That makes college players less risky than high school players.
Also, players from the Sun States, from the West Coast and the South,

have played a lot more baseball and tend to be a safer bet than players from the colder climates of the Northeast and Midwest. When you see kids from the Sun Belt, you have a better idea of what you are going to get, of how they are going to turn out. But the kids from the North may have just as much potential. But because they haven't had the opportunity to play as much, they haven't realized it yet.

Besides the kid's physical tools, you also have to be concerned about his psychological makeup. Is he coachable, does he have confidence, is he a hard worker? In the old days before the draft, scouts spent a lot more time with prospects. They got to know them better than they do today. They had better knowledge about the kid's character. But now with the draft, there is less need to romance the kid, to sell him on your organization, and to convince him to sign with you. Consequently, you don't get to know any of the kids as well as scouts once did. Instead of knowing them personally, today we ask them to take an ISM, a personality profile test. I am not a big believer in it. Although it can tell you some things about the kid's mindset, it's not too useful in ranking kids, in deciding where to draft them. Sometimes, for the minor league people, it's a valuable tool in figuring out how to deal with the kids. For example, it may tell you that the kid doesn't take well to criticism, and that you are going to have to pat him on the back and explain something to him differently than you are to other kids. If you jump in this kid's face, you may ruin him. He might hit .120 for the first month in rookie league because he is scared of you. Or the personality profile might tell you that he is a loner. So when the manager sees him sitting in the back of the bus by himself or going to a movie by himself, he knows he needs to get a little closer to that kid and try to draw him out a little bit.

You can watch how much a kid hustles and get some idea of what kind of desire he has, but for the most part the psychological dimensions can't be detected from the stands. I try to go in and interview every kid I think I might recommend for the draft. I give them the personality test and an eye test. These are basically small tools, and are often more of an excuse for me to get into the kid's house and meet the family, to have some coffee and sit down and spend an hour-and-a-half or so with them. In that time, you also get a feeling for what the chances are that he will sign if you draft him. I have walked out of houses this year after giving the test and lowered the kid on my list because I knew I couldn't sign him. I knew from that hour-and-a-half conversation, from the way the kid came across, that this kid wasn't going to sign, and that he was determined to go to college. Now, that hour-and-a-half is a valuable chunk of time because we don't get stuck with a losing draft choice.

When you see a kid you like, you have to be patient. You don't want to tip your hand. You do everything you can to talk with him without other scouts seeing you. Don't be too obvious. Some of the younger scouts, when they see a kid they like, they jump up and walk right down there and start talking to the kid to get information—address, phone number, and everything else. I like to wait and hang around, let everyone leave, go to the parking lot and read a newspaper, and maybe get the kid before he gets on the bus to go home. Or if I can't do that, I see the manager of the club and ask him, "Say, Tommy or Bob or whatever, do you mind if I call you tonight? I am going to talk to you about John." The only problem with this is that coaches can talk too much. A coach may tell four or five other scouts, "Yeah, Hep said he likes this guy." "Hep is calling on this guy."

When I go to the kid's house and visit with him and his folks, I try to find out how much they know about the draft and about the college scholarship plan that Major League Baseball has. I don't want to spend an hour explaining something they've already heard five times. By the time I leave the house, I want to have given the family some sense of what to expect when draft day comes. Sometimes they just don't have a clue. You go in there when the kid is a possible fourth-round pick, and the family says they expect a million dollars. Well, obviously, they are way out. I give them some figures from last year's draft. Let's get realistic. I add 10 percent for inflation. So if the kid is in a round that went for, say, about $60,000 last year, that means they might expect, more or less, $70,000 this year—not a million. Sometimes the parents will say, "I don't care what the average is. My son is not going to sign for less than $500,000 or else he is going to Stanford." Well, that visit saves you time because now you know not to draft him. He is one player we won't waste a draft pick on.

Every once in a while, you get a father who knows the picture. He may have played minor league ball or know somebody who works for the White Sox or whoever. But basically, most parents don't know what the catch is. Probably seven out of every ten don't realize that the decision between pro ball and college doesn't even have to be made for many draft picks, that they can do both and have it all paid for. When you tell them the plan Major League Baseball has, they drop their mouths open and say, "What do you mean?" I have to explain that their kid can sign and we will pay for room, books, tuition fees, and everything, guaranteed for four years. Even college athletic scholarships can't do that. They only guarantee one year. I tell them to tell me what the tuition is. I will write it down and times it by four. I tell them that we will set aside that amount for the kid's school [as part of the signing bonus]. Yes, it will take six or seven years to graduate, going one semester per year, but most kids don't graduate in four years anyway. You'd be surprised at how many parents are confused by what they read in the papers. They see where somebody who hit .250 signed for two million dollars last year. They forget that money is for guys in the major leagues, guys at the very top, and not for high school players.

Before the draft, you make up a final list of the kids in your territory in rank order by their OFP ratings. The scouting director and the national cross-checker get lists from all the area scouts like me. Then they combine all the rankings and come up with a master list to use in the draft. To do that, they have to know the area scouts and know how tough they grade. No two scouts grade exactly alike—some are low, some are high. When they collate the rankings, they take everything into consideration. Once they come up with a master list, they usually follow it pretty closely in the draft. Sometimes they deviate a little. Let's say we've taken six pitchers straight, and it's the seventh round and the next guy on your list is another pitcher. But maybe one point below him is a catcher. So they jump the catcher ahead of him.

Who you get in the end depends a lot on what the other clubs do. This year, from my list of twenty-one kids, we drafted a third rounder, an eighth rounder, and a twelfth rounder. All three were high school pitchers. We could have the same exact list and do the draft over tomorrow and we might get none of them because someone took them right before us.

After the draft, it's your job to contact the kids in your territory whom your club drafted and begin negotiations to sign them to a contract. A lot depends upon what kind of education the parents have. You walk into a home that has both a father and a mother, and the father is a lawyer and the mother is a doctor. Well, even though they may not have a lot of baseball savvy, they have been out asking the right questions and they have gotten a good picture of what their kid's chances are of getting X dollars. Then you go into the middle of Tennessee someplace and there is no father [in the household] and the mother works at McDonald's. They have no chance. I mean, they don't know. I am not giving out any secrets when I tell you that baseball doesn't like agents. But sometimes, when you see a situation like that, there is a place for somebody. It doesn't have to be an agent, but the family should at least find a lawyer in town who is willing to sit there and listen so that the kid has a chance of getting what he deserves. The mother and the seventeen- or eighteen-year-old son sitting there trying to negotiate a contract without any help are at such a disadvantage compared to the doctor-lawyer family.

Overall, I think the kids who are easiest to sign are the ones who see themselves playing in the big leagues. They tend not to be interested in spending a month negotiating or going through another year of school and doing the draft all over again. With the guys who are really tough to sign, sometimes I say to myself, "Back off. This guy doesn't have enough confidence in himself." You wonder how badly he wants to be a professional player. Is he just in this to get as much money as he can? Is he going to take your money and then run away from baseball in a couple of years? I like it when you ask a kid if he wants to play and he says, "Yes, sir. I am ready."

⚅

Scouts are often identified by and have reputations based on the players they signed who became major league stars. I [George Gmelch] remember being introduced to Detroit Tigers superscout Ed Katalinas during my first spring training. I knew Katalinas by reputation as "the scout who signed Al Kaline." Likewise, when I was first told that Baltimore scouting supervisor John Stokoe lived in my town, it was "John Stokoe, the man who signed Mike Flanagan." Cronin finds these attributions embarrassing and inappropriate.

⚅

It's amazing the respect you get once some of your players begin to perform. You happen to get lucky one or two times and all of a sudden people will say, "Oh, this is Hep Cronin. He signed Dave Justice." It makes me feel a little goofy when I hear that. It doesn't take a genius to see that a player like Dave Justice has great potential. Like when I saw Chipper Jones play. I knew he was going to be a top pick and that he had a good chance of making it. The same with guys like Dwight

Gooden. These are the easy ones. The scout who deserves credit is the guy who discovers someone the others missed or underrated, like our guy in New Jersey who recommended Mark Lemke. We got him in the twenty-seventh round. Nobody else seemed to have him on his list, and yet he made it to the big leagues.

It used to be that the scouts who had been big-league players were looked up to. Everybody gathered around them. But I don't think it means a whole lot anymore. There are so many guys out here now who only played one or two years in the minors or were just college baseball coaches and later went into scouting. Our new scouting director, Chuck LaMarr, was just a junior college baseball coach.

Today's big league players are not going to be interested in scouting when they retire. With their pensions and their investments, why would they? Tomorrow I leave here and drive eleven hours to Youngstown, Ohio, to see a high school tournament. Then I have to come back here to see two pitchers. Tell me, if you had a pension of $100,000 a year, would you want to come out here on the road for $25,000 and drive, drive, drive all over the place and sit through rain delays? Do you think Barry Bonds is going to want to scout some day for $25,000? No, he's not going to want to drive from Alabama to Ohio when he can sit back in his living room in a million-dollar house. You're not going to see today's big leaguers down here in the trenches. These guys are well-heeled for life and they have had their fill of traveling—four or five years on the buses in the minor leagues and then ten or more years traveling all over through airports in the big leagues. The scouts of the future will be former college and minor league players—guys like me.

THE FIELD

Those who work on the field are team personnel: players, coaches, and managers, and their supporting cast of trainers, batboys, ballgirls, groundskeepers, umpires, and the mascot. For all of them, the playing field is their workplace—the stage on which they perform their jobs. Their roles, like those of the workers in the stands, are easily identified by their dress—the white baseball uniform of the home-team players and coaches; the nonwhite (usually gray) uniform of the visitors; the blue blazers and pants of the umpires; and the khaki or forest-green trousers and white shirts of the groundskeepers.

For spectators, the field is the focal point of the ballpark. Their gaze is usually fixed, even as they talk and eat, on whatever activity takes place there. Whoever walks on the field, even during pregame activities, is noticed: fans even observe with interest the batboys and ballgirls.

The field's expanse of emerald-green turf and the dirt insets of the batter's box, pitcher's mound, and infield, all lined in white chalk, are the aesthetic center of the ballpark. For the groundskeepers, the field is the showcase of their skills, a visible indicator of how well they do their work. Brown, bare, or thin patches of grass; dirt that is too loose around the pitching rubber; or uneven edges around the warning track are bad marks on the groundskeeper's report card and are readily seen by both fans and management. The condition of the field—its turf and dirt—is of vital importance to the players, as it can influence their performance. Infield dirt that is too sandy or damp will slow a base runner. An uneven surface in the infield can cause a bad hop. Grass that is only slightly longer than usual will slow down ground balls and potential base hits going through the infield.

The field is protected, separated from the grandstands and spectators by a wall or railing and secured by sentinels of ushers and security guards. In Yankee Stadium, for example, there are over one hundred Burns Security Guards in brown uniforms who guard the boundary at every game, to maintain order and to prevent anyone from trespassing onto the field.

The clubhouse, reached by a tunnel from the dugout, is also part of this setting. It is the backstage, the area where the teams and the umpires, who occupy separate quarters, dress, eat, relax, and mentally prepare for the game. Clubhouses in the major leagues are spacious and well appointed with carpeting, sofas, televisions, and oversized lockers. Food, spread on large tables, is plentiful. Minor league clubhouses, in contrast, are often cramped, have bare concrete or linoleum floors, and lack the amenities found in the major league clubhouses. Whether in the majors or minors, however, the clubhouse is a sanctuary, a place where the players are sheltered from autograph requests and other demands of an adoring public.

QV Lowe

MANAGER, JAMESTOWN EXPOS

QV Lowe, who went from a being player to a pitching coach to a manager in the Cubs, Yankees, and Expos organizations, has spent all but one of his twenty-six years in professional baseball in the minor leagues. I first met QV Lowe in 1991 when he was the pitching coach of the Jamestown Expos in the Class A New York–Penn League. When a follow-up interview was done the next summer, QV was managing the team. In the first half of the narrative, QV talks about his life as a minor league player and coach in the 1960s and 1970s; in the latter half he describes managing professional baseball players today.

QV, age forty-eight, is a little under 6 feet tall and has the look of a marine drill sergeant—close-cropped hair, thick chest and arms, conservative dress, and a no-nonsense manner—which belie the open-minded, sensitive, and thinking man that he is. A sportswriter described him as "a man you wish you had time to know." QV is his actual first name, not his initials. His father wanted his children to have names nobody else had (QV has a brother named FE). In baseball QV is usually referred to simply as Q.

QV Lowe, age two, in arms of his older sister, with his siblings at their Florida home in 1947.

My dad died when I was two. My mother raised us seven kids in Ocala, Florida, by doing washing and ironing; the Baptist church gave us space in an army barracks to live in. When I was in elementary school I would play baseball in the yard. It was then that I began to realize that I was better than most of the other kids. I was about nine years old when one day the principal, who was also the Little League coach, saw us playing. He asked me why I didn't play Little League. I told him that my mother didn't drive and I had no way to get there. Besides, I really didn't know anything about it. The principal drove me home that afternoon. He told my mother that if she let me play, he would come get me and take me to the games.

I was a shortstop and an outfielder. At the tail end of the season I pitched for the first time. We had some pitchers on the team, but they couldn't throw strikes. The coach called the whole team together and asked if anybody could throw a strike. I told him that I often threw in the backyard with my brothers and that I thought I could get the ball over the plate. That day I became a pitcher. I pitched well and I've been a pitcher ever since. I suppose that was the start of my pitching career.

I made the All-Star team when I was eleven; and my older sister, who was a senior in high school, went out and bought me a new glove. I'd never had a good glove before; I think her doing that was one of the proudest moments of my life. It still stands out in my memory. You see, my sister worked in a grocery store after school. She didn't make much, probably just fifty cents an hour. She spent fifteen dollars to buy me that new glove. That was the kind of support my family gave me all through the years of my playing ball. When I was in high school and college, they would pack up and drive to see me play. We were a very close knit family, I suppose because of the bracket of poverty we came through.

I was pretty successful in high school. I studied hitters and I kept a little book on what hitters could hit and what they couldn't. Some folks thought that that was weird. But by studying them, I knew how to pitch them. I set up a table in the yard and drew spots on it and then threw baseball after baseball so I could hit the spots. And I studied pitching mechanics when nobody else thought much about it. I knew exactly what I had to do to be in sync after I strided—the ball would hit the mitt as my right foot would hit the ground. If it hit too soon or too late, then I wasn't in sync yet. Since I wasn't that big and didn't have an overpowering fastball, I knew, even back then, that I had to get every advantage I could.

When I was a senior in high school, a Dodger scout started coming around. I didn't notice him at first, since back in those days, scouts didn't have radar guns or blue books. But after a ball game one day he walked up to me and introduced himself. He told me he was with the Dodgers and gave me his card. My heart was pounding. He said he was ready to offer me $10,000 to join the Dodger organization. I was stunned. I was excited to get home and tell my mom. That was more money than I had seen in the world. But having him want me was as important as the money. My girlfriend's dad was an educator, the school superintendent. He was like a father to me and he said that $10,000 was not big time, that once I had spent it, it would be gone. He said I would do better going to college. I talked to my uncle, Mel Wright, who was Bill Virdon's pitching coach. He used to stop by and see us in Ocala on his way to spring training. He told me how difficult it was to get to the big leagues, that many who signed [contracts] ended up with nothing, no job and no education. So I didn't sign.

Coming out of high school, I wanted to go to the University of

Florida. We lived only 30 miles from the university, and I thought that with the kind of seasons I had in high school, they would offer me a scholarship. In my senior year I was 10 and 0, and we had won the state championship. I was dominating, so I figured they'd surely offer me a scholarship. The [University of Florida] coach came to the championship game. Afterwards he said he wished he could offer me something but felt I was too little to win in the SEC [Southeastern Conference]. Here the Dodgers had offered me a contract of good money, and he says I'm too little to pitch in the SEC. So I went to Raxly Gulf Coast Junior College. I was All-American there both years and that got me a full scholarship to Auburn. At Auburn I was All-American again. The first time we played Florida, I pitched a perfect game against them. The adrenaline really kicked in. There was no way they were going to beat me. After the game their coach came up to me and said that he had made a mistake about me. I was never so proud. Florida never once beat me in my college career.

The Cubs drafted me from Auburn, but I really didn't want to be with the Cubs. They were losers, and I wanted to be with somebody who was competitive. The Cubs offered me just $1,000 to sign. I was an All-American, and they only offered me $1,000. I said no. They came back and offered $3,000. I was a senior; my college career was over, so I really didn't have much choice. I signed and they sent me to Lodi in the California League. That was 1967.

Immediately the manager has me room on road trips with a black guy. I was never exposed to blacks. In Ocala we lived on our side of town and they on theirs. We had our high school, and they had theirs. We were happy, and we assumed they were happy too. I had never even played with or against a black player in my life until the College World Series when Auburn played Ohio State, which had one black player. So this was a new experience for me. I remember neither one of us sleeping that good. His name was Jim Atterbury. He finally broke the ice and said, "QV, is it true down there in the South that you whites carry guns and go around shooting blacks?" I said, "No." Then I asked him, "Jim, is it true that you black guys carry knives and run three or four in a pack just to attack a white guy?" He said, "No." Right there, the barrier between us came down, and by knowing him, I started to see what blacks were going through. They wouldn't let them live in Lodi; they had to live in Stockton, about 20 miles away.

There were places on the road where blacks couldn't stay in the same hotel with us.

I often remember baseball through the songs that were popular. The song that summer was "Oh Lord, I'm Stuck in Lodi." I was put in with a bunch of guys who had been in baseball for three or four, maybe five, years. Very few guys in baseball in those days had a college education. In the 1960s the big-name ballplayers signed out of high school. The organizations wanted to get their players early and mold them into the kind of ballplayers they wanted. My manager hadn't gone to college, and the few college players in our club took some abuse from him. He would needle us; he liked to say, "You're not so smart after all." You'd go out and pitch, not do so well, and come back to the dugout, and the manager would say, "Yeah, not as easy as all that damn college stuff that you're playing." A lot of those kids played for seven or eight years and never made it [to the big leagues]; they had three or four kids, no education, and no place to go. They were locked in. But I wasn't locked in and I think that caused some jealousy.

In those days organizations were looking for hard throwers, the Bob Gibsons and the J. R. Richards. You had to really throw hard or you weren't considered a prospect. Because I didn't throw really hard, the Cubs organization labeled me no prospect. Of course, they don't tell you that. But I could see the writing on the wall. The guys who got all the attention threw hard. It didn't matter if they could throw strikes or win: the hard throwers moved up to the next stage.

Pro ball was so different from what I'd experienced in college. Winning was not important. You played for yourself, not for the team. It was nice to win, but that wasn't the most important thing. I remember my second start in pro ball. I warmed up in the bullpen and started to the mound when a pitcher, a teammate who had been around four or five years, said to me, "I hope you get your tits ripped."

I said, "Pardon me?"

He said, "I hope you get your butt killed out there."

I said, "Why would you say that to me?"

He said, "If you do good then you are going to pitch on my mound. So I pull for you not to do good." I might also have moved ahead of him.

That was the stark reality right there.

The next year I went to spring training and had a great spring and made the Double A club, which was San Antonio in the Texas League. Looking back on my career, I wish that I hadn't made that club. I would have been better off going back to Lodi with a new bunch of players and having a good year. At San Antonio we had a terrible team and were thirty games out of first place by July. And the club didn't care. Winning wasn't a priority with them. I never had a losing record in my life and now I was stuck in this mess where everybody is losing and after a while you start to accept it. Nobody wanted to go to the ballpark. That almost destroyed me. For the first time in my life I didn't love baseball. The only good thing that happened that year was that I got married to my girlfriend from Auburn.

The next year I was sent back to Double A, San Antonio. I got off to a pretty good start, but then I broke my finger trying to catch a line drive. I couldn't pitch. So I taped my finger and tried to use a knuckleball for the rest of the season. Statistically, I had a horrible year, and I started having nightmares about being released. The organization might act like they care about your injury but they really don't care—not unless they have a lot of money invested in you.

The next year—it's now my fourth year out—they tell me in spring training what I had always known, that I am not a prospect anymore. They asked me to go back to San Antonio as a player-coach. I thought that was great. They offered me more money, and I had always wanted to coach, even back in high school. So I accepted.

I had a good year pitching and enjoyed the coaching. At first it was difficult to walk that fine line between being a coach on one hand and a player on the other. Your teammates have a hard time accepting that you are with management, sitting in with the manager and making decisions while still being a player. There were the same jabs intended to upset me. But after I explained my situation, that I was still friends with them but was now also in management, most of them came around.

The Cubs asked me back the next year to do the same thing. I was now twenty-six and it didn't look like I was ever going to make the big leagues. But a break came when the big league pitching coach died during the winter. The Cubs didn't have anyone else in the organization who knew the pitching system. So Leo Durocher asked me to come to the big leagues, not to play but to help with the pitching—mainly to be a bullpen coach. A friend of Leo's, Larry Jansen, was to be the pitching coach, but we would share a lot of the duties since I knew the system. That was 1972, the year I hung up my playing shoes and started coaching for good.

First, they flew me to Chicago for a press conference. I was standing there beside Leo Durocher and Ernie Banks and some guys who were my idols. I was a small-town guy from a poor family, and I always had to work hard for everything I got in life. Suddenly, being there in Chicago, it was quite a shock—the big people at that press conference and all the little hors d'oeuvres they put had out. It was megabucks. I had never seen anything like it before. It stunned me. Some of the writers fired questions at me, almost to intimidate me: "At your age, aren't you going to feel out of place?" "You weren't a successful pitcher in the minor leagues, how are you going to be a big league coach?" I stood up there and I handled myself well in the interview. I told them that I wasn't here because of my knowledge of pitching but that I was here to supervise and help out and do whatever I could. I never once acted like I knew big league pitching, or even that I was intelligent about pitching or anything else. I told them that I was there because the coach had died and I knew the system a little bit and that I was going to do anything that I could to help the team. I tried to be humble about it.

When we got to spring training, I was nervous about the work that Leo was going to give me and how the older players would react to me. On the third day, Leo told the group that we were going to go over bunt defenses and that I was going to run it. I went through the defenses like Leo had drawn them up and it went well. I never stumbled or acted nervous about it. I just did it, and that got my feet on the ground. As spring training rolled on, the players saw that I could throw an hour and a half of good BP [batting practice]. I made sure that the pitchers did their running every day. I organized their schedules. I made it clear that I wasn't there to teach them how to pitch, but that I was there to help them. The older guys—Kessinger, Hickman, Santo, Beckert—those guys respected the fact that I worked hard. The only one who was kind of disrespectful was Burt Hooten, who was a young, hotshot rookie. He felt that with my background, I had no business being there.

The road trips were outstanding. All chartered flights. You fly into a city and the bus is there waiting for you. You don't touch your bags. You don't even take them up to the hotel. All that's done for you. You go to the hotel and all your bags are there in your room. Most hotels had bourbon and scotch in the room, complimentary for the coaching staff. I didn't know if Leo ordered it, if the Cubs asked for it, or if it was a gift from the hotel. But that was always the way it was.

All the coaches were big drinkers. I had never been a drinker, other than beer, and I'd never even had a beer until I was twenty-two years old. My folks were teetotalers. But because of the situation—going to dinner with Leo and the other coaches every night—I got into drinking.

They have a way, just like kids have, of making you feel guilty if you don't. By mid-season I was drinking scotch. And by the end of the season it wasn't one scotch, it was four or five. If I am ashamed of anything in my life, it is that I fell into that and didn't have the courage to go against those folks, to say that I'd had enough to drink.

⚉

Like most players and coaches, QV didn't see much of the cities in which the Cubs played, except their restaurants and ballparks. All team personnel were expected to be at the ballpark by 4:00 P.M. at the latest. QV routinely got there by 1:30 P.M. to get everything organized. By the time the game was over and everyone had showered and changed, it was after 11:00 P.M. The men then typically went out for dinner and returned to their hotel rooms to watch television and wind down from the game. Most slept late into the morning and had only a few free hours to do anything before heading back to the ballpark. Here QV describes his life on the road.

⚉

I mostly stayed in the hotel, watched TV, and did my paperwork—keeping up with the pitchers, recording how many pitches they had thrown, who was to throw on the side, and so on. I was nervous about going out and walking the city streets by myself. The other coaches were much older than I was, so there was no common bond there, and they certainly weren't interested in going walking. Being a country boy, I wasn't going to walk the streets of New York City by myself. Even the subway scared me. Most of the players had this same fear of getting onto the streets, unless they could go in groups of five or six. But it wasn't like that in every town. In Houston we stayed at the Marriot in a suburbia-type setting. People out there were different from downtown and it seemed a lot safer. The guys liked that better.

Most guys liked to go to San Diego because it was clean and had great weather and good restaurants. They didn't like San Francisco because of the ballpark—cold and very windy. We almost froze to death. We liked going to Los Angeles—nice hotel, great ballpark. We didn't like Philadelphia because we stayed downtown. Atlanta had a new stadium back then. Since it wasn't too far from my home in Florida, a lot of my friends came to the ballpark to see me and that was really special. St. Louis was good because the Cubs had a rivalry with the Cardinals and they have great fans there. Cincinnati was always a challenge because they had those great ball clubs, the Big Red Machine. Montreal was a big deal for me because I had never been to Canada before. But often what's most important to players and coaches is not the city but the ballpark and the hotel.

There are certain ballparks that guys really like to play in—usually it's the places where they have been successful or else they like the fans, the style. That's more important than the city they're in.

The thrill of seeing those ballparks from the inside for the very first time was something. It gave me goose bumps. My first time to the Astrodome, I thought I must have died and gone to baseball heaven. There were beautiful red seats, great big dugouts, gigantic locker rooms, where everyone is comfortable, and the place was the same temperature all the time. What else could a guy ask for? It was a different world from what I'd known. Yes sir, I thought I had died and gone to heaven.

But it wasn't going to last. About a month before the end of the season, Leo [Durocher] was relieved of his duties. John Holland [Cubs general manager] called me up to his office and told me that they liked me, that they wanted to keep me in the organization, but that none of Leo's coaching staff would be brought back next year. Now, when I took the job with Leo I knew I'd be second in command, but I thought that if I did a good job I'd be able to stay in the big leagues. I was naive in that regard. It's a tight fraternity. It's a friend-takes-care-of-friend type of business. It doesn't matter how good a job you do or how hard you work: if you don't have friends you ain't got a chance. But I didn't know that then, and I had worked my tail off. Leo often said that he couldn't have made it through the year without me. But when Leo was gone, new people came in and I was back to nothing, back to square one.

Holland said he wanted me to scout for the Cubs and then manage their rookie team in the Gulf Coast League. He thought that he was doing me a favor; most folks have to go out and find their own jobs when a manager is fired. But the new job put me back in the minor league system where I was no longer answering to John Holland. The minor league director was fairly new. He had no idea of my background and had no feelings for me.

The next two years I scouted for the Cubs. I had Georgia, Florida, and Alabama. I'd be on the road for the high school and college season, from February through May. Occasionally I'd come back and say hi to my wife and baby before I would have to be off again. That put a strain on my marriage. After the free-agent draft in June, which meant the end of the amateur scouting season for me, I'd report to Bradenton, Florida, to manage the Cubs rookie team in the Gulf Coast League.

Having been a pitching coach, I was now learning to be a manager for the first time. There was a lot more paperwork and I had a different kind of relationship with the players. I had to keep some distance from them, whereas when I was the pitching coach I could joke with them and get closer to them. And I didn't mind if they took a few liberties. But a manager can't do that. I was somewhat hotheaded back then, as most young managers are, and I had some difficulty with umpires. When an umpire made a call that didn't go my way, I often felt that he was screwing me. I had a lot of maturing to do.

In 1975, midway through the season, the Cubs asked me to take over the Key West team in the Florida State League. That assignment brought the end of my relationship with not only the Cubs but also with my wife.

We had a player on the team who got $90,000 bonus money. The farm director wanted him to bat third. When I took over the club I pulled out all the stats and saw that this kid had struck out 56 times in 68 at bats, all the time being third in the lineup. The team was losing 3–2, 2–1, 4–3. I kept the lineup that the other manager had been using, and this kid night after night was striking out. So about the fourth night I moved him down to eighth and put somebody who could help the club in the third spot, somebody who I thought was a prospect as well. He drove in some runs and we got a couple of wins. Then the farm director called me and said he wanted his kid batting third. I asked why. And he said that it didn't make any difference. I told him that if he wanted me to run the ball club, then I must have some say in the batting order for these kids to have a chance to win. He said, "You play them like I tell you to play them." We had some pretty strong words. I said he needed a robot, not a manager. He said, "If you value your job . . ." And I said I don't, that I would be glad to leave today if he could find somebody to replace me. And if not, then I would stay for the rest of the season but that I wasn't going to work for him anymore.

As far as my wife was concerned, my being in Key West was like me being in Cuba. It was far away and I didn't see her and the baby much. My wife started saying, "It's time you get a real job. How much longer are you going to be away from home? When can you be home with us?" That put a real guilt trip on me because I knew I should be there with them. No one can be a father and be away all the time.

The season was just awful. We went 12 and 57 the rest of the season. The only thing that could have turned that team around would have been Jesus himself coming back to earth. To get to the other towns, we had to travel back and forth across forty different bridges over more than 50 miles. That really took its toll. We'd get in at three in the morning, and the next day we'd be off again. After awhile the players lost interest in playing. It was a real struggle to keep them positive and to get them to work.

That season cost me my marriage. As soon as I got home, we got divorced. All the things that I had loved most in life: my wife, my child, and baseball had all become a nightmare. None of it fit anymore. I was twenty-eight years old and I felt like my life was a total failure. I went to take my life three or four different times. I couldn't deal with the fact that I was a failure. I had a son that was not yet two years old and he was gone. And I was a guy who wanted to have twelve kids and live on a farm. Several times I got in my truck—I'd had my insurance made out to my son so he could go to college—and with tears running down my face I'd start going 100 miles an hour over a bridge, so it would look like an accident. But I couldn't do it. I couldn't go over. I'd park in the woods somewhere and cry it all out. I went from a healthy 200-pound guy to 145 pounds trying to deal with my life. I blame baseball for all of that.

I decided to get out of baseball totally and never to get back in. I took a job teaching physical education at an elementary school. For a while I thought that this was where I really belonged. But when the baseball season came along, being out of the game began to gnaw at me. I started getting an itch to be back on the ball field.

Then I got a call from a junior college in Andalusia, Alabama, that wanted to start a baseball program. It sounded interesting; and besides, my ex-wife and kid had moved back to her hometown in Montgomery, Alabama, so I wouldn't be that far away from my son. The next year, the Yankees called me about working for them in the summer, coaching Oneonta in the New York–Penn League [a short-season A league]. I was paying child support and my salary wasn't particularly good. I needed the money, so I got back in with both feet. I drove from Alabama to New York. The countryside up there was beautiful. It was real country, and I'd ride around up in the hills. It had a strong German influence and also close-knit Italian folks, which you don't have in the South. I was around the community a lot, and the folks enjoyed my southern accent. A lot of them thought that I was putting it on. And then when I went back to Alabama at the end of the year, folks there thought that I was talking like a Yankee. That's how diverse the two languages are.

In Oneonta I lived with a family—Sam and Alice Nader—and became very close to them. My son would come up for the summers, and they were like grandfather and grandmother to him. Alice was always there to help me and to take care of my son when I was at the ballpark. When he was old enough, my son became our batboy. Once a week we'd have a big cookout, with hot dogs and pizza, in their backyard for all the players. It was a family thing, and it made those summers extremely enjoyable.

After playing and coaching in leagues and having to go on really long road trips, Oneonta was nice. Since it was kind of central, our furthest trip was to Jamestown; five hours was the longest we had to go. It made me think that maybe baseball had changed, that they [front-office management] were trying to make life more enjoyable for the kids [players]. I was the pitching coach [at Oneonta] and the front office wasn't telling me how to coach or who to pitch. The manager and I made the decisions. Things were working out really well. We won the championship in 1977.

The next year the president of my college in Alabama asked me if I could stay for the summer and help with financial aid. I said that I would, but all summer long I was knocking my head against the wall thinking that I should be on the ball field. It was a long summer for me. So after that year I went back up to Oneonta in '79, '80, and '81. Then the Yankees asked me if I would go full time. Baseball had been

Ballplayers in the dugout. (Photo by Darren Mrak)

good to me during this period, so I accepted. In 1984 I was moved up to Triple A to Columbus [International League] and was considered Yogi Berra's guy at the Triple A level. He took me to spring training every year to be with the pitchers and help out.

Those years with the Yankees were extremely enjoyable. They [front office] left you alone. They wanted to win at the minor league level and they let you coach the way you thought best. At the top, Steinbrenner would hire and fire new guys every year, but at the lower end of the totem pole—especially in A ball—he didn't have much effect. They let us go about our business of trying to develop the kids. When I got up to Triple A, I started to feel the heat from Steinbrenner's changes at the top. To remain on his good side you had to be a puppet. Whatever he said or did or wanted, you had to say yes. Steinbrenner drew power from the fact that he had money. He wanted everyone around him to be subservient. Billy Martin, although most people see him as a hothead, kissed Steinbrenner's butt over and over. Billy always made peace with him and did what he wanted. Yogi [Berra] wouldn't do that. I was at a meeting once where Yogi kicked a chair through the wall of a hotel room when he got angry at something Steinbrenner said.

The end of my association with the Yankees came in 1985. Columbus was having a good year; we were tied for first place. Then one day in July I walked into the clubhouse and Stump Merrill, the manager, said I had a phone call. It was the director of the farm system. He was very cold on the phone. He told me that George [Steinbrenner] had decided that I should be replaced. I was in total shock. At first I thought that it was a joke, since I knew the farm director and we often joked around. He said that he was serious. I asked why, and he said that he couldn't discuss that. I asked him what this meant, and he said it meant that I didn't have a job anymore. To this day I'm not sure exactly what happened. The only thing that I can figure is that I was considered part of Yogi's crew. When Yogi was fired, Billy Martin [the new manager] wanted Yogi's people gone. Steinbrenner let Billy have his way, and that meant me and some others lost our jobs. There were people in the front office who should have stood up for me and said, "QV is not Yogi's man or anyone's man. He is a Yankee's man." They betrayed me by not standing up and saying that.

Anyway, I was still on the phone with the farm director, and I said "Okay, I'll finish up tonight." "No," he said, "we don't need you in the uniform anymore." I told Stump [the manager] that I would go to my apartment, get my things packed, and come back to the ballpark to tell the kids good-bye. I remember Stump saying that I didn't need to come back to the clubhouse. I said, "What do you think I'm going to do—put a bomb in the clubhouse? These are not only my players, they are my friends." I came back to the ballpark and watched the last five or six innings in the stands. By now the fans had heard the news and many were upset about it. I wanted to sit there like a man and take it. Newspaper and TV people came up and talked to me. At the end of the game I went to the clubhouse. I especially wanted to see Jim Deshaies, whom I had coached since A ball in Oneonta. He had pitched that night. He'd just come off the DL [disabled list] and pitched a one-hitter for seven innings and got the win. When I went to the locker room, he had saved the game ball for me and hugged me. I told the guys goodbye. I had tears, and they had tears. It was very difficult for me. I got in my car and headed south. I had to get home and get myself together. After all these years of baseball, here I was leaving again, being fired for no fault of my own. I felt betrayed by people who had been my friends, or had pretended to be my friends over the years.

I got home and got together with my son. He cried, and I had to go over all of that again with him. I still found it hard to see the positive side of it. I tried to console myself with the thought that I was now at home and would be able to watch my son play ball for the first time. I could be part of his season.

But I wasn't home long when I got a call from Montreal. The Expos wanted to know if I would be interested in being the pitching coach at Jamestown [New York–Penn League]. They told me that I would first have to get my release from the Yankees. When I asked for it, the Yankees told me that they wouldn't give it to me, that Steinbrenner didn't actually fire me, and that he was going to reassign me. Pure bull. I told him that I would never go back and work for the Yankees again. When the Yankees still wouldn't let me go to work for Montreal, I called the commissioner's office. They stepped in and made the Yankees give me my release. So three weeks after I'd left Columbus to go south, I was driving north, right through Columbus on the way to Jamestown. Very strange, but it did patch up my ego.

In some ways going from Triple A down to A ball was good too. The kids at that level need you a lot more. They are just getting into pro ball and they have a very big adjustment to make and are not at all certain if they can do it. They need you to help them through it. The high school player has never been away from home before. He starts to rely on the telephone, calling back to mom and his girlfriend, who he worries may be seeing someone else. He runs up a $500 telephone bill before he knows it. The college kid has already been away from home, so he has gone through all this before and is finished with it. But for the high school kid this is the first time away, and he is like a tiger out of a cage. He doesn't understand what's out there. He is liable to get into drinking and gambling. He doesn't have to answer to mom or dad. I've seen a lot of kids who couldn't handle the freedom. You need to talk to them, set them straight, put some sense into their heads. Most kids [rookies] are receptive to everything that we talk about, and that made me feel more important.

The Triple A players, guys who had been playing five, six, or seven years, think that they have all of the answers, so it's more difficult to help them. As they move up, they rely less and less on you. By the time they get to the big leagues, they are making one or two million dollars a year—and the manager is making a tenth of that, while the coaches are only making 40 to 50 thousand. Well, it's an entirely different re-

QV Lowe, manager, Jamestown Expos, 1991.

lationship. It's the players that put people [fans] in the park; at that
level [Triple A], some players have more clout than the coach. In a dispute, it might be the player who stays and the manager or coach who
goes. When players have that kind of clout, you lose a lot of your control over them. You just hope that you get good kids that respect you
for the man that you are and for the job that you do.

Here [in the New York–Penn League] I am managing kids who are entering their first season of pro ball. I like to form my own opinions about them. I don't want to know what round they were drafted in. I don't want the farm director telling me how much [money] the kid got. Most of the time, I don't even want to see the scout's report. I don't want anyone coloring my opinion of a kid before I get a chance to look at him carefully myself. I've seen an awful lot of kids who got big money and didn't go anywhere, and a lot of kids who didn't get any money but made it all the way to the big leagues. I don't want my mind to be confused by a scouting report that says that his character or work habits aren't good but that he has a good arm. In pro ball people are quick to put labels on kids. Pro ball is very big on labels. I cringe when someone labels a kid "gutless," a "pussy," or whatever. I can't stand it. Let me decide for myself. Let me look the kid over and see what direction we need to go in. At the first meeting I tell the kids that I won't make any changes [in how they play] until I've had a really good look at them. I want the pitchers to pitch the same way that they did wherever they were before they came here. For their first two or three times out [pitching], I tell them to do what they've always done, then we'll review the situation. I never tell a kid that he must change; I only make suggestions that he can accept or reject. It is his decision. He can try what I suggest and if it doesn't work out, we will try something else.

I want them to enjoy the summer but also to understand that pro ball is very different from college ball. I tell them that we will have to make decisions that may not be aimed at helping the team win, but that we must do them because the front office expects certain things. I tell them that we [coaches and managers] have to follow orders just like they have to follow orders from us. There is a chain of command and the orders always flow down. We try to explain what the season is all about. We tell them that we would like to win a championship and that our main purpose is for them to get better and to go out and do the best they can, so we can see where they stand and what their chances are of playing in the big leagues. That's our primary purpose for being here, and that's hard for some of them to understand, coming from college or high school ball where winning was everything.

I tell the pitchers we have ten or eleven of them on the staff and that all of them aren't going to be able to pitch often enough to stay sharp.

Most of the pitchers were starters in college or high school, and now some of them are going to the bullpen. That's a big change. It's difficult for them to learn to get up, get loose quick, and come through in tough situations. You've got to teach them that once you get loose, you back off and play easy catch. You don't take everything out of your arm all at once so that you can't pitch again tomorrow night. All these lads were stars in high school or college and now some are on the bench or in the bullpen. That's difficult for them.

It is a big adjustment for the hitters too—especially switching from aluminum to wood bats. It takes a while for kids to make the changeover. Some never do. But the biggest adjustment is playing every day. When you play every day, week after week, for an entire season, you've really got to discipline yourself—to stay in shape, eat right, and to get to bed at a decent hour. You can't stay up playing poker or running around till four or five in the morning chasing women and sleeping till two the next afternoon. If you do, you'll be sluggish and you won't perform well. You tell them that they need to get some fresh vegetables, green salad, and all that, but you still see a lot of kids eating burgers and fries all the time. It's like a mother or father talking to a child; you can tell them all you want but that doesn't mean it's going to sink in. It takes them a while to catch on. I feel good that today we at least try to offer the kids some guidance. When I first came into the game, you only had a manager. There was no hitting coach or pitching coach or anything. You were pretty much left on your own. Either you did it or you didn't, and the manager didn't care much if you were out all night. He didn't check curfew, he didn't explain how the system worked, and often he didn't much care.

Today we are also doing a better job of controlling our ballplayers. We tell them to clean out the bus so it won't be a mess when we get off, and that we will check their hotel rooms and make sure that they've picked up the papers and cleaned up after themselves. Years ago bus companies wouldn't rent to ball clubs and hotels wouldn't let teams stay there. When I started out at Lodi, we never stayed at a nice hotel. You had three or four guys to a room, stacked in, in cheap, crummy hotels with pull-out sofas and roll-away beds, the cheapest things you could rent. Now, by controlling our ballplayers, we stay in nice hotels and travel in good buses. We make sure that our players aren't rowdy, that they are not up until the wee hours making noise, tearing up the place, and waking up other guests.

Most of the kids come from college where they've been kept busy with their classes, homework, and practice in the afternoons. Here they've got a lot of free time and that can be a problem. Many of them don't know what to do with that free time, and a lot make the wrong decisions. They spend it chasing women and hanging out in bars. They think chasing women and booze is the way it is in pro ball. They don't want to do it, but they get drawn into it and the next thing they know they're hooked. Some of them never get out. I tell them that there are more good ballplayers taken down by their nightlife or their drinking, than by anything else.

The kids also have to learn how to deal with umpires. In pro ball you see the same umpires over and over. You can question a call but you've got to do it in the right way, without making the umpire look bad. If you show them up, they are never going to forget it. So don't do it. The basic philosophy is you catch more flies with sugar than salt.

You've also got to help kids through their slumps. All players have slumps, but kids coming into pro ball often have a more difficult time with them because they haven't been in pro ball long enough to have had much success and to know they'll come out of it. The rookie is not yet sure that he has the tools to play pro ball, even though he might have been a great college player. When he goes into a slump, he gets down on himself much more than the Double A player. At the Double A level the kid can remember back to when he was successful; he can say to himself, "I may be struggling now but I've been successful in the past and there is no reason why I can't get that back." But the first-year kid here has not yet been successful in pro ball, so he starts thinking that he doesn't deserve to be here. He starts thinking that maybe he was successful in college because they used aluminum bats, or because the hitters weren't as good. Soon it becomes a mental thing. The more he lets himself get beat mentally, the deeper the slump is going to get and the more difficult it is to pull out of it. Slumps are natural, everyday occurrences in baseball, just like the sun going up and down. If he carries on, he will eventually work his way out of it. But if he starts worrying, starts dwelling on it, it will only get worse. We've got a kid on this club [Jamestown Expos] who hit .400 for Wichita State, played on a couple of College World Series teams, and he hasn't had a hit in the month of July. I see him with his head down, thinking his baseball career is over. I'm trying to stay positive with him, but his head is in a hole. He never hears you. He is so mired in self-pity that he's not hearing anything. He's not wanting to hear anything. The total dream that he has had all his life is coming apart. You do your best, but sometimes it's really hard to reach a kid when he is in that state.

Every organization has rules governing the behavior, conduct, and dress of its players. It's the manager and coach's responsibility to communicate those rules to the players at the start of each season— especially to the new players. Then you have to enforce the rules. For example, we have a curfew—1:00 A.M. when we're playing at home and two hours after the game when we're on the road. So if they leave the clubhouse at 11:30, then they have got to be in their rooms by 1:30. We have a dress code—collared shirts, long pants, and no sandals when we're on the road. We have a clean-shaven rule: you can have a mustache but otherwise no facial hair. And, of course, there are rules for things like throwing a helmet. If you throw a helmet down hard enough that it bounces and could hurt somebody, it will cost you 10 dollars and I'll take you out of the game. Our starting catcher the other day, in a tie game, tossed a helmet and I took him out.

And there is to be no foul language where the fans can hear it. We don't want you using the F-word or the G-D word or something that is unacceptable to society, at least not where the fans can hear it. No women in your room or that will cost you $50. And one of our big rules is being on time. I'm especially strict on that. The other day I had two kids come in ten minutes late—that was $50 a piece. I said, "Fellows, I'm not going to fool around with you. Every manager expects you to be on time. We stretch as a unit. So if you are late you're going to miss out, and we can't allow that." I don't like to have to fine the kids, but it is important that we live by the rules. I tell them right up front: "I won't ever be taking you out of a game, but if you break the rules you will be taking yourself out of the game. I'm not fining you, you are fining yourself." It's very simple. Most kids understand the rules and it's not too often that we have a problem.

At this level, coaches and managers throw a lot of BP [batting practice]. You try hard to have every hitter come out of the cage like he is the best hitter in the world. You want to build up his confidence and have him carry that attitude into the ball game. BP is not like pitching where you are trying to get movement on every pitch you throw. In BP you want to straighten things out, make it easier for the batter to bust the ball out of the park. You don't want to fool the hitter the way you do when you pitch. It's just the opposite; it makes you feel good when the guys hit everything hard. When a hitter is having trouble handling a particular pitch, like low and away, we'll work on that in a special session but not in pregame BP. In BP you want to pitch to their strength. You want them to leave the cage thinking that they are good hitters.

I'm not a big meeting guy. Except for our daily postgame meeting to review the game, I have gotten the team together only twice this year for one of those speeches where you say that you think they're much better than they're showing, and that if they want to stay in pro ball and make the big leagues, then they're going to have to do things differently and work harder. Mostly I try to be positive and pick them up as much as I can. My managing philosophy is a lot like that of Walter Alston [former Los Angeles Dodgers manager]. He was a low-key manager that let his team play; he didn't act like he was the only one who could win or lose a game, like Billy Martin did. Billy thought that he—not the players—was the guy who was solely responsible for winning or losing. Walter Alston knew better.

One of the big frustrations in managing in the minor leagues is not having control, not being able to make the moves and play the kids that you need to win, and not being able to do the things that you know are best for the kids. We had a kid out there on the mound last night, a kid to whom we [Expos] had given lots of money. He gave up six runs in the first inning and was really struggling. I took him out in the fourth and put in a kid I thought could give us a chance to win. We did win. But then the front office gets on me for not giving the bonus kid one hundred pitches. I know that it's important that the kid get his pitches in, but it is also important to the rest of us that the team plays well, that we have a chance to win. I speak from experience, from having been on losing teams where morale got so bad that kids lost their desire to play. You take a great player and a team that always loses and after a while he is going to feel like a loser himself. Besides, it doesn't do the kid any good psychologically to leave him on the mound when he is getting shelled. But the front office isn't here. They can't see the whole situation. They only see the damn numbers. So many times I have seen organizations make decisions with no regard to the kid, almost as if his welfare didn't even cross their minds. There is too much of the [front office] dictating things from a distance.

The single most difficult task in all of pro ball is having to release a player. I'd rather take a beating than have to release someone. It is devastating to you and to the player. All kids are crushed; they feel like their life is over. I have worried that every kid I've ever released would run out of the office and commit suicide. Generally, you do it in a private, closed room—your office or the coach's office. I try not to let it go on too long, but you can't cut it too short either. I try to put a good face on. I tell the kid that there is no need for him to hang around in this game not making much money and not having a chance to be successful, and that the best thing is to go out and get a job and get on with his life. I never tell him that he couldn't play. I might tell him that he doesn't fit into this organization, which is often the case, but I would never tell him that he can't play. There have been too many that have hooked on with somebody else and made it all the way to the big leagues.

After I tell him, he goes into the clubhouse and packs up his gear. The other players usually try to console him, shake his hand, that comradely thing. When one of their own has been wounded, most will try to soothe his feelings. They will say something like, "Hey man, give me a call when you get back home." Or they'll tell him that he is lucky now that he can go home and go fishing and lead a normal life. But they don't really mean it; they are just trying to help ease his feelings. They feel sorry for him, but they're really glad it wasn't them. The organization gives the kid a plane ticket home. It's best that he leave the same day. You don't want him going out that night, drinking to drown his sorrows, and getting into trouble. That's when something gets torn up and you've got real problems. So it is best to get him out of town the same day you release him.

Most released players try to catch on with another team, but it's awfully difficult. It may be a month or so before they realize that it's hopeless and that it's time for them to get on with their lives. Some of them will go a year trying to hook on with another organization, and some do. But 90 percent don't go far; usually the decision was right in the first place.

I now earn a pretty good living between my college job and coming up here to coach in the summer. But I've come a long way. In 1984 I was making $14,000 a year as a Triple A pitching coach, and in 1986 I was making $16,000 as a Double A coach with the Expos. I asked the guy [in the front office] if he could live on $16,000 a year. He said, "No." I said, "Well, then, how do you expect me to live off of that?" He said, "All I can tell you is that I have a long list of guys who want your job." That's how they always do it in baseball. They always tell you that they have nine thousand resumes of guys who want your job, who will take my job at the salary I am getting now. That's why in 1986 I quit being full-time and accepted the coaching job at the Auburn University in Montgomery. Until a few years ago, most organizations treated you worse than a construction worker. They wanted you to think that what you did was nothing so that you'd be happy with the money they offered. There were some exceptions, like the Dodgers, who always took care of their people, paid them well, and flew their families down for spring training. Most organizations are better now, but they still have a long way to go. They've got to start realizing that to keep good coaches, they have to start paying them better. They've got to start realizing that good coaches aren't just baseball men. At this level [Class A], we are guidance counselors too. We help the kids with their lives, not just their baseball.

At the end of the year I have to write up a report on each player for the front office. I grade each player: definite major league prospect, chance or fringe prospect, a "hold," which means a blank, and no prospect. Every kid gets put into one of those categories at the end of the season. He can change categories the next year by playing better, or he might be graded lower if he plays worse. Of the twenty-one players on last year's team, we probably had five or six of whom we categorized as definite major league prospects, about four or five who were chance or fringe prospects, and most guys in the hold category, which means that it is too soon to tell. And then we had two or three guys who we labeled no prospect and who were released out of spring training. I have to explain the grade or categorization to each player. In grading a player, I discuss each of the five skills—running, fielding, throwing, hitting, hitting with power—and I talk about his character and his mentality, and all the things that you've gotten to know about him over the season that contribute to your assessment.

⚾

EPILOGUE

At the end of the following season, QV told the Montreal Expos that he would not be coming back. The long bus trips were "killing" his back, and coaching a full college season on top of his duties for the Expos in the New York–Penn League was causing him to feel burned out. He said, "I find myself complaining about a lot of things, and that's not like me. I don't like the person I'm becoming, so maybe it's time to stop, to take a leave of absence for a while." QV thinks he will return to managing for the Expos, but he is firm about never working full-time in pro ball again. "At the college level you have some security and you can have a life apart from the game. In pro ball, when the front office changes, so do the personnel up and down the line. Having been fired for absolutely nothing that I did wrong has made me a little scared. You want to feel that if you do your job and work hard, that you will be taken care of, that it won't be taken away from you. But it's hard to find that security in professional baseball."

Mark Letendre

TRAINER, SAN FRANCISCO GIANTS

Every ball club has its own physician, often an orthopedic specialist, who cares for serious injuries but does not travel with the team nor is present in the ballpark when injuries occur. However, the athletic trainer is the first line of diagnosis and injury care. He is also the supervisor of the team's strength and conditioning program and one of the least noticed team members on the field. All that the average fan knows about trainers is that they wear white pants or shirts and run out to administer first-aid when a player gets hurt during the game. Yet, as Mark Letendre's narrative reveals, the trainer's role is critical to the team's health and success. He oversees the conditioning of the players to enhance their performance and to reduce the likelihood of injury. When injuries do occur, he provides immediate treatment and then, with the help of the team physician, prescribes a rehabilitation program to speed recovery and get the player back into the lineup.

Athletic trainers are the only ones in the dugout who must have college training. Today, most are also certified by a national board. Like Paul Zwaska, the Oriole's head groundskeeper, Mark Letendre reached the pinnacle of his profession at a young age, becoming the head trainer of the San Francisco Giants at age twenty-nine.

I came from a large Catholic family in Manchester, New Hampshire, and sports were a major diversion for us. Manchester was a mill town, so it wasn't known much for culture. Either you played sports or you worked. I was a gym rat. I got involved in sports early, through the Catholic Youth Organization and later the Boy's Club. I really liked playing sports, but by the time I got to high school, I wasn't physically able to compete because of my size.

How I got into sports medicine really goes back to my sophomore year in high school when I hung around the gymnasium a lot. One day a PE teacher who was busy taping an athlete before a football practice challenged me to give it a try. It wasn't as easy as it looked, but I kind of liked it. It was a challenge to be able to do it right. That summer I decided to attend an athletic-training youth clinic at Northeastern University in Boston, and there I learned the minimal skills of being a trainer. When I went back to high school in the fall, I volunteered to be the student manager-trainer for the football, basketball, and baseball teams. By the end of the school year I had gained enough experience to know that training was something I wanted to do. At that time, athletic training, although it had been around for more than twenty years, was just beginning to be recognized as a health profession. People were just beginning to realize how much it could contribute to athletics. I knew this was what I wanted.

☙

The following summer Letendre attended another clinic for athletic training, this time at the University of Maine. There he met Wes Jordan, a leading figure in the field. The University of Maine offered Letendre a scholarship. Each summer during college, Mark worked in the university's athletic training room. By his senior year, he had set up his own training program at a local high school in Orono, Maine, and volunteered to be the school's trainer. It was other voluntary work that eventually got him his first job in professional baseball. When his hometown hosted the American Legion World Series in 1976, Mark returned to New Hampshire and volunteered to be the trainer. He was seen by Pete Gebrean of the New York Mets, who offered him a position as trainer for the Mets' farm club in the New York–Penn League. Mark declined but began to think that a baseball life could be exciting. After graduating from the University of Maine, he was hired by the New York Yankee organization on the recommendation of

*Stump Merrill, who had seen him work as a trainer in American Le-
gion baseball.*

⚉

Fortunately the Yankees didn't have a lot of certified trainers in the minor leagues. I had just taken my certification exam when Stump became the manager of the Yankees Double A team in West Haven, Connecticut. Stump went to bat for me and I was hired as their trainer,
fresh out of college. My family has this guardian-angel theory about
me always being in the right place at the right time. It does seem like I
have always gotten good direction from people. The following year,
the Yankees' trainer at the Triple A level—Columbus, Ohio—got a job
in the big leagues, and the Yankees decided to move everybody up one
notch. So I wound up in Columbus in 1979, and three years later I
was summoned to the big leagues to be the assistant trainer under
Gene Monahan. Three years later, in 1985, the new management of
the San Francisco Giants cleaned house and fired their two trainers.
After some phone calls by my boss, Gene Monahan, to an old Yankee
colleague, Al Rosen, who was the new GM [general manager] in San
Francisco, I was offered the head trainer's position with the Giants.
[While most major league teams carry two trainers—a chief and an assistant—the San Francisco Giants, following the example of the National Football League, has a team of three trainers.]

Unlike years ago, most of today's players realize trainers' importance to their careers. They know that good care can not only improve
their performance but also extend their careers. A guy in the early
1980s who had rotator-cuff surgery was destined for the scrap pile.
Today we can bring him back and maybe keep him out there so that
he is able to play longer. With the average salary over a million dollars
a year, if he plays an extra year that is big money for him.

There is a lot more to baseball than meets the eye. When an injury
occurs the trainer usually understands the mechanics of how it happened, which is one reason one of us is always on the bench watching
every play. I don't watch the game in the same way as the players,
coaches, or spectators. For example, if there is a slide at second base
on a double-play ball, my eyes may linger on the slide rather than
looking to see if the throw beats the runner at first, because on that
play if there is an injury it's most likely to be on the slide. Trainers are
just conditioned to watch the game in that way; even when I am a

spectator at a sporting event I find myself doing the same thing. I remember an incident in 1989 after we had just defeated the Cubs to go to the World Series. Everyone was running onto the field, and out of the corner of my eye I saw Dusty Baker holding someone. It was Dave Dravecky who in the player celebration had gotten thrown into the pile and refractured his arm. Those are the types of things that are almost a sixth sense for trainers.

I had some great teachers. Tony Bartirome of the Pittsburgh Pirates taught me that the eyes are windows of the soul in more ways than one. If a pitcher is injured, I will run out to the mound and stand at 45 degrees to him. I scope right into the eyes, because if he is pain he will either wince, tear, or blink. There will be something unusual going on in the eyes. I have always used that as a diagnostic tool and it has never let me down. Even the best warriors who will fib to stay in the game cannot conceal what their eyes show.

Trainers often say they look for little odd behaviors or idiosyncrasies that are not usual to a player. Say there is a second baseman who usually taps his mitt three times but all of a sudden he stopped tapping it, and he had recently got jarred at second base. To me, that is a possible hint that something is going on. Or an outfielder may have run down a ball in the alley; he is typically a guy who sets his leg up parallel in the outfield before the pitch but now his legs are staggered. That tells me that perhaps one of his leg muscles was slightly pulled and that he is trying to compensate for it. Or, take the catcher who just got a foul tip off his foot. I'll watch how he throws because if he starts favoring the foot that was not hit, he may jeopardize the integrity of his shoulder or his elbow. So at the onset of any injury, you have to think about what the possible ramifications may be.

The manager always has the ultimate say in who comes out of the game because of an injury, but usually it is a decision by committee. We provide the medical information that the manager and the player need in order to make an intelligent decision. We kind of walk the manager through the equation as best we can. If it is a broken bone, it is pretty obvious what you do. But usually it's not that clear cut. In today's game, with the tremendous salaries, there is a lot of pressure to keep the athlete on the field for as long as possible. Even playing at 80 percent, Barry Bonds may be better than his backup who is playing at 100 percent. If we can give the coaching staff the knowledge that Barry is going to be only 80 percent, but with little risk of reinjuring

Mark Letendre tending to injured Barry Bonds. (Courtesy of the San Francisco Giants/Stanton)

whatever the ailment is, then the manager can make an intelligent de-cision. At no time do we get into this godlike complex of the medical profession where we think we have all the answers. We don't.

If there is any doubt about the seriousness of the injury, you err on the side of conservatism. You always try to think of the player first, but you also have to look at it objectively. And sometimes you need to ask yourself if the guy has some psychological hang-up. Does he have a fear of failure, for example? Say it's the eve of a rubber game of a very important series with the Braves. We are one game out, and the player is the pitcher for the next day, but all of a sudden his arm is cranky. Once in a while it may be something more than the arm. Maybe it's in his head. I've seen athletes go to the brink of stardom and hit a wall. It's like they don't want to break that barrier. They're great ballplayers. They have the world by the balls. And yet when they get to that threshold, they just can't go any further. They chalk it up to injury. To me an injury should always have a medical component, but sometimes it's just not there.

Each day I give a written report to the manager and coaches concerning the injury situation and who might need a rest. We also keep a record of the treatments that we are giving each player. They're pretty detailed because the records could be subpoenaed in a court of law—say, if there was a grievance by a player—or someone wants to consult them when considering a trade for a player. The industry is now working on a standardized medical information form to be used for all players by all teams, so that when a player moves to another team, his record will go with him and it will be the same one used by everybody.

Every day as I drive to work I try to collect my thoughts about the day's work. I know we're going to have X amount of treatments. In the case of an injury, I am going to have to deal with the media, the front office, and maybe somebody's wife or agent, as well as the coaching staff, the manager, and the player himself. Often you are dealing with an injured player who really wants to be in the lineup. It's always been important to me to be truthful. With the injured player, I want to walk him through what would happen to his injury if he were to play. I explain to him in layman's terms the diagnosis and the potential problems if he were to play on it. I take into account how the injury is going to affect the stability of the team. For example, if he is a team leader, we may need to keep him playing. These are some of the daily challenges that I deal with.

When I first came to the Giants, the biggest thing I thought we needed was more attention given to conditioning. The athletes that were left over from the previous year were poorly conditioned. It wasn't that they didn't want to work, but that the Giants simply didn't have the technology and equipment needed. I wanted to put a system in place that would bring the best of every possible discipline to the job of looking after the players. If you cut down on injuries and treatment time, then everybody wins. Fortunately, Al Rosen, the general manager, was progressive and gave me the freedom to do what I thought we needed. The result is that today we have a training team that includes a physical therapist, Stan Conte; an assistant trainer, Barney Nugent; and myself. Most major league clubs only have two trainers. Most don't have a full-time physical therapist.

While trainers know the mechanics of injuries and how to care for and prevent them, physical therapists have extensive medical background in rehab. They were in medicine long before trainers came along. In fact, for a long time trainers and physical therapists were at opposite ends of the health spectrum, and they never saw eye to eye. They're still territorial creatures. But when they leave their egos at the door and work together on a project—on a player—the results can be phenomenal. Here the three of us put our heads together to formulate a treatment plan for the player, and sometimes it involves other disciplines, such as chiropractic care or psychological care. By collaborating, we expand the size of our medical tool chest. You might say we have more finesse today. We're no longer trying to drive in every nail with the same sledgehammer.

✺

When Letendre came to the Giants in 1985, he brought with him a training-room system that he had learned in the Yankee organization. Everything from Q-tips to liniment has a specific place. On a long table in the training room are a wide array of sprays, powders, ointments, and lotions, each in its own section. In one section, for example, all lined up perfectly parallel to one another are rubbing alcohol, tape remover, baby oil, peroxide, astringent, Listerine, medicated powder, baby powder, various anti-fungal potions, tape adherent, and collyrium for fresh eyes. Beside those are tongue depressors, various applicators, bandages, gauze, cotton, Q-tips, Band-Aids, plastic gloves, and even dental floss.

Also part of the training table is a row of sixteen different types of clippers, cutters, nail files, and scissors. The players learn to put things back exactly where they found them. "Mark's philosophy," explained assistant trainer Barney Nugent, "is that a training room that is disorganized, with stuff out of place, reflects on the staff and that affects the attitudes of the players toward the staff. Whereas if the training room is always organized, then the player knows he is going to get a systematic, organized approach to his injury."

The training room is busiest a few hours before batting practice, when the players come in for different treatments, such as moist-heat treatments, stretching routines, and liniment applications to loosen the muscles of pitchers. The activity and the trainers' workload lightens a bit as the game approaches and all the players have been treated and prepared to play. By the fourth or fifth inning the activity increases again as pitchers who have been relieved come in to get a full-arm massage, ice packs, and a reminder to eat correctly to help their bodies repair the microtrauma caused by pitching. Finally, there is a rush of work again as the game ends and all three trainers become occupied with evaluating old injuries and prescribing and administrating treatments.

I wondered if baseball organizations ever attempted to measure the job performance of their athletic trainers. Could they, for example, compare injury and rehabilitation rates of their personnel with those of other teams? Would that be an accurate indication of how well their trainers were doing their jobs?

⚾

Unfortunately for us, for years and years the Giants have been decimated by injuries far above the average. Lots of thought has been given to the cause of them. Most say it's the ballpark and the weather. We do sit down at the end of the season and look at what our most common injuries were. Some things you can't prevent—like Robby Thompson getting hit in the face by a Trevor Hoffman fastball. That's simply a part of the game and there is nothing we can do to prevent it. On the other hand, there are lots of preventable injuries such as muscle strains and foolish tendinitis from overuse. These are the things that we as medical professionals need to pay special attention to and ask why they are happening and what can we do to reduce them.

One thing we have done in San Francisco is to individualize our training programs. We no longer have a single generalized program for all twenty-five players. Rather, we have a program for each individual. You can't cookie cut baseball and get good results. Pitchers, for example, need good trunk stabilization to pitch. Outfielders, who need to be fleet of foot, require repetitive fast-speed work. And infielders need to develop lateral-movement capabilities.

West Palm Beach Expos training room. (Photo by Jason Getz)

It used to be that when the season ended the players went home to winter jobs to pay bills. They didn't do much to keep in shape, which is why spring training is so long. Today athletes don't need winter jobs. And with the free time they have during the winter, some of them over condition themselves. Some guys over develop the duty muscles— you know the big biceps, triceps, and big shoulders. These muscles don't have any place in baseball; that is not what baseball is about. Baseball is a worker's type of sport in that the actions are repetitive; it's not like football where you have one explosive type of action. It's our responsibility to make sure our guys don't ever overtrain these muscles. So we lay out a year-round conditioning program that is individualized to the person and sensitive to his weaknesses or deficiencies. We make sure that we don't add something to his program that he doesn't need.

Today strength, conditioning, and rehabilitation are all grouped together. You work on strength and conditioning to prevent injury but also to enhance performance. When a player gets injured, you start him on a rehab program that usually involves a progressive exercise program that not only repairs but strengthens the injured area and becomes part of a total-body conditioning program. A lot of times you'll talk to a player who has gone through rehab and he'll say, "Yeah, I learned these exercises when I hurt my shoulder, and I just keep doing them all the time now. They have actually helped my pitching even though I am no longer hurt." So you really can't separate the two.

Proper conditioning is important to the athlete as well as to everyone else—especially with so much money on the line these days and with the average major league career being just four years and seven months. Conditioning affects how long players are going to be in the big leagues and in a position to make a large salary.

✪

I was curious about what trainers do to encourage their players to eat properly and, in general, to adopt other fitness and health behaviors.

✪

It's hard to change an individual. I always say you can't change the animal in the jungle, but you can change the jungle a bit. We try to do that by providing more nutritious snacks, better airline food, and, especially, more fruits and vegetables in the postgame spread. Besides making fruit available in abundance, we also put out supplements that Gatorade provides for us. You try to avoid the saltier things like peanuts, potato chips, and any kind of processed meat or hot dogs with high fat content. Rehydration is also very important because when you get dehydrated your taste buds become suppressed and you don't have an appetite.

In terms of meals, we try not to let them beef up. If it's twelve o'-clock after a night game, we like them to have light pasta and then come back early in the morning for a nutritious breakfast. I won't say this happens all the time, but we try to do it ourselves and hope that they'll see our example. There are other little ways too. Like if I find a can of smokeless tobacco in the training room, you can bet that I'm not going to return it to the player. He'll never see that can again. If a player feels that tobacco is something that he needs, then I'm not going to stand in his way. But I do try to make it uncomfortable for the guy who comes in the training room with dip in his mouth. I don't want him to think that it is okay, but I'm not going to preach. I might let him know what happened to Don Zimmer and some of the others so that he realizes he is dealing with a demon.

As a trainer, you walk a thin line between management, and the players. You're part of management, but to do your job well you have to get close enough to the players to know what's going on in their lives. And that's where good listening comes in. It's really kind of a high-wire act because you owe it to management to keep them informed of what's going on in the players' lives, but at the same time the players have to know that they can tell you things in confidence, or they won't come to you.

I try to let the players know that the training room is not a pipeline to management. If they come to me with a problem, I'll help them solve it without going to management—unless the problem is going to affect the players life or his ability to play baseball. If the problem is going to be detrimental to the organization, then I'm obliged to go to management.

Sometimes a player will say to you, "I have to tell you something. But if I do, are you going to tell management?" I tell them that if they violated some rule, I would have to tell. If what they say is going to put the player in a bad situation, I might say, "Don't tell me, but let me help." That leaves the door open, and most times he'll say, "Okay, here's my situation . . ." But if he starts talking about illegal substances, then I have to say, "Wait a minute. If you are going to tell me what I think you are, then you need to understand what my responsibility is so you don't back yourself into a corner." I don't want him to think that I'm like a priest, that he can tell me whatever and it won't go any further. I can't guarantee that.

In my ten years with the Giants I've dealt with several ballplayers who had drug problems. Drugs are difficult because they are injurious not just to the player but also to his family. And by affecting the players' performance, they hurt the team as well. Usually I'll tell the player there are two routes to go: the first is for me to give him the phone number of the wellness coordinator; the second is for me to make the call on the player's behalf. I'll do whatever I can, but the player has to take responsibility. The player only has himself to worry about, while I have twenty-four other guys to look after, plus the coaching staff, who are all aging ex-players themselves with ailments of their own.

Part of being a trainer in the big leagues, unlike the minor leagues, is knowing how to deal with the media. They have a much bigger presence up here. You've got to have some understanding of the way the things you say are going to come out in the papers or on TV. You've got to think about how the front office is going to interpret what you say. Will you hear from the player's agent? Will his wife be upset with you? So you temper things. There are ways that you can give honest answers without divulging too much. Think how often you've heard the words "cautiously optimistic." The beat writers with the Giants often tease me because just before I'm going into my report, particularly if it is a sticky situation about an injured player, the writers will mimic me, saying: "day-to-day," "cautiously optimistic," or "We'll see how he is tomorrow;" and I'll just nod my head in agreement. I don't believe a trainer or doctor should be the focus of any newspaper article about a player—unless there is a catastrophe like a career-ending injury. As medical professionals, trainers shouldn't be looking for headlines. I didn't get into baseball looking to read my name in the paper. Actually, it's a bit of an embarrassment if I see my name too much because that means we're having an injury-filled year.

I have tremendous respect for the old-timers who did this job without the training and technology we have today. They did it all with their hands and their minds. There are still a lot of wonderful, very experienced old trainers around like Bill Buhler with the Dodgers; Gene Monahan with the Yankees; Dave Pursley with the Braves; and Jim Warfield with the Indians. Warfield's club had never sniffed third place until recently; I wonder how in August he is able to psychologically get his players out of the training room when you got guys using medical excuses to stay out of the lineup on a loosing team; or how Dave Pursley, who was with the Braves when they were in Milwaukee, is able to relate well with kids who are probably younger than his sons. I also wondered how Gene Monahan survived in the Yankee organization longer than anybody. Gene is the only one left from the day George Steinbrenner took over. I look at their careers and I know how much easier they've made my life as a trainer today.

I often draw upon my family for the strength to get through all the travails of baseball. We don't have a normal lifestyle but we do try to make the most of my off-season time. The job requires a tremendous amount of sacrifice on the part of your family. You ask a hell of a lot of them and that's true for anybody in baseball. When we're at the ballpark, it's easy to forget about the people at home who are nurturing and raising the kids, while paying attention to our careers and anguishing along with us. I was home sick with a virus for four days recently. It was humbling to be reminded that while I am in my own little world, my wife, Judy, runs the household twenty-four hours a day, 365 days a year, and never has a break. It reminded me that while baseball has an off-season, the life of someone who runs a household doesn't. In my moments of despair, I try to remind myself of that.

Bernie and Waleska Williams

CENTER FIELDER, NEW YORK YANKEES, AND
BALLPLAYER'S WIFE

This chapter, unlike others in this book, combines two narratives, that of husband and wife Bernabe "Bernie" and Waleska Williams. When I first interviewed Bernie Williams, the New York Yankee's center fielder, I was not expecting to interview his wife too. As Bernie made frequent references to his wife during the interview, saying that she might know more about a particular topic than he, the idea of including her emerged. By including Waleska, we could explore not only the life and work of a ballplayer but also its impact on his family.

Bernie and Waleska were both raised in Puerto Rico in middle-class families. Bernie's mother was a school principal and his father served in the merchant marines; Waleska's father was a businessman and her mother, a housewife. Waleska was educated at an exclusive private school, the Wesleyan Academy; Bernie attended Escuela Libre de Música High School, where he learned to play classical guitar, which aside from baseball is his passion. Bernie and Waleska met in biology class at the University of Puerto Rico, where they were both premed students. At that time, Bernie had just finished his second year in the Yankee organization and was attending college during the off-season.

Bernie, 6 foot 2 inches, is bright, sensitive, and soft-spoken. One reporter described him as the perfect opposite of the swaggering Deion

Sanders. His shy, quiet demeanor earned him the nickname "Bambi" from his Yankee teammates when he first arrived in the big leagues. At first some New York sportswriters thought him an unlikely heir to what is probably baseball's most glamorous position: center field, Yankee Stadium—the old turf of Joe Dimaggio and Mickey Mantle—for the highest-profile team in baseball, if not all professional sports, the New York Yankees. Bernie's performance has quelled all such doubts.

⚾

BERNIE WILLIAMS

When I was a little kid, the only thing I could do really well was run. But that really had some eyes looking out for me. You can always teach someone to throw and hit, but you can't really teach someone to run faster. When I was playing Little League I was always wanted because I could run fast, but I wasn't a star in any other way. I was never a power hitter and I didn't have an outstanding throwing arm. As I got older some of those skills began to develop. Around my second year in high school some scouts were beginning to watch me. And the next year, when I was a junior, I signed with the Yankees.

I didn't start playing professional baseball, however, until after I finished my senior year of high school in Puerto Rico. They [Yankees] sent me to Sarasota, Florida. I was just seventeen years old but making money—it was only $700 a month, but back then it seemed like a million.

Sarasota was all a shock at first. We lived in a motel down on Siesta Key, right on the beach. I slept a lot, watched a lot of TV, played the guitar, and didn't have much else to do except baseball. I wasn't old enough to go to bars. But we always had a lot of girls following us around. I didn't know anybody there. All my friends were either players or in baseball. I didn't have any contact with the real culture. Everything was baseball. It was a great experience, just being away from Puerto Rico, away from home for the first time. It was wonderful. I had all this time to myself. I didn't have anybody to account for in terms of the way I behaved. My parents were a thousand miles away.

I suppose I could have gone astray, but my mom and dad brought me up always stressing strong moral values. That upbringing is important when you find yourself in a place where you are by yourself and you have got to make choices between doing the right thing and

Bernie Williams at bat, 1995. (Photo by Steve Crandall)

doing the something that might be fun but not good for you in the
long run. I've had to make a lot of difficult choices in terms of hanging
out, drinking, drugs, staying out late, and not taking care of my body.
I think I've always been able to make the right the choices, and for
that I give a lot of credit to my parents. They always stressed our education first and sports second. We never had much leisure time to run

around and do bad things or hang around with the crowd and stuff like that. You might say I was raised in a shell.

For the first couple years in baseball I mostly hung around with Latino guys. Some of the them were older and had been in baseball a lot longer than me, but I knew the language [English] and could help them talk to coaches, order food in restaurants and talk with girls— stuff like, "This guy likes you very much and would like to meet you." Since they were older and had been around a lot longer than me they knew the system better and could help me there—like helping me to understand the importance of being on time. Americans, I discovered, like to stress being on time, and they take pride in it. That's not the way I was brought up in Puerto Rico. Down there you can be ten or fifteen minutes late or you can even postpone it to the next day. We are kind of relaxed about time. But here in the U.S. people come fifteen minutes before the time they have to be there. That took some adjusting for me. If practice starts at four o'clock, I want to come in here at twenty to four, just time enough to get ready and go out and do what I have to do. I don't like hanging around doing nothing. Some of the American guys here come in at noon and just do nothing until they have to be on the field. I would rather be home talking on the phone, reading a book, playing my guitar, watching TV, or doing just about anything other than sitting here doing nothing.

⚲

WALESKA WILLIAMS

In 1990, after his third year in the minor leagues, Bernie and Waleska married. Waleska, 5 foot 7 inches and thin, with dark eyes and a pretty face, speaks English with hardly an accent. On her first trip to America, she arrived in Albany, New York, in April 1990. She joined Bernie, who was playing there for the Double A Albany–Colonie Yankees.

⚲

We lived with this great lady, Maureen, who rented us a bedroom in her house. She was very nice to us and gave use of the whole house. Because we were a recently married couple, she would sometimes leave for the weekend so we'd have the whole house to ourselves. We're still friends with her and she has come down to Puerto Rico to visit.

In Albany, unlike here [Yankee Stadium], you have a lot of contact with the fans. It is very personal, and you get to know some of the fans who go day after day. I remember this lady named Marilyn, a die-hard Albany–Colonie fan, and there was a guy, Ed Haber, that used to call Bernie "Big Man." He still sends us Christmas cards. We made some really good friends in Albany and later in Columbus, too. But that changes when you move up to the big leagues. Up here, the fans look at ballplayers as something you don't touch.

Coming to the United States was easier for me than for some of the women from the Dominican Republic and other places in Latin America. The language wasn't a problem for me like it was for some of them. In Triple A, Columbus, one of the wives was from the Dominican Republic. I felt so bad for her. She had been a pediatrician at home, but because she didn't know the language here, she was so helpless. She felt so useless. Whenever the team was on the road, she had to depend on me because she couldn't even go and buy milk by herself. That is very hard. There were other women just like her. What are they supposed to do when their husbands are on the road for fifteen days if they didn't drive, don't speak the language, and don't know how to get groceries and stuff like that.

I really think the baseball organization should pay more attention to the players' families when they come from a different country. It's not only the player that has to get along in this country. He comes with a wife and sometimes kids. Some wives don't even come to the games because they don't understand the language. They could use some help in getting to know the area better too. It's hard to know where to live—for example, knowing which districts have good schools for your kids and which don't. When you make it easier for the wives, you make it better for the player too because it takes off some of the pressure at home.

🏀

BERNIE WILLIAMS

It was in Albany, 1990, Bernie and Waleska's first season together, that Bernie first realized he had a good chance at making the major leagues. He had made the Eastern League All-Star Team and was named by Baseball America's postseason poll as the second-best prospect in the Eastern League.

When you are talking about your chances of making the big leagues, there is a big difference between the guy who is a high draft pick and gets a million bucks and the kid like me who signs at seventeen years old for a whole lot less money. Of course every guy who signs thinks he is going to play in the big leagues someday. But the opportunity to get there isn't always equal. The guy the club has invested big money in is going to play every day no matter what, even if you have more ability than he does.

The other thing—in terms of your chances of getting to the big leagues—is who else is playing at your position. When I was starting out with the Yankees they had an outfield of Ricky Henderson, Dave Winfield, Gary Ward, and Mike Easler—some really big names. And in Triple A they had Roberto Kelly, Henry Cotto, and Jay Buehner. I was wondering how I would ever get a chance to play up there. But a lot of things can happen in one year. I had a great year in Prince William [Class A, Carolina League] and won the batting title. That kind of put me on the map. The next year I was invited to the big league camp for the first time. I just kept making the cuts—cut after cut after cut—until I finally got sent down toward the end of spring.

After that I realized maybe the big leagues wasn't so far away after all. The next year [1989] I was close to making the big league roster again, but I got sent down. Then in 1990 I was in Triple A for the whole spring training. And just before the season was to start, they sent me down to Double A for the year. It was kind of hard going back to the same level, the same team I had played on the year before. But they explained to me that in the long run I'd be better off to take it slowly, step-by-step, and not be rushed. I guess it was a good decision because I am here now, and you never know what could have happened.

I had enough confidence in my abilities to know that sooner or later I would be given a chance to play in the big leagues. I put my heart into it and I was doing all the things I was supposed to do. I was improving at each level, so I knew that eventually something was going to happen. A lot of guys have this state of mind where they believe if they hang around long enough and stay healthy things will open up for them.

Looking back on it now, minor league baseball was a lot harder than I had thought. At the time, I didn't know any better. In fact, I had thought I was living a great life. But once you get up here to the big leagues and look back you realize how hard it was down there—the low salaries, the long bus drives, the long workouts day after day, the living conditions, and even the playing conditions. It's all hard. A lot of what you have to do here—like getting enough rest, eating right, getting through the slumps—is even harder in the minors. Nevertheless, I really had a great time. We won a championship and I was on a winning club for most of those years. But it was still hard. You think of riding eight hours in a bus from Albany to Canton, Ohio, and then a few days later getting back on the bus for London, Ontario. When you get off your body is so stiff you can hardly walk straight.

⚉

Bernie got his first call-up to the big leagues when Yankee outfielder Roberto Kelly sprained his right wrist and went on the fifteen-day disabled list. At the time Bernie was hitting .294 in Triple A. The Yankee front office believed that although Bernie, who was just twenty-two, wasn't quite ready for the big leagues full-time, putting him there temporarily would give him a taste of that experience and allow the club to get a reading of his progress before returning him to Triple A when their injured outfielder came off the DL. Bernie recalled his first trip to the big leagues.

⚉

We were playing in Louisville. My wife was there too, because after the series against Louiville, I was going to stay to play in the All-Star Game. It was our second day. And I had just finished taking BP when I wandered over to this little fair that was going on behind the stadium. I didn't have much to do after BP and thought I would just check out the fair. When I got back, everybody was looking for me, saying, "Man, where have you been? We have been looking all over for you. The manager is looking for you." When I went into his office, he said, "Pack your bags. You have a plane in an hour. You are going to New York." When my wife got to the stadium, I was already gone. I gave her a call from New York. She always has the worst of it. Every time I've been called up or sent down she is the one left behind with all the moving arrangements and taking care of the kids. It's not a lot of fun for her.

[In New York] I was kind of overwhelmed by all the attention. I was used to playing before ten thousand fans at most. And now all of the sudden, overnight, there are thirty thousand people watching me. It was a lot—especially the first couple days when I was trying to get used to the playing conditions, trying to get settled in. It was really exciting, but it made me nervous too. I remember wondering if I was going to be good enough to play in this league. Was I ready to make this step? But once I got to bat it was all fine. My first at bat was against Jeff Baller, a lefty for the Orioles. I hit a fly ball with a man on third and got an RBI. Later that game I drove in another run with a single.

⚉

During the first few days after he arrived in New York, Bernie told the New York sportswriters, "I really never expected to be here so soon, I am just trying to take everything slowly right now. Everything is happening real fast. I am just going to perform to the best of my ability, and hopefully I will stay here a long time." A writer for the New York Post, *Joel Sherman, noted that Bernie, "enjoying the novelty of the major leagues, still watches the between innings highlights on the big center field screens and is a bit dazzled by the sheer size of the crowds."*

Although he hit and fielded his position well, Bernie, in the words of one writer, "makes a mockery of running the bases, causing management and teammates to question his baseball IQ and instincts for the game." He was good-naturedly razzed by some of the veteran Yankees for his boneheaded, baserunning mistakes. Each time Bernie was razzed, players stretched out his first name in a sing-song manner. The sound, "BE-E-E-E-R-R-R- . . ." would mean the abuse was about to start. Although the hazing was good natured, Bernie heard it all, and it hurt. On one occasion, he stormed out of the clubhouse. There was enough harassment that manager Buck Showalter ordered the tormentors to knock it off.

⚉

One thing I noticed right away was the travel. After the game there are buses waiting; you go straight from the ballpark to the airport to the plane. And the planes are all charters. So they are just sitting there waiting for you to arrive. In Triple A we flew commercial flights and had to wake up like at five in the morning to get to the airport for the first flight—and that was after playing the night before and not getting to bed until midnight. On the charters up here we have first-class seats from top to bottom, first-class service—steaks, lobsters, any kind of food, you just name it. It's a lot easier than in the minors, where sometimes you get off the bus and you are so stiff you can hardly walk.

But even so, the trips can be a burden—moving every three or four days, going to the West Coast, living out of a suitcase for two weeks, and eating in restaurants all the time. And you are away from your wife and kids. But then I think, too, that this is a privileged opportunity—being able to travel, to see different places, and to meet people that I probably wouldn't have the chance to if I weren't a baseball player. It would be a lot nicer if I had time to do some things in these cities.

People think that ballplayers have a lot of free time. But you're always thinking about the game, trying to prepare yourself mentally. That and eating and resting are the vital things. Much of the way I perform relies on the energy I have. So I try to get a lot of rest. I really watch what I eat—a lot of pasta, rice, and fish. I do a lot of visualizing too, like seeing myself hitting the ball right on the button, making a good throw, gliding through the bases. I look at some video too but not as much as I should. We have all the equipment here. We pay a guy, Karl Taylor, to film us hitting and he puts together a highlight tape for each of us with just the good swings and the good at bats in order to give us positive reinforcement, to show us what we are doing right when we're hitting the shit out of the ball. There is so much new technology now that helps us. I'm still working on keeping up with it all.

The hardest thing for me is being both mentally and physically ready to play every day. Over a 162-game schedule there are going to be many times when you are not quite there, times when you don't feel good enough to play at a top level. But when you are facing the kind of pitching you see in the big leagues, you have got to be at the top of your game at all times. It is a constant struggle to stay mentally alert—every pitch, every out, every hit. If I know that I am not at my best, I'm going to be stepped on. I think the great players, the Hall of Famers, find a way to get the job the done even when they are not quite 100 percent.

Sometimes something will happen that really makes me focused and determined. Like one time I had gotten a two-RBI base hit off Roger Clemens in my first at bat, and the next time up he plunked me right in the head. I knew he did that kind of thing, trying to intimidate people. Getting hit got some kind of rage going inside me. If I hadn't been so groggy from the beaning, I might have charged the mound right then. I knew that to get back at him, I was going to have to be at the top of my game, physically and mentally. By staying really focused, I ended up getting a couple more base hits, I had a diving catch, I was all over the place, and I was chosen player of the game. It's hard to explain, but Clemens hitting me made me that much better of a player. I wanted to get back at him so bad.

But baseball is a very humbling game. Just when you think you are on top and feel like you are big and nobody can get you out, you go into a slump and everybody gets you out. You are always dealing with failure it seems. In a single game you can go from feeling exhilarated, excited, feeling like you are bigger than the whole world, and then end up feeling like dirt. But I also think that's what makes baseball a great game.

What gives me the biggest high is being a determining factor in the outcome of the game. It means a lot when the fans like what you do, but it means a whole lot more when your teammates congratulate you and realize that you were a factor. It's great having guys that are already Hall of Famers, like Mattingly and Boggs, saying, "Good job, man, way to go!"

I work on all aspects of my game, but hitting is the toughest, the one you have the least control over. You can be hitting the ball hard, doing all the right things, and still not get the hits to fall. When I go up there, I just want to have a good at bat—to be able to see a good pitch, swing at a ball that I can handle, and hit it hard somewhere. If I hit it hard and it goes right at somebody, what can I do? It's out of my control. But if I swing at a bad pitch, then I'm mad because that is something that I can control. Sometimes you have to give the pitcher credit for setting you up and making you do things you really didn't want to do. I used to get too down on myself. Sometimes even when I had a good game I wouldn't enjoy it because I thought I could have done better. I've learned to realize that when I've had a bad at bat that I am going to get another chance to redeem myself. I now say learn from it, don't dwell on it.

There are a lot more things I can control in my fielding—like getting a good jump, charging the ball hard, keeping the ball in front of me, going to the fence and not lollygagging, throwing the ball to the right place, hitting the cutoff man. Those things are under my control and I can take pride in doing them well.

Baserunning is another aspect of my game. There is a lot more to baserunning than just getting a good jump and stealing a base. You've got to learn how to read the pitchers and to read the outfielder's positions so that you know when you can take that extra base. You have got to know the game situation too. Some of this stuff the coaches can teach you, but a lot of it you just learn from experience, from game situations. You are always learning. It's a never-ending struggle.

Being on a winning team, like we [the Yankees] have been the last couple years, makes a big difference; it makes the job a whole lot easier. I get a good feeling knowing that when my team arrives in a new town, they say, "Here come the Yankees. We got to play hard." People are talking about you, talking about how you play, and trying hard to defeat you. I played on some winning teams in the minors—like at Albany where we won the championship—and it was really special. When you are on a losing team, the season seems to go on and on. Everything you or the team does gets magnified. When you are winning, little things pass unnoticed. But when you are losing, little things can mean lots of finger-pointing—they start trying to teach you to do things a different way. It's not a good experience and it is not good for your own development as a ballplayer.

⚘

WALESKA WILLIAMS

People on the outside don't realize how much of a ballplayer's life revolves around baseball. Tonight when Bernie comes in, the first thing he will do is recount the game. Then he will turn on the TV to see if there is another game that he might watch. That is part of his job because he wants to watch other pitchers and batters to see how they do what they do. He will stay up maybe two hours more watching baseball. If he sleeps until 11:30 in the morning and has to leave for the ballpark at 2:30, what time does that give me? Only about three hours to be with him, and then he is away on the road for half the season. Sometimes I stay up and watch baseball on TV in order to be with him, but often I fall asleep on the couch.

I went into marriage thinking it was a fifty-fifty thing, but now I find myself doing lots of things that I thought we would share. With road trips and all, Bernie is not always around to help. I remember the first time the Yankees called him up from Triple A. He wasn't sure how long he was going to be in New York, so he had me stay in Columbus and stand by. I was waiting there a whole month not knowing where we were going to be. It was like my husband is in New York, I'm in Columbus, Ohio, and my family is in Puerto Rico, and after a while I wondered, what the heck am I doing? Then when he did call me to New York, I had to move everything by myself.

When you are married to a ballplayer, naturally all the attention is on him. He is the center of everything. When Bernie is here, I go to the games and stay up late. Then I get up to look after the kids and then to cook him a good breakfast and lunch because he likes home cooking. Sometimes, when he doesn't get a ride with another player, I drive him to the stadium, drive back home, and then drive back to the stadium again that night at seven o'clock for the game. Back and forth. I watch most of the games in the wives' section. When the team is on the road, I watch the games on TV.

A ballplayer gets so used to people treating him well and looking after him that he begins to expect that at home. I was just telling Bernie today that he can't expect the same treatment at home that he gets out here at the ballpark. He might be a successful ballplayer but at home he has other responsibilities. His being a baseball player is only 20 percent of what he is to me. Yes, I'm married to a baseball player, but I need him to be other things as well. I really want at least a few hours each day just for us, with no baseball.

Even though I like baseball and it is Bernie's career, I try not to let it be too big a part of my life—especially if he is having a bad streak. He gets very quiet when he is in a slump, like 0 for 15. Then I really notice it at home. It changes how he interacts with us and the time that he spends with us. He's normally a quiet person anyway. But when he is not playing well, he gets extremely quiet. Sometimes when he is on the road, it is actually more relaxing at home, although I do miss him. It is at these times that I can enjoy just being with the kids and going out and doing things, like visiting friends from Puerto Rico.

⚾

Some ballplayers who have been in the big leagues a few years become recognizable to fans away from the ballpark. Many take steps to conceal their identity and to protect their privacy when out in public. I asked Waleska how she felt about the loss of her anonymity.

⚾

When we are out in a shopping mall or in a restaurant often someone will recognize him. Sometimes Bernie wears a hat and his prescription glasses so that he will be less likely to be recognized. It's funny because sometimes people will say, "Hey, you look like Bernie Williams." Some people come up and make small talk. Often I don't mind and I just keep on my way, but there are times when you we in the middle of something, like a conversation, and we really don't want to be interrupted. We get a lot of people coming up and asking Bernie for autographs. Again, it is the timing. And usually I don't mind it if they are only asking for one or two. But when they want him to sign a bunch of things, then I think it's too much.

One thing I don't like is the groupies. One time in Columbus this girl called Bernie's room and I picked up the phone. He didn't know her. If you know the name of the player you want, anyone can call the hotel and ask the desk to ring his room. We have a strong relationship right now, so I don't worry much about groupies. But if things were wrong at home, you know, then I would have to be concerned. I think some of the wives whose husbands make really big money like to travel with their husbands, maybe because of all the stories they hear about groupies on the road. If the young women that have these fantasies about being with ballplayers really knew what it was like being married to one, they might not be so eager. They don't know that you don't have your husband around for half of every year, and that there are times that you wish he were in some other profession so he would be home every night. I think a lot of the groupies don't have big self-esteem themselves, so they have to be with someone who is successful to make themselves feel good or important.

⚾

At the end of the interview I asked Waleska if there was anything that we had overlooked about being a baseball wife. In response, she told the following story.

⚾

When Bernie was sent to Triple A [Columbus, Ohio], I got there on a Friday and started to get sick. I went to the ballpark anyway on Saturday and I heard this lady talking Spanish, so I went over and introduced myself. We had a nice chat and she gave me her phone number. Two days later I had a very high fever and they had to take me to the hospital. My firstborn, Bernie Alexander, was only seven months old at the time, so when the doctors wanted to keep me in the hospital I said, "No, no, I have no one to take care of my baby." Bernie couldn't take care of him because he was at the ballpark and the next day they were leaving on a road trip. And it would take my mother, who was in Puerto Rico, two days to get to Columbus. I didn't know anyone in town except the lady, Lilet Martinez, whom I just had met briefly at the ballpark. So I called her. Here I was bringing my baby to this lady that I had just met. She stayed with my son for two days until my mom came. To this day I am so thankful to her; she is still my friend and we still call back and forth. I was in the hospital for a whole week with a high fever.

I think going back to college and getting my degree has been very helpful. It shows I have accomplished something and I'm not just Bernie's wife. Not many of the wives have finished college, and sometimes it is tough on them to be married to men who are so successful. I am really thankful to Bernie for letting me go back to college [University of Puerto Rico] after we were married. His playing baseball meant we wouldn't be together for several months at a time. He could have said, "No, I want you here with me." But he didn't do that.

⚾

What will Bernie and Waleska do after baseball? Coming off the best season of his career, Bernie hasn't given a lot of thought to what he might do after retirement—except that he would like to do something in music. He talks about playing the guitar and perhaps studying music at University of California, Berkeley. Waleska talks of getting her masters degree and working as a nutritionist.

Paul Zwaska

HEAD GROUNDSKEEPER, BALTIMORE ORIOLES

"I always had an interest in grass," recounted Paul Zwaska, head groundskeeper of the Baltimore Orioles. Zwaska, who became a head groundskeeper at age thirty-one, oversees a crew of seven full-time workers and seventeen part-timers. At Camden Yards the grounds-keeping operations are based beneath the right field grand stand. The area is divided into a warren of rooms and storage areas. The command post is Zwaska's large office at field level with a large plate-glass window offering a view down the right-field line. Meteorological instruments, a computer, and a couple dozen switches and dials in Zwaska's office suggest that caring for grass and dirt is a scientific enterprise—at least at Camden Yards.

Just outside Zwaska's door is an equipment-storage area with a quarter-million dollars worth of turf-maintenance equipment. At the back of the room is a vacuum pit that is connected to drainage lines that run beneath the field and pumps that suck moisture from the turf during or after a rain. There is a workshop with air pumps for pneumatic tools and stainless-steel-top working benches. Another room houses pesticides and fertilizers, and another area has large bins containing different types of soil. There are two locker rooms, a full

*kitchen, and a lounge with couches for the crew to relax during their
sixteen-hour days. The grounds crew wear uniforms, one of two different sets: tan or khaki shirts and pants during the day or white aviator
shirts with epaulets, black pants, and black shoes during game time.*

⚘

How I got to be a groundskeeper goes back to when I was ten years
old and growing up in Madison, Wisconsin. The Brewers didn't exist
yet, so the Chicago Cubs were the big team up in the Midwest and I'd
watch them on TV. I fell in love with Wrigley Field and the Cubs at the
same time. Eventually my dad took me down to Wrigley Field. It was
that visit, and later trips as well, that made me think about becoming
a major league groundskeeper.

It was a magical feeling just walking into Wrigley. If you've ever been
there, you know what I'm talking about. You walk up the ramp into
the seating bowl on a beautiful, sunny afternoon, with the breeze blowing and the ivy waving. And out there across a big expanse is that nice
green grass. What a sight. I thought, boy, I'd love to take care of this.

As years went on and I got a driver's license, my friends and I used
to drive from Madison down to Chicago ten or fifteen times a year to
watch ball games. We'd be down there getting autographs. They'd be
taking pictures of the players, and I'd be out taking pictures of the
grounds crew and all the different types of things they did—from
dragging the field to hosing it and putting the tarp on when it rained.
I still have those pictures today. From the time I was young I made
money by mowing lawns all around the neighborhood. So, I suppose I
always had an interest in grass.

As I went through high school and college the idea of being a
groundskeeper stayed in the back of my mind. For the first two-and-a-
half years at Madison [University of Wisconsin] I majored in meteorology. But I had a hard time getting through calculus. In three at-
tempts, I never made it past the sixth week of class. I said to my parents, "This just isn't working." You had to have calculus to do
meteorology. My mom said, "Well, why don't you see if they have
anything on groundskeeping." I said they don't have stuff like that in
college. You don't go to college to learn how to cut grass. She said just
go down to the agriculture department and see what they've got there.

I went down there and talked to Dr. Jim Love in the soil science department. He was in charge of all of the students specializing in turf and grounds management. I couldn't believe it. He said it was a shame that I wasn't just finishing college because the Milwaukee Brewers just had an opening for a new assistant head groundskeeper and none of his students wanted it. That really shocked me. Most of his graduates in the turf management program wanted jobs in the golf course industry. There are a lot more golf courses than major league ballparks, so I guess it's natural that they leaned in that direction.

Anyway, I switched my major to soil science, with a specialty in turf and grounds management. During my final year (1984), I had an internship with Harry Gill, the head groundskeeper for the Milwaukee Brewers. That gave me a good idea of what taking care of a major league baseball field was all about.

When it came time for me to send out my résumé, Harry advised me to wait until the end of the year and to send two copies to each ball club—one to the general manager and one to the groundskeeper. I sent résumés to only six major league clubs—both Chicago teams and Detroit, Boston, Baltimore, and Cleveland. I wanted to stay on natural turf and, because I was from the North, I wanted to stay in that region.

Graciously, every one of the six ball clubs answered back, saying, "Thanks but no thanks; there's no room for you in our organization at this time." I got a letter from the general manager of the Orioles, Hank Peters, saying the same thing. But shortly after, I got a phone call from his head groundskeeper, Pat Santarone. He said he was looking for somebody to become his assistant because he was going to be retiring in several years. He invited me to come for an interview. It was the last week of the 1984 season.

I flew to Baltimore and went to Pat's office in Memorial Stadium. We weren't talking more than five minutes when Pat said I could have the job. He never asked any questions about my experience and the things that you would expect. I was shocked; he had already decided that he wanted to hire me. Years later I found out that after he had gotten my résumé, he had called one of my references, Harry Gill. And Harry had said, "He's your man, if you two can get along." Harry knew Pat. He knew that he was very meticulous and therefore hard to get along with. He also knew that I was meticulous and a lot like Pat. So it came down to whether Pat felt he could work with me. After talking to me for five minutes I guess he decided that he could.

You know how kids out of college send out hundreds of résumés

Paul Zwaska and his mentor, Pat Santarone, when Zwaska first came to work for the Orioles in 1985.

and never get a job or even a bite. If you consider major league base-ball and count how many teams have natural turf and figure my chances—well, it was like winning the lottery. I just happened to be at the right place at the right time, and I knew the right people. That's all there was to it.

I worked as Pat's assistant from 1985 until he retired in 1992. I then took over for him as head groundskeeper.

As groundskeeper, my main worry has been making sure that the field is playable and safe, and that we get the game in if there is in-clement weather. To be a groundskeeper you've got to be a weather-man, a janitor, and a mechanic. It's not just cutting the grass and putting down the foul lines. It's a lot more involved than it sounds. And with a crew of seven, plus myself, it means sixteen-hour days when the ball club is playing at home, and eight-hour days when it's on the road, and that's usually seven days a week. The grass doesn't stop growing just because it's the weekend or a holiday. Once March 1st hits, there are very few days off for a grounds crew until the end of the season in early October.

On a typical game day, we start work between seven and eight in the morning. After the crew gets in and they change into their uniforms, we sit around and talk for a few minutes about what needs to be done and where I want everybody to start. There are a lot of jobs to do that people don't even realize, such as washing the dugouts; washing the outfield track; vacuuming the track; cleaning the bases; painting the outfield foul lines with latex paint; cleaning the bullpens; repairing the batter's boxes and the pitcher's mound; and repairing and vacuuming the batting and pitching tunnels in the clubhouse—all of which have to be done every game day.

But most of our time is spent maintaining and repairing the grass and dirt. No aspect of a ballpark or the playing conditions changes the game of baseball as much as the surface. Tall grass will slow down the ball. The type of dirt and its firmness influences the speed of ground balls and their chances of getting through the infield for hits. But the grass is always on my mind. Baltimore is in what we call the transition zone, which makes it the worst part of the country to grow grass. You've got cool-season grasses and warm-season grasses. Either way, you're going to have trouble at this time of the year in this region—the transition zone. Cool-season grasses are prone to funguses, so we're constantly spraying fungicides. And with a warm-season grass, like Bermuda grass, you have problems in winter. A lot of these grasses are cut very short. When they get covered with ice, as they did six or seven times this past winter, they can't breathe and they suffocate. There's no easy answer. And then you have disease to deal with as well. We're a lot like farmers, at the mercy of Mother Nature. It makes you insecure sometimes. Whatever happens to the turf—whether or not you could have controlled it—is going to be seen as your fault upstairs [in the front office].

The front-office people don't understand this kind of thing. You tell them that our grass has this disease and that we can't do a lot about it, even when we put down the proper chemicals. Unless you have some knowledge of soil science and turf management, it's hard to understand. The front-office folks say, "Well, how come they aren't having that problem in this ballpark or that ballpark?" Well, each ballpark is in a different location in this country. The variables are countless—soil types, turf-grass varieties, climatological conditions, warm-season versus cool-season grass.

When we hosted the All-Star Game—national TV and all—our field was in awful bad shape. We had eight straight days of 100-degree temperatures, and never got lower than 85 degrees at night—and here I am with a cool-season grass. Soil temperatures in the nineties can burn off all of your roots. I was lucky to have any field left. And on top of that, the day before the All-Star Game they had a giant party on the field. It was almost 100 degrees and there were eight hundred field passes for all the dignitaries, players, corporate sponsors, and everybody else. They were all out there, scrunched into my foul territory, which they totally annihilated in just a few hours, from fungo circle to fungo circle. We lost a lot of turf. At that high of a temperature, bluegrass can't take that much stress—especially when you throw in a herd of elephants walking all over it for several hours. But there was nothing I could do to stop it. Major league baseball was not going to allow me to rope it off the day before the All-Star Game. And then we had another seven days of home games after that. Made me sick having to look at this ugly, chewed-up area behind home plate.

Players sometimes create extra problems—like when they take their warm-up swings on the grass instead of in the on-deck circle. Often they don't realize what they're doing. Last year, Mike Pagliarulo used to tear up the turf real bad when taking his swings. He'd dig a rut that deep [he spreads his fingers two inches apart]. I finally had to say something to him. I said, "We can't keep this place in sod with you around here. You're going to have to start learning to take your swings on the warning track because you are killing us down here." Sometimes it just gets to the point where you've got to tell the players.

When the club is at home, we cut the grass every day. When the team is on the road, we try to give it a rest and go every other day or sometimes every three days, depending on how fast the grass is growing.

In foul territory we use a rotary mower; and in fair territory we use a reel mower—like the old-time mowers that you pushed as a kid. They do very different things to the grass. The blade of a rotary mower creates a suction that lifts the grass up and holds it up while the impact of the blade cuts it off. So it's ideal in foul territory where it's not crucial to keep the grass cut short. The higher you keep the grass, the healthier it is.

On the playing field we use a reel mower, which sheers the grass.

Sheering, rather than cutting by impact, provides a better quality cut and creates those nice mowing patterns you see in the ballparks today. The mower creates patterns by having rollers in the front and at the back, so that as the mower passes over the grass, it lays it down in the direction that you're going. The way the grass lays down determines how the sun reflects off it and the particular shade or color of green you get. When you crosscut, you get four different colors or shades of green.

We rotate our mowing patterns each home stand. We have three cuts or patterns: a foul-line cut, a center-field cut, and a radius pattern. The foul-line cut is where you cut parallel to the first-base foul line and go back and forth all the way across the field. When you get done, you parallel cut the other foul line back and forth all the way back. The result is a grid pattern. For the next home stand, we'll switch to the center-field cut, which starts at second base and heads straight out toward the center. We'll mow back and forth, and then we'll crosscut that by going foul pole to foul pole. The radius pattern is where we cut following the back radius of the infield, going back and forth. It creates an arch pattern as opposed to a crosscut pattern. Because it doesn't show up aesthetically, we often save that cut for when the team is on the road. During home stands we mostly use the first two patterns.

But we no longer put a crosscut pattern in the infield. The players complain that it makes the ball snake. For example, a ground ball will hit the different grains and spin in different directions. When you stand behind a batting cage, you can actually see the ball zig-zag as it goes into the outfield on the crosscut grass. That's not crucial to the outfielder because the ball has slowed down tremendously by the time it gets out there. But on the infield, where the ball is moving very fast, you don't have time to make quick adjustments.

The guys who work on Astroturf don't have to worry about any of that stuff. But they've got other problems to deal with, like trying to get bubble gum and tobacco-juice stains out of the carpet. Overall, they have things a little more under control than we do. In working with grass, we are dealing with a living, breathing animal. You have to have your hand on its pulse every minute.

Besides the grass, we also have the dirt to worry about. Every major league groundskeeper has his own ideas about how he wants to keep the dirt—whether to shade toward sandy so it drains well or toward more firm. Ballplayers like it firmer. When the dirt is sandy, ground balls tend to skid rather than bounce. With firm soil, the bounce is more predictable, and therefore the ball is easier for the infielder to play. Although looser dirt drains better, it's more important, in my opinion, to give the players what they want and not worry about rain. Rain is what you have a $30,000 infield tarp for. If it rains, you cover it. Or if it's raining lightly, you throw out soil-drying compound.

I've had infielders tell me that this is the greatest infield they've ever played on. Last year Sparky Anderson sat me down and told me that it was the best infield that his club had ever played on, and then he introduced me to Alan Trammel, who is very particular about what he wants on the field. He just ranted and raved about our dirt.

George Toma, the Kansas City groundskeeper, likes to say, "If you can't work infield dirt, you're not a major league groundskeeper." Anybody can grow grass, but getting the dirt the way ballplayers want it is the real trick. Of course you've got twenty-four guys on the club and you're never going to satisfy them all, but you try to satisfy as many as you can—especially the important ones, the big-dollar players.

Usually by noon we pretty much have the field ready to go. Then after lunch, from 1:00 to 2:30, it's last-minute things that need to be finished up—maybe some hand watering of turf and watering the dirt again, which you do all day long. At 2:30 you set up for early batting practice. [This involves putting up the batting cage and the screens—which provide protection from batted balls—and putting down mats and protective blankets on the pitching mound and home-plate area.] Lastly, you put water on the dirt just before you let them hit. The visiting team is allowed to hit for an hour, then our club comes out and hits until 5 P.M. That's early BP. The regular batting practice starts at 5:15 and lasts until about 6:55.

After batting practice and infield practice end, about 7:10 P.M., we take the field and prepare it for game time. The game begins at 7:30, and it is usually a three-hour game. During that time my crew is split up. Some of the crew is down behind home plate in case there is a problem that needs to be taken care of at the mound or at home plate. I'm usually here in my office watching the game from my window or on TV, or both. And the rest of the full-time crew is over in the lounge area, eating, relaxing, and watching the game. If we have rain, everybody has to be on the field to give a hand.

In addition to my three teams, I have a seventeen-man tarp crew. They're mostly sixteen- to twenty-year-old kids who we recruit every year. They come in for every game, whether the weather is good or

Grounds crew dragging the infield at Yankee Stadium. (Photo by Steve Crandall)

not. You never know when a forecast is going to be off. The tarp crew is my rain insurance, to make sure we've got enough people to cover the field quickly in case of rain. The tarp crew sits out in a cage in right center field. They watch the game, but they also do odd jobs, minding the bullpens, opening and closing the gates for pitchers and catchers, and covering the mounds. At the end of the fifth inning they drag the infield.

A lot of tarp-crew members apply for the job because they want to be in the ballpark and near ballplayers. You have to be careful about who you hire. You don't want somebody who is going to be hanging around the players, bothering them. A lot of the guys like the job because they are able to say they're around the ballplayers. They like to be able to say to their friends, "Hey, I talked to Lee Smith last night and he said this and that." When you're sixteen years old, you want to impress. So you can imagine working here is a pretty big deal for them. I allow them to talk to players in the bullpen but they can't get autographs. That would be taking advantage of the job.

Once the game ends, my full-time crew goes back onto the field to do the postgame repair work. It usually involves patching holes in the mound and home plate, dragging the infield, raking off the lips at the edge of the dirt, and things like that. Then we put the tarp on the mound and home plate, or on the whole infield if the weather prediction calls for rain. We usually don't get out of here until after midnight. By the time you travel home and get into the sack, you only get four or five hours of sleep before you are heading back here the next morning. But during game time, the guys do get a chance to catch up on some sleep, which is why we work in shifts.

The only other time we catch up on lost sleep is when we have a day game and get out of here at a reasonably decent hour. That's when I recharge my batteries and feel great the next morning. But that doesn't happen too often.

Even when there is no night game, it's sometimes hard to get away early. If rain is forecasted, you have to wait around to put on the tarp. You can't put it on when the sun is still out because you will burn the turf underneath it. So there are times when we will sit here for three or four hours just waiting for dusk to put on the tarp. To a wife sitting back home with kids, that's three or four hours when you could be at home with them.

On this home stand we've had ten night games, and most days the temperature has been in the nineties. You're drained after the second or third day and you are pretty much running on automatic pilot, just trying to keep going. It's not all the glamour that people think it is. We're out there under a blazing hot sun from the moment we get here, sweating like crazy, drinking water to keep hydrated. And then you hear these other people complain about how tired they are from working nine to five in an office. I say, "Come on, try my job for a while."

It's not an easy life—especially during the heat of July and August when you're really struggling to keep the grass alive.

Whenever I go upstairs to the front office, where you can look out the windows, I always stop and look down at the field to see what it looks like from above. I like baseball, but even more I like how a baseball field looks—especially when it's in its prime. And when I watch a game on TV, I'm always looking at the other guy's field. I think all groundskeepers do the same thing.

It was tough on my wife the first couple of years, before we had kids. But once the kids came along, they gave her company and something to do. She wasn't always thinking about where the heck I was. Baseball life, in general, whether you're a groundskeeper, player, or in the front office, is never a nine-to-five job. Over the years I've seen a lot of families break up. My kids don't see me during home stands, except for ten or fifteen minutes a day, so it's like I'm on the road and gone for ten days at a time. I miss a lot of holidays. This year we're working every single holiday this summer, starting with Easter and including Memorial Day, the Fourth of July, and Labor Day—you name it, we're working. That's real tough on my family. On the other hand, at Christmas and Thanksgiving, which are big holidays in my book, I'll be home. Think about the groundskeepers who work at multiuse stadiums where they've got both baseball and football. I don't know how those guys do it and keep a family together. If they're lucky, they get two months off between the end of football and the start of baseball. They're never home for anything. They've got to have awfully strong women behind them.

I don't want to miss my kids growing up; I don't want to be someone who fifteen to twenty years down the road is saying to himself, "Why didn't I spend more time with them when they were younger?" It's not easy, and when you are home, there are all those other things that have to be done, things you've been putting off because you've been at work. You end up telling your kids that you've really got to do this or that and hope that later in the day you'll have time for them. You feel bad for the kids because it's like they don't have a father, because the father is never around.

One thing that I've noticed is that baseball groundskeepers are behind the times. There's a lot of guys in major league baseball who came up the old-fashioned way, through the minor leagues, where they learned it as they went along without any professional training. I think some groundskeepers feel intimidated by the people who have been through college. I think that in the old days groundskeepers never wanted to share their secrets. There was this notion that you might lose your job if you told somebody else a secret and they then used it to do one better than you. It's all wrong.

In my opinion, you can never stop learning. I'd like to see a little more unity among groundskeepers, more sharing. There's no occasion when we all get together and have dialogue about how to make things better. In golf there is an association of golf course superintendents. They have all kinds of educational information, research data, and that kind of stuff. They provide support when members have turf problems and need help. You don't have any of that in baseball. At the baseball winter meetings they have a seminar for the trainers, one for the directors of stadium operations, and so on, but nothing for groundskeepers. It's kind of crazy when you consider they put their million-dollar ballplayers on our fields.

Scott Jaster

BALLPLAYER, BIRMINGHAM BARONS

At 6 foot 5 inches, and with power and speed, Scott Jaster is a superb athlete. From early childhood, he has wanted to follow in his father's footsteps and become a major league ballplayer. He has played at all levels of the minor leagues for three different organizations—Mets, White Sox, and Royals. He was released twice, and today at age twenty-nine his dream is beginning to fade.

I first met Jaster in 1992 while traveling with the Birmingham Barons. I interviewed about half the players during the ten days I spent with the team, but I only did multiple in-depth interviews with Scott and one other player. I chose Jaster because I found him to be uncommonly thoughtful in talking about his life. Also, I thought his setbacks in baseball, mostly brought on by injuries, had caused him to reflect about his career and profession more than most players. During the four years that have elapsed since the first interview, I have kept in touch with him to track his progress in the minor leagues.

His story begins with recollections of childhood spent in ballparks with his father, Larry Jaster, who was then pitching for the Atlanta Braves. About one in every ten professional baseball players today have fathers who once played professionally themselves, an incidence of "foot-stepping" comparable only to farming and the medical pro-

fession. In Scott's narrative, we glimpse some of the advantages of being in ballparks and around professional players while still a youth. Above all, his story shows the degree to which the player's life revolves around his profession. Everything else is secondary.

⚉

The first memories I have of baseball are in St. Louis, when my dad was with the Cardinals. I can just remember a few brief moments, like my baby-sitter, Grandma Miffort, throwing me Whiffle balls. I must have only been three years old, but I can remember wanting to hit those Whiffle balls. That must be when it all started.

I have clear memories of Atlanta when I was five, six, and seven years old and dad played for the Braves. By the time I was eight or nine, we were in Richmond, the Braves' Triple A team, and my skills were developing. I was at an age where I could be on the field and actually shag fly balls. I would go to the ballpark early with my dad and hit on the field. That's what I lived for when my dad went to the park. Everyone there knew who I was—I practically lived there. I would just go to the concession stand and get free hot dogs and cokes. I can still remember how other kids looked at me: "Wow, why is he out on the field?" I can still remember the feelings inside of me. It wasn't arrogance. I didn't look at those kids and think, "Yeah, I am down here and you are not." Actually, I didn't like the feeling and I kind of kept my distance from them. It was uncomfortable for me because I felt privileged and I knew that these kids wanted to be where I was and they couldn't.

Driving to the stadium was like one of those things where as we got closer and closer, I would get more and more excited. While in the locker room waiting for my dad to change, I would get even more excited to get out on the field. Being on the field, watching the crowds come in, the perfect green grass, the infield dirt exactly level, the fresh chalk on the foul lines and batter's box, the sun setting, and the air still warm gave me a real high. I've heard people talk about drug addicts—the highs they get. Well, that is kind of what it was like, I guess. And the great thing was that I knew that I was going to get the same high when I came back the next day and the tomorrow after that.

During the games I ran around and played cup ball with some of the kids—that's where you wad up a paper cup, use your hands to bat it, and then run the bases. But whenever my dad would come in to pitch,

Scott with his father Larry Jaster in 1967. (Photo by Alfred Fleishman)

I'd sit right behind home plate where my mom was. We had seats there. I remember really being into my dad's performance. If he did well, I would be pumped up; and if he had a bad outing, like if he got taken out, I would be down and upset about it.

⚱

By the time Jaster reached high school, his father had retired from professional baseball and was coaching. Scott played on his father's team at Coronado High School in Colorado Springs and then again at the University of New Mexico, when his father became their pitching coach. Since he had not been drafted out of high school, Scott went to college to play baseball, and hoped to be noticed by the scouts.

⚱

In my first year at the university, I didn't do too well academically—skipping class, you know. Looking back, I realize that it wasn't hard to get up and go to class, but I just wasn't into it. I was there to play baseball and have fun, and that was it. My dad busted me a few times for going duck hunting when I should have been in class. He knew a coach in Colorado at Trinidad State College, where it would be easier on me as far as grades went. He talked to the coach, Rick Zimmerman, and my attending that school sounded pretty good. It was a small school of about 1,500 students in a small town up in the mountains.

All I wanted to do at college was to play baseball, and that was pretty much all I did. The entire baseball team lived together in one dorm. We formed a tight bond and had a great team. We ended up just dominating—we won the whole northwest region, which was Idaho, Montana, and Colorado, and we went to the Junior College World Series. I had a pretty good World Series, and there had been tons of scouts there. The Mets had already drafted me in the second round of the winter draft. So as soon as the college season was done, I could either sign with the Mets or hold off and go to the June draft. I talked to my dad and the Mets over the phone on a conference call. The Mets offered me a $50,000 plan that included my school and incentives. It seemed good and I signed. There wasn't any negotiation at all.

The Mets sent me to Florida a week later to their extended spring program [each organization runs an extended spring training that lasts until June, when the short-season Class A leagues begin to play]. I was working out, getting used to wooden bats. The ball wouldn't quite get out of the park like it did with an aluminum bat, but I was still hitting the fence—and that was in Florida, where the parks are big and the ball doesn't travel well because of the humidity. I could tell that they were impressed.

They sent me to the full-season team in Columbia, South Carolina (Class A, South Atlantic League), instead of the short-season team in Little Falls, New York. Looking back, that was probably a mistake. When I got there the guys had already been playing for almost half a season. They seemed older and a lot more experienced. I got tight and tense and didn't hit well, about .190. I didn't really lose faith in my ability but I kind of forgot what got me there. I got wrapped up in the fact that I was now playing pro ball. The pressure and tension set in and it was like a stranglehold.

After a month, they sent me down to Little Falls. It had mostly rookies, and I had a pretty good year. Little Falls was a small town with one main street and two bars, but it is beautiful country up there with some really good trout fishing. I lived with a young couple in a two-bedroom house. I shared a room with a teammate who ended up getting released and stealing all of my underwear, socks, and T-shirts the day he left town. I came home after the game and my clothes were missing. He didn't take any of my nice shirts—just underwear and socks. But the couple was real nice and they cooked a meal for me every day, so it was a great deal.

One of the bars in Little Falls gave us free pitchers of draft beer every time we won a game—and we had a pretty good team. Finally they had to stop doing that because we were drinking them dry. Being young and having our first taste of freedom away from our parents and families and rules and restrictions made us pretty wild, I guess.

The next season they sent me back to Columbia for the full year. We had a great team, Gregg Jefferies was there, and we ended up winning it all [the championship]. I had a good year, averaging about .250 but with almost ninety RBIs and fifteen home runs. That fall the Mets invited me down to Florida to the Instructional League. [Major league organizations invite their twenty-five best young prospects to Florida in the fall to play in a league in which the emphasis is instruction.] There, you get up early in the morning, play in the afternoon, and have the night off. It was a pretty good routine. And there were lots of fun places to go out. It seemed like there were always nine or ten of us hanging out, going to the beach, or hanging out at a bar in the evening.

The next year I moved up one level to the Carolina League, where I had a pretty good year. I was showing them a lot of good things and I thought I would get a chance at Double A the next year. But I didn't. With about a week to go in spring training, I was expecting to go to Double A, but they told me I was being sent down—to Port St. Lucie in the Florida State League. The next day I got hit by a pitch—a 0–2 fastball that came up and in on me and hit me in the hand. It didn't break it, but I was out for a week and I never got going again. At Port St. Lucie I only hit .200 or .220—something like that. It was terrible. I couldn't understand it. For the first time in my life I was really struggling. It became a mental thing. I had been successful the year before in the Carolina League and now in a similar league I was a failure.

At mid-season they sent me back down to Columbia, where I had played two years before. That was a blow. Right then I started saying to myself, "You are in trouble now." I had gone from being one of the top-ten prospects in the Carolina League by the managers' and coaches' vote to this—a demotion. It was very hard to deal with—my wanting to make it to the big leagues so badly and then being sent back to a league I had left two years before. When I got there, I didn't do much. I had my good moments where I tore it up but then leveled off and played like everyone else in the league. At the end of the season, the Mets didn't invite me back to the Instructional League. That told me that in their minds I was no longer a prospect.

Looking back at that period now, I think I began to fail because I took my ability for granted. The better you do, the harder the opposition works to bury you and you have to rise up to the challenge. I had done well, but the next thing I knew I was looking into the pitcher's eye and he was just super intense, determined to get me out.

Also, I may have lost some of my focus and concentration. I would go 0 for 4 and I would go out to the bars at night to escape the bad time instead of just dealing with it. If you are going to make it in baseball, you have to eat, drink, and sleep baseball. Some people say you can go to the field and turn it on when you want and then turn it off when you take the uniform off. I think that even when you take your uniform off, it stays with you. When I am lying in bed at night falling asleep, all these pitches start coming at me or I see line drives hit down the line in a tight game situation, and I am there having to make the play. That's the way it should be, but I got away from that.

When you get into a downward spiral like that it's really hard to pull out. I had a good hitting coach, Tommy McCraw, who tried to help. But when you are struggling, you get so frustrated that you don't know what the heck is going on—even though you had been successful in the past. Before you know it, a huge monster is created and builds inside of you. Pressure. You just can't break out of it. I experienced a little bit of that last night in the game. I struck out with runners on second and third and one out. A fly ball would have tied the game and a base hit would have won it. But I struck out looking for sliders and the guy had just pumped two fastballs by me. I was really mad at myself because I am a fastball hitter. Why did I look for a slider when I hit the fastball best? Why did I go away from my strength, especially early in the count? I outsmarted myself.

Today I was thinking about it again, wondering if I was so dumb after all. I had looked at the charts when they brought in the reliever and saw that the pitcher had thrown me slider, slider, slider, curve, forkball, slider, and slider in a previous game. Not one fastball. I had faced him twice and had gotten not one fastball. So, maybe I was right in going up looking for a slider. I still don't know. What can you do?

Even when playing came naturally to me, I was slow to understand the importance of the mental aspect of the game. My dad was always telling me to keep on an "even keel"—don't get too high or too low. All the great players naturally keep that even-keel mode. My dad was always drilling it into me. I can hear his words now. But until you experience it yourself, you don't truly know what it means.

Okay, so now I am back in Columbia. Wake-up call. I am playing and hustling harder than I ever have. Almost ridiculously. I am trying to show the coaches and front office that I still want to play. Maybe I was trying to show them too much. Maybe I was always trying to show these guys instead of going up there and going, "Okay, it is you and me, pitcher. Let's go. One on one." Maybe I just needed to do it just for myself. I finished the season in Columbia, but it was the worst year of my life. I was bummed out.

I came into spring training the next year all ready to go, ready to show them that I had come out of my slump. I'd gone to Florida early to workout with my dad when a weird thing happened. My arm went bad. I have no idea what happened, but I couldn't even throw the ball from left field to second, not even a good one-hopper. I didn't play much. The Mets ended up sending me to an independent team in the Carolina League, the Peninsula Pilots. [Independent teams are clubs that are not affiliated with any major league organization.] My dad was in the league coaching the Durham Bulls. Our manager told me that I'd be playing every day, that I didn't even have to look at the lineup card, that I'd be in there. That took a lot of pressure off me right there. Before, the first thing I would do when I got to the yard was to look at the lineup to see if I was in there. That was the peak of my day, seeing if I was in the game or not.

Being on an independent team meant that there was no organizational pressure. I was away from the Mets. If I failed, I failed. I didn't feel like they were looking over my shoulder all the time. That was the feeling I needed and I took off. Boom! I was hitting about .300, going great guns. Then the Mets brought me back to St. Lucie because a couple of their outfielders had gone down [had been injured] and they were in a race for the first half title. On one of my first days down there I was in playing right field. It was the top of the eighth, man on second, and two outs. We're up by one run. Their guy hits a flare [soft fly ball] down the right-field line. I was running full speed, and the ball kicked back to my right, so I bare-handed it and made a perfect throw to the plate, cutting down the runner. During the next inning, still pumped from that play, I hit a home run off the first pitch. We won and clinched the title.

I hit a couple more home runs and things were going well, but the outfielder I had replaced got healthy again. I asked the Mets to send me back to Peninsula where I could play every day. They agreed. I was excited. There was lots of camaraderie, and team morale was intense. We were a bunch of scrappers. We were tough and playing well. We were beating people's butts.

We were four games out of first place, behind the Indians. They came into town for a three-game series, and we swept them. We were just one game out of first place when the Mets wanted to send me to Jackson, their Double A team in the Southern League. This happened just as we got back from a road trip. I had eaten a sub sandwich and had gotten food poisoning. I was out for a full week and had lost fifteen pounds. I have never been so sick in my life. I thought I was going to die. I was in my apartment all by myself with no one to take care of me, sick as a dog. As soon as I got my strength back, I went to Jackson and I played okay. Things were looking up. I thought I was back on track.

The next spring training was going well. Then a freak thing happened. I swung hard through a pitch on a 2–0 count, expecting a good pitch to hit. I swung and came down on my back knee and hurt it. The trainer told me that it was just a bruise, but the next morning I could barely walk. A few days later I still was not playing. "Just a bruise," they said. There were maybe five days left of spring training and the doctor said, "I hope it's not cartilage damage." That is all he told me. The next day I was released. I can't say that it was just the injury, but not being able to play for the last two weeks of spring training sure didn't help.

When they called me into the office to tell me that I was being released, the first thing that went through my mind was: "Okay, this is just the break I need. Somebody will pick me up. My talents and skills are good, and I am not too old yet." Sure enough, I was home packing when the Orioles called. They said, "We have an outfielder down with a bum hand. Why don't you come over for a few days?" I played three days there and did okay. The day before spring training was to break,

I still hadn't signed a contract with them. The injured player came back. They said, "Sorry, we have to let you go." That's when it hit me. I got back to the hotel to get my stuff together and realized I had no idea what I was going to do. I called Dad and I couldn't even talk; I was so upset. It was the first time that I realized I might never play again. When I thought about that, I couldn't even deal with it. I couldn't function. I couldn't talk to my dad on the phone; I just hung up.

I drove around to all the spring training camps that I could—from nine in the morning until dark. I think I went to eight camps—the Yankees, the Reds, the Tigers . . . I just drove all over the place and talked to all the minor league directors that I could. They all said, "Sorry, it's too late. Our teams are already set for the season."

I was bummed. My mom called and asked me to come out to Fremont, California. She had some work around the house that I could do and I could try out for one of the independent teams, Salinas or Reno, in the California League.

Reno was full, but Salinas invited me down to take some BP. I talked to my dad on the phone and he encouraged me to go. He said it was the only way I would get back into the game. I went down there and worked out with them, and they signed me for $500 a month. The money was brutal. The environment was very wild. The team was Japanese-owned so there were a bunch of Japanese players, as well as a Japanese coach and manager.

The Japanese were good players, but communication was pretty bad because they hardly spoke English and we didn't speak any Japanese. Steve Howe and Leon Durham were on that team too. I was commuting 70 miles each way from Fremont to Salinas, not making much money and not knowing where this was going to lead me.

Before in my prayers I had always said, "Okay, Lord, I will do whatever it takes to play baseball." I tried to remember that promise, to do whatever it took. But the situation kept getting worse and worse and worse. I was going into debt. It was getting so hard. After thinking about it for a long time, I finally decided to quit. What finally told me it was time to end it occurred when I was in right field in the middle of the game. I had gotten two hits but I just wasn't into it. My mind was somewhere else. I thought if I can't be committed enough to be intense and concentrate, then I shouldn't be here at all. I got three hits that night, but it didn't make any difference. I went into the office and told Heidi Koga and Kono, the coaches, that I was quitting. They were both so upset that they cried. They were good, sensitive people. Their crying made it even tougher on me. I almost broke down right there too. Baseball was a sacred thing to them as it was to me, but the situation had become impossible.

I went back to Fremont and packed all my things that night. My mom and stepdad were out of town, so I left them a note telling them what had happened. I was driving down the highway, heading east, and had driven for about fifteen minutes before I stopped. I sat there on the side of the road thinking about what I was doing, and then turned around and went back to the house. I sat there for a couple of hours and decided to leave again. I drove for about an hour. Then I sat on the side of the highway for about three or four hours. I just didn't know what to do; I had no idea where my life was going to go from here. Was I going to be able to handle it? Could I handle being out of baseball?

I finally decided that I was definitely leaving. I drove a couple more hours down the road. Now, I was about four or five hours outside of Fremont. I pulled over and called my agent to tell him what I had done. He said, "I have been trying to get a hold of you all day. The Milwaukee Brewers want to pick you up." He told me to go back home. So I ended up driving the five hours back to Fremont. During the whole trip back I was still indecisive, not sure what I should do. I got there and waited around for two or three days, calling my agent practically every hour to see if he had heard anything definite. The Brewers were having trouble coming to terms with Salinas, who held the rights to my contract. I couldn't see the point. This was my life that they were bargaining over. What is a couple of thousand dollars to a millionaire when someone's career is at stake? That is how I looked at it. I was more than a little bitter. I didn't sleep for three days. There was no night or day for three days. It may sound pretty dramatic, but that's how it was. They couldn't agree on a price, so the owner of the team put me on suspension for the rest of the season so that I couldn't get my release. Finally, I just left and drove east. The hardest thing was being out of the game when I knew that I could still play well.

I got a job working for a conveyer company in Alta Vista, Virginia. It was hard work—especially when you are not used to getting up and being at work at 7:00 A.M. every day. We did a lot of work for Georgia-Pacific, installing and fixing conveyers for their corrugated-box plant. We would often be on the road, putting in long hours, really hustling. I was working with good people and the work was keeping my mind occupied.

In the fall I started talking to my dad about getting back into baseball. He told me that if I wanted to, we could both make some calls and at least get a tryout. The White Sox invited me down to Sarasota for spring training. By then I had been back in school for a month and knew it was going to be a huge risk to go to Florida on a trial basis, but I went for it anyway. The next day, I was packed up and gone. I had a month to get back into shape for spring training so I could show them what I could do. My dad was living in West Palm Beach, and the Braves were letting us use their batting cages and facilities. Every day we were out there—hitting, running, throwing, catching fly balls. We probably took only four days off all month. After that I would go lift weights. I was putting in eight or nine hours a day. It was really intense.

My attitude was that I am going to work harder than I have ever worked before in my life. Before all of my energy and ambition was directed toward making the big leagues and anything short of that just wasn't acceptable. Now my attitude was just to go out there and do the best I possibly could. If I didn't get to the big leagues, then I would get out and accept it.

When spring training started, I went over to Sarasota and had the best spring of my life. I worked with Pat Rossler, a great hitting coach. I was out there at 7:00 A.M. every day in the batting cages when the other guys weren't even up yet. Pat was always out there early too, always willing to work with me. The White Sox have their own structured way of hitting and they want every player in the organization to hit the same way. They teach you to swing down and inside the ball, to keep hitting through the ball even after you have made contact—down and through the ball and then follow through. Most organizations believe hitting is more of an individual thing and that you can't teach everyone to hit the same. But I learned the White Sox approach.

I played with the Double A team [Birmingham] all spring. Every day I knew the situation was do or die. I knew I couldn't relax. It was nonstop busting my butt, and it paid off. I had a great spring. When we played the big league team, I was their designated hitter for the first few innings and then played right field. It was a good feeling knowing that there was a place for me.

The last few days of spring training, the front office bumped two outfielders down from Triple A, so I knew I wouldn't be playing every

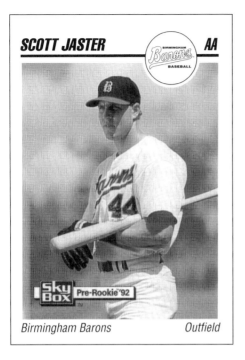

A Scott Jaster baseball card.

day. When we got to Birmingham, they platooned me against left-handed pitchers. My intensity would just build on the bench for the two or three days of waiting to play. Then when I got in, I would be super intense and focused. Shoot, I started out the first month hitting about .370. They moved a couple guys up and another guy got hurt. That gave me an opportunity to play every day. I kept it going.

When I wake up in the morning, the first thing I do is my visualization drills. Some days you wake up and it is just right there, you begin to visualize. Other days you have to make yourself start to think about it before it starts to flow. I try to visualize hitting against the pitcher I am going to face that day: visualizing past at bats that I have had against him and defensive situations, and plays coming at me and how I handle them. I do it for about ten to fifteen minutes or however long it carries me.

Then I get up and try to get my body going. You are often a little stiff, so you have to get up and do something—maybe go to the mall or do some sort of activity. I try to get to the ballpark early every day. I like to take my time putting on my uniform and getting ready. I don't want to feel rushed. I use the uniform as a concentration lock-in. Once I get it on—boom—I am in, I am focused. I am ready to go out there and do my work. Some days I am super intense, other days I feel a little bit lazy and have to force myself to get into it. It's a mental and physical roller coaster, but I have to try and make it a straight ride as best as I can. Some days you are on a straight ride. You get your hits, you make the great plays, and the day is great. Other days, for some reason, you just can't do it. That's why baseball is so difficult sometimes.

After the game, I get something to eat. Sometimes, if the game was good, I go out with the guys. It's good to get out and get the game off my mind for a little bit. I need a break to change the subject for a while. When I go to bed, I try to visualize again. I put another fifteen minutes into it. Then I say my prayers, and the next day it starts all over.

⚛

The next year Jaster was again sent to Birmingham, where after hitting .290 for the first half of the season, he was promoted to the White Sox Triple A team in Vancouver, British Columbia. There he continued to play well. Toward the end of the season he made plans to join his uncle in Alaska. But during the last road trip, he learned that the White Sox expected him to play winter ball in Venezuela.

⚛

I didn't know anything about it until some of the guys asked me if I was looking forward to winter ball in Venezuela. They said they'd seen my name on the list and that I was one of the five or six guys the White Sox were sending. I'd already made plans to go to Alaska to work on a mining claim with my uncle. I had my plane tickets, and everything was worked out. I was going to be leaving in a few days, the day after the season ended. So when I heard about Venezuela, I called up the minor league director and he said, yeah, they wanted me to go. With one day's notice I had to contact my uncle to tell him I wasn't coming, which was hard to do because he was living in the bush. I went home to Midland [Michigan] for a week and then down to Florida for some training at the White Sox complex in Sarasota before the five of us were to leave for Venezuela.

I was a six-year free agent and they hadn't signed me to a contract yet. [After six years with an organization, minor league players become free agents and may sign with any organization they wish.] The day before I was to fly out, the front office said they wanted to meet with me. I went upstairs to the office. They asked me to sign a new contract, offering me a thousand dollars less per month than what guys with my experience were making. The game was sacred to me. I loved this game. I didn't need to make a million dollars. But I did need to make enough to start paying some bills. The six-year free agents my agent was handling were making between five and six thousand a month. I was twenty-six years old, had been in the game for six years, and had put up some good numbers. And they were offering me a thousand dollars less than what my agent said was reasonable?

I asked them for $500 more per month—that was only $2,500 over the course of the season. They refused and said that I was squeezing them and a lot of other crap. I got mad and walked out. I called my agent. He said their offer was unreasonable and that if I wanted him to, he would have no trouble getting me more money with another team. I just couldn't accept the way the White Sox were treating me. So I walked out—no winter ball. A month later I signed with the Kansas City Royals.

𝕕𝕠

Jaster went to spring training with the Royals in 1993 and was assigned to the Memphis Chicks of the Double A Southern League. He was now playing for his third organization. It did not work out like he had hoped.

𝕕𝕠

I missed the White Sox training program, especially having a hitting coach on every team. The Royals have only one hitting coach for the whole minor league system. With the White Sox, having a hitting coach that I could work with every day kept me sharp all year long. He was like a video camera or a second pair of eyes. He could see what was working and keep me swinging the same. Plus, the White Sox had an excellent conditioning program that kept you strong all year so you didn't get tired in August. The Royals don't have a conditioning program and they don't believe in lifting weights. With the White Sox, we had a weight facility right in the clubhouse. With the Royals, I had to go on my own to a gym every day—forty-five minutes away—come back home after my workout, eat lunch, and then go to the park, which was a half-hour drive away.

In Memphis I got off to a good start and was hitting close to .300 when I hurt my wrist sliding. I didn't feel much pain at first and kept playing. Then I could feel it and I started struggling at the plate. Your bat control and your mechanics change all on their own when your brain is trying to protect an injured part of your body. I was hooking a lot of balls, couldn't stay through the pitch and drive the ball the other way. I went on the DL [disabled list] and rested it for awhile. But when I came back it wasn't any better. Finally, they sat me down for the whole month of July to see if my wrist would come around. It didn't, and I ended up seeing three doctors over the next couple of months. Finally one of them scoped it and found tears in the cartilage. The doctor—a Royals doctor, not the specialist I wanted to go to— made some repairs and cleaned it up a bit. He made me think it was going to be alright and that I'd make a full recovery. I was in rehab for it all winter and went to Florida to work out with my dad two months before the start of spring training. I got back to where I could do everything that I had done before, but my wrist felt different. Knowing that I had to put the surgery behind me and be positive, I made myself believe that I was 100 percent.

During the first game of spring training, I hurt my wrist again. I didn't realize it until that night. I had all the same symptoms—locking and heat flashes—and the wrist swelled up. I was afraid to say anything. I showed it to the trainer and told him I didn't want anyone else to know because this spring was do or die for me. My career was on the line. So I played on my sore wrist, and over the next nine games I got only one hit. On the tenth day they called me up to the office and told me they were releasing me. I told them my wrist was bothering me, and they kind of looked at me like I was making excuses, like they didn't believe me. When you can't produce, you're gone! I was feeling long gone, and I was wondering where the humanity and compassion was. I packed up and left the next morning for the long drive back to Midland, Michigan.

⚉

EPILOGUE

When I called Scott a year later, he was at home in Midland. He said, "I am sitting here on the sofa trying to figure out what I am going to do with the rest of my life." Since his release from the Royals, he had been to orthopedic specialists in Michigan, Kansas, and Virginia, hoping that someone could heal his wrist so that he could return to baseball. It took almost a year and some legal help before he received any of the workmen's compensation he was entitled to. The Royals had not been cooperative and had balked at letting him see an outside orthopedic specialist. Scott was bitter: "When you're doing well and success is all clouded around you, you don't see the crap. The thing of it, though, is that when you're on the field, under the lights, and the crowd's energy is beating on your back, it's magical out there. It's a swing back to those days growing up. That's what keeps you going, when the magic outweighs the crap."

No longer attached to any major league organization, Jaster talked about going to play in the Mexican League, if necessary, hoping that doing well there would lead to an invitation to spring training next year. Meanwhile his agent was looking for an organization short on outfielders in which Scott might fit. At age twenty-nine, after two "surgeries" and no big league experience, Scott recognized that it was going to be an uphill struggle.

✺

If I am healthy and go back, believe me it will be 100 percent, full tilt, total dedication! If I am not healthy, and this is the end of my career, I still have to get this wrist fixed so that at least I'll be able to chop wood, pound nails, or swing a golf club someday. Right now, I can't even get a job. And I am getting married soon, so there will be more than just me to look after. I can't expect Jennifer to endure the hardships I seem almost immune to. But she has already accepted the fact that I may go back to baseball.

Pat Young

Every professional baseball team has a clubhouse manager who looks after the players and the coaches. Major league teams have a small staff performing that function, while the low minor leagues have a single individual. For the Hickory Crawdads of the Class A South Atlantic League, that person is Pat Young. Young has been a "clubby" for three years, having started with the Greensboro Hornets in 1991. A friend in the Yankees organization got Young the job after he had become bored with being a layout artist for a newspaper. The Crawdads' clubhouse is also Pat's home. At night he pushes two training tables together to make a bed. Young's view of his work and of ballplayers is different from that of most others in this book.

☫

When I found out I got the job, it was great. I thought, "Now I'm going to be making forty or fifty thousand a year." And I was like, "Yeah! I won't have to work in the off-season, and I can take seven months off and do nothing." I told everyone that I was quitting my job as a layout artist because I was going to work for the Yankees. I thought, "What a great career decision this is going to be. My life is going to be baseball. And I'm going to work with the players and work my way up to exercise physiologist and work in Tampa. And isn't this going to be great?" When I got there, it was nothing like I thought it would be. It was horrible.

It was real culture shock for me. The players knew that I was a rookie and kept trying to take advantage of me. I'd tell them to pick their stuff up from the floor, and they would say, "Hey, we pay you. We take care of you. Don't tell us what to do." That's the way it was with those guys. They pushed me at every angle to see if I'd give. I was too easy on them, and I still have that problem today. I just don't like getting in somebody's face.

When I took this job, my boss didn't tell me that it was going to be a fourteen- or fifteen-hour day. I've learned how to wash and dry pants: you've got to wash them right side out in hot water, then you pull them inside out to let the pockets air out when you hang them up to dry. I've learned how to get stains out. Until I learned the right way to remove stains from uniforms, the batting coach would look at me and then look at his pants that had a big stain on them and say, "Mmmmmmm." I've learned the system, but it's been rough.

One day when I was there for seventeen hours, I thought, "There has got to be a way to cut back." I figured that while the game was going on, I could wash the practice uniforms and shine some of the shoes so I wouldn't have to be doing it till the wee hours of the morning. But I still couldn't get this job done in under fourteen hours a day when the team was at home. There was so much to do.

The first few months I had a lot of temper tantrums. I punched the wall. You should see my car. It's got a big hole in the dashboard where I punched it. I busted the windshield. I slammed the driver's side door and busted it out. Our trainer joked that he was going to get me some Valium to calm me down. But he helped me out. He told me not to take any crap from the players.

I got a nickname the first day on the job. It's an honor, but I didn't realize it at first. I thought, "Nickname? I don't want no nickname. I'm Pat Young." They said, "Well, we've already got a guy named Pat on the team. We can't have two Pats. Let's see, Pat Young, huh? Sort of like Youngblood. Joel Youngblood, yeah. Youngblood. Hey Youngblood!" That kind of stuck. Then the manager started calling me Plasma or O Positive.

My friend Shawn came to town a month into my new job, and I begged him to get me out of it. I told him I was going to quit. He said,

Pat Young, clubhouse
manager.

"Don't quit. These guys can be jerks, but they're not bad. They've given you a nickname. You should feel honored. 'Blood?' That's a good nickname. They could have called you something horrible."

On a day-to-day basis, I'm responsible for the players' laundry. I hang up their gear, put their mail in their lockers, clean the clubhouse, mop the floors with disinfectant, clean the toilets, take the pass list up to the ticket booth, make sure the baseballs are taken to the umpires, and shine the coaching staff's shoes. If the players pay extra, which most do, I'll do their shoes. Shoes are a big part of the job. I've never liked doing them. It takes an extra hour to do it right. Today I didn't use any polish, but I'm going to leave the polish out there to make it look like I shined the shoes. They won't know that all I did was clean the shoes because they look fine.

I'm given a dollar a day by each player, which includes home and road games. So I get thirty dollars a month from each of these guys. The coaching staff pays me double. I could have charged $1.50 a day, but these guys don't make very much. A dollar is the average for this league. If you go below that, you're a fool because you won't make any money. The dues make up 80 percent of my salary. I get a small supplemental check from the GM [general manager] and, like the players, meal money on the road. It's not cheap anymore to eat on the road. When the bus stops, you have no choice but to eat right there.

I post on the bulletin board the date that the players are supposed to pay their dues. If they are real late, I can tell the manager. I haven't done that yet. But I have a real problem enforcing my dues. Sometimes I'll let them slide until the next time—like if the guy is just plain broke. Sometimes they'll say, "I owed you from last week. Here's an extra five dollars. Sorry about that." So they'll give me $35 and sometimes $40. A lot of them are really good about paying up front. Pitchers—I don't know if it's because they've got a lot of spare time—always treat me the best. They always tip me and always pay me first. The Latinos are the worst on paying, but that's probably because they send a lot of their money home. The players think I'm making a killing. I'm not. I'm making less here, where during a home stand I work ninety hours a week, than I made at the newspaper job, where I worked thirty hours a week.

Some of the guys think everyone is going to roll out the red carpet for them just because they're ballplayers. Well, I'm not. I'm not impressed. I just want to do the job that I've got to do. Now if they take care of me—tip me and things like that—well okay, I'm going to take care of them. But, I'm not going to go out of my way to do an extraordinary job for a guy who pays me just the normal stuff and doesn't treat me with any respect. I have to beg a lot guys to get my dues, and they treat me like dirt sometimes. They think, "You're working for the players, buddy. If it weren't for us you wouldn't have a job."

The players try to get as much out of a clubhouse manager as they can. They might say, "Can we get some Gatorade in the cooler?" Gatorade is a big expense, and I would be crazy to go out and buy it for those guys. So I might say, "I don't have any Gatorade." "Well don't be afraid to go out and buy some. That's what we pay you for. We take care of you. You're killing us." Or they might say, "Can you go up and get me some fried chicken?" Then I might say, "Wait a minute. I, who worked fourteen hours yesterday, you who worked seven—I can't see how I have the time to buy you fried chicken. I don't think so."

The players also seem to think that everything is free. It's not. I should know. I've asked for free stuff for the players. "If it's free, it's for me." I hear that all the time. All their lives they've been given things and they expect things to be free after that. They've been patted

Inside the clubhouse of the West Palm Beach Expos. (Photo by Jason Getz)

on the back and told, "It's okay. We'll take care of it. You shouldn't have to do that." They've got that mentality of "What do you say I play a round of golf for free because I'm a ballplayer and you should be honored." They get a lot of things for free in this town. This town has opened their arms and the women have opened their legs to these guys.

Our concession guy came in here with some leftover burgers. There was enough for everybody to have one burger. They were complaining about not being able to get two apiece. The concession guy told them, "You're kind of lucky to be getting these." And one of the players says, "What does that guy mean by saying that? He's lucky he's got a job. If it weren't for us, he wouldn't have a job." Since I was in a bad mood, I went storming upstairs and told him not to feed these guys again because they don't appreciate it.

You can't piss on somebody and then hand them a hundred dollars and say you're sorry. And it happens in this league and it happens later on in baseball. But it doesn't work like that with me. I'll be thirty this year and this isn't the kind of job for me. I never have time for myself. I know it's only five months. But I never have time for myself. It's just grueling sometimes. Five months where you have no patience, five months where you just want to take something and throw it, which I have done.

The only way the skills I use for this job could transfer outside of baseball is if I became a kindergarten teacher or a camp counselor. I'm raising children. I can't believe some of the things I have heard and seen from these guys. It's amazing how impatient they are. "I want this" and "I can't find my pants" and this and that. You get sick of it. They can't take care of themselves. If they were responsible for washing their own uniforms, it would never get done. Here's a typical scenario I deal with: "Okay, well I went out last night and got drunk, got home about four in the morning, got up about two o'clock, and came to the ballpark. Can you go get me some food?"

I tell people in the real world that players are like that and they look at me like I'm crazy. "They're such nice guys. They sound so nice on those interviews." Well sure, who doesn't? The players don't respect very many people outside baseball—except maybe other pro athletes like football and basketball players or golfers. Anybody outside of the realm of baseball is nothing to them. You owe me everything because I'm a ballplayer. You should worship me. I know I'm painting a really bad picture of these players, but a lot of ballplayers at this level are like that.

EPILOGUE

By his own choice, Pat Young left baseball after this season and returned to his old newspaper job in St. Louis. But one year later he got "the itch to work for another team" and took a job as clubhouse manager for the Boise (Idaho) Hawks of the Northwest League.

Jim Leyland

MANAGER, FLORIDA MARLINS

When the Pittsburgh Pirates announced in 1985 that forty-year-old Jim Leyland was to be their new field manager, the reaction of the Pittsburgh media was cool. Although Leyland had been the third-base coach for the Chicago White Sox for the four previous seasons, he had never played nor managed in the major leagues. At the press conference to announce Leyland's appointment, general manager Syd Thrift explained that in hiring a new manager the Pirates wanted someone who could relate to younger players, who was receptive to new ideas, and who reflected the strong work ethic of the Pittsburgh area.

As field manager for the Pirates, Leyland turned around a team that had lost more than a hundred games the year before and had finished last. In two seasons the Pirates were playing .500, and in 1990 they won their first of three National League East championships. In a Sep-tember 15, 1990 Sporting News *article, writer Tom Barnidge de-scribed Leyland in these words: "In a sport populated by Porches, Mercedes, and Jaguars, Leyland is a pickup truck, and the side panels are dented and scraped. The engine is a V8 but the model is stripped down. No power windows, no reclining seats . . . You get yourself a Leyland to do a job not to impress your friends."*

Leyland's success with the Pirates soon ran out, however. Strapped for cash, the small-market club was forced to sell off, or lose to free agency, their best talent. After two last-place finishes, Leyland quit in 1996. Offered managing jobs with four big-spending teams, he eventually signed a five-year contract with the Florida Marlins. He led them to a World Series in his first season.

Jim Leyland grew up in a small town, Perrysburg, Ohio (population 12,551). At Perrysburg High School, he played quarterback, sang in the choir, edited the yearbook's sports section and was voted the most popular boy. A standout high school catcher, he was signed by the Detroit Tigers after graduation. In the minor leagues he was a strong catcher and a weak hitter, and in seven years of playing never got beyond Double A. I was his teammate on two teams in the mid-1960s— in Jamestown, New York, and Rocky Mount, North Carolina.

When I met Jim in his clubhouse office at Three Rivers Stadium in 1992, I hadn't seen him in twenty-four years. I was eager to catch up and hear of our old teammates, some of whom Jim still heard from: Gene Lamont was managing the White Sox; Jim Rooker was the color commentator for the Pirate broadcasts; Dave Bike was a college basketball coach; and Jon Warden had won the Ohio state lottery.

As Jim and I talked, I thought about how different our career paths had been. We were exactly the same age; and in our early twenties, we had been at the same place with the same ambition of making the big leagues. Although I had always been pleased with my decision to become an anthropologist and a college professor, seeing Jim's world from the inside made me nostalgic for the baseball life.

⚾

When I started managing in the minor leagues, I never had any thought of going to the big leagues. That wasn't why I managed. The Tigers offered me a job as a coach at Montgomery [Double A, Southern League] in 1970 and I thought, "Well, I'll try it. It's a job." I wasn't doing anything better at the time, and I didn't have a lot of education. I thought I'd try it and see if I liked it. The next year they offered me the manager's job at Bristol in the Appalachian League. It never really dawned on me that I would ever be a candidate for a major league position—at least not until 1979 when I was managing Toledo [Triple A, International League] and our club won the pennant and everything. At that point I had already managed eight or nine years in the minors. That year I managed against Tony La Rusa and he got the big league job with the White Sox in August. I stayed in Triple A two more years, thinking that I might have a chance to at least get a coaching job in the big leagues. But really, up until 1979, I had no idea that I'd ever get a shot at the big leagues.

A lot of people say that when you make it after all those years in the minors, you paid your dues. Yeah, I did pay my dues. I rode buses much of those eighteen years. [He also changed addresses many times during his tenure in the minor leagues. He has lived in Cocoa Beach and Lakeland, Florida; Jamestown, New York; Rocky Mount, North Carolina; Montgomery, Alabama; Bristol, Tennessee; Clinton, Iowa; Evansville, Indiana; and Toledo, Ohio. His teams won three league championships, and he was voted manager of the year three times.] But a lot of other people in the minor leagues also paid their dues and never got a chance. So I've been very fortunate. And if I never managed another day, I'd still say it's been great. It was all worth it.

Managing up here is more difficult than in the minor leagues because here it is win or you're out. Down there, there is no pressure on you to win as long as you are developing the players, seeing to it that they are getting all the work they need to make that advancement to the next step. If you do that and keep your nose clean, your job is never in jeopardy.

Up here, you can be managing your ass off and if you don't win, sooner or later they get you because there is pressure from fans and the media to win. The front office may like you and may even think you're a good manager, but they may still give into fan and media pressure. Often your fate is in your players' hands: either you're a beneficiary of your players' successes or you're the victim of your players' failures. That's what you have to realize. You can't take yourself too seriously. That's very important. Yes, it's the players who mostly determine your fate. I've been lucky.

Don't think you're going to outsmart Joe Torre or Jeff Torburg, because you're not. Usually you're not going to outfox anybody. You make a move one night that pays off and the very next night you get humbled doing the same thing. You just hope that your guys outplay their guys.

⚾

Jim Leyland is one of baseball's most popular managers, in part because of his modesty. When he was named National League Manager of the Year by the Baseball Writer's Association in 1992 for the second time in three seasons, he gave credit to others: "I really believe anybody could have managed the Pittsburgh Pirates in 1992 and won. I don't think I had a whole lot to do with it."

When you go from the minor leagues to the big leagues the game doesn't change. It's still four balls, you walk; three strikes, you're out. That's not going to change; that's the great thing about baseball. But so many other things are different up here—like all the media. One big thing you must do differently here is handle the media and learn to manage your time. You have to make time for reporters, along with everything else you do. I've learned that I've got to come to the ballpark early each day just to have some time to myself before the barrage starts. Down there I could come to the ballpark at 3:30 in the afternoon and have plenty of time to do whatever I needed.

I learned from my parents not to lie, and that's the best way to get along with the media. It's the best way to get along with people, period. All you have to do is tell the truth. And when there are issues that you can't talk about, you politely say, "Fellas, I'm not at freedom to talk about that right now." Everything you say is the truth, because that's the way you were raised. The other advantage I've had is that when I coached in Chicago, Tony La Rusa [manager] allowed me to come into his office after every game and listen to him be interviewed. I used to sit in the corner and just listen. That was a great experience because Chicago was a large media city and there were lots of people there, lots of writers, with lots of questions. That really put the finishing touches on me—on top of my grade-school philosophy that if you tell the truth, you'll have no problems.

Up here you got players with big salaries, making big, big bucks. That's real different from down there. But it doesn't make any difference when it comes to how I treat my players. I've always tried to treat people the same, from the first day I've managed until right now. It hasn't changed. You treat them the way that you'd want to be treated. You treat them like adults. I think it's a very simple but very wise philosophy.

From the players I expect effort and preparation, and I usually get that. I like my players, and that's an advantage. I have no animosity about the money they make. In fact, I'm proud of them. I disagree with people who say that they're overpaid. It always rubs me a little

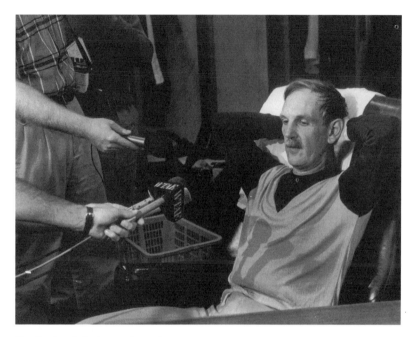

Jim Leyland during an interview. (Courtesy of the Pittsburgh Pirates)

bit wrong when folks say, "Geeze, these guys are dumb jocks and they're making all this kind of money." You got to remember that the owners that are paying the big money are successful businesspeople. They're smart people; they're college graduates. When free agency came in it was their decision to pay those big salaries.

⚂

In the major leagues the manager and coaching staff have access to a great deal of statistical information about opposing teams. I asked Leyland what difference that made in managing in the big leagues.

⚂

I get computer printouts of all the players in the league showing what they do against each of my pitchers—how many hits, how many fly balls, how many ground balls, where they hit the ball. Some people think you manage by the computer, but that isn't true. Computers produce basically no more information than the good old-fashioned paper and pencil gave you. It's just that computers are much quicker. You can put this in, and within five seconds you have your answer. You are not sitting down with paper and pencil figuring it all out. That takes forever. But basically, the statistics that are made available today were always there. It's the time element that's different.

I normally look over the stuff before the game. I come in at 1:30 or two o'clock in the afternoon and look at it. I try to use it to program my mind. For instance, today I saw that Lonnie Smith [of the visiting Atlanta Braves] has hit .627 with three home runs against Bob Walk, so I know this is not the ideal matchup I want, and that knowledge may help me make a decision during the game. Although I look into that stuff before the game, I do take it with me to the bench just in case of an emergency where something slips my mind and I think, "Gee, I'm not sure." Then I look at my data real quick and alter or confirm my decision.

A lot of people think we use computers because it provides an explanation after the game for a decision you made. That's wrong. That's not the reason at all. There is one thing about managing in the big leagues that is very important. If you make decisions based on what you're afraid of, you'll have to answer for that after the game—and then you're a horse-shit manager. You do what you think it takes for your club to win that game, and you have to care less about what some reporter asks you afterwards.

Some writers ask legitimate questions and some ask the dumbest things you've ever heard in your life. But that makes no difference. Your responsibility as manager is to answer them—whether you like them or not. I say I made my decision because I felt that it gave the Pittsburgh Pirates the best chance to win the game. For instance, the other day in New York we had a one-run lead in the ninth inning; they managed to get a man on first; and my pitcher went three and two [in the count] and I changed pitchers. That pitcher got the batter out, and we won the game. A lot of people questioned my call, saying they didn't understand it. It does not matter what they have seen or haven't seen. You as the manager have got to be thinking all the time about what gives your team the best chance to win. I don't give a damn if some sportswriter from the *Stony Ridge Gazette* thinks that we should have bunted, hit and run, or whatever. I can respect his opinion, but it's irrelevant. You have got to do what makes sense to you, and that may not always be what people expect. I don't want to be sitting home someday after I get fired saying, "Geeze, I wish I'd done it my way." So I make decisions based on what I feel.

Up here we use a lot more video than down there [minor leagues]. We have a regular video guy who travels with us. It's outstanding. There isn't any question that video has been one of the major breakthroughs in baseball. It makes our preparation a lot better. We have tapes of all the pitchers who pitched against us, which enable us to watch those tapes when we play against them next. Even if they're using a new pitcher that we haven't seen, we can still see him on tape and see what he throws. It is definitely an advantage for our hitters.

But there is a limit to how much of this new technology you can use. A lot of different stuff has been tried—like different bat weights, different machines, and all. I think it has maxed out. Baseball will never be played by robots. One thing that you have to remember as a manager is that your players are human beings. They're not mechanical men. There are always going to be errors. You can have all the technology that you want, but when the players go out to take the field, they are on their own. The human element will always be there, and that will never change. That's why it is such a great game. You can computerize batting averages on printouts and all that, but you'll never computerize the game.

When I was a youngster, and even when I started playing professionally, I wasn't really aware that baseball was a business. I never ever thought about players' contracts, arbitration, free agency, TV contracts, or the money the owners were making. It just never dawned on me that NBC or CBS had a contract that was worth millions of dollars to the teams. I thought of it totally as a game, but as we got into the nineties, I began to realize what it was all about. I don't think I really ever realized it until I got to the big leagues in Chicago, where we had some guys under big contracts. That was 1979, a time when salaries really started to skyrocket. Then it dawned on me: "Hey, thirty or forty thousand people in the park, concessions, programs, TV contracts—this has got to be a billion-dollar business." As a kid, baseball was a taped-up bat, an old ball, taking batting practice, and sliding into a sawdust base. That's what I thought, and then all of a sudden I realized that, "Hey, there is big money involved here."

In eighteen years in the minor leagues, I was never involved in any kind of real money. You made ends meet, and that was it. But at least you always had a buck in your pocket. You could always buy a new pair of shoes and that made you happy—but it wasn't like money. It was like survival. Then you get to the big leagues. In my second year in the big leagues we got into the play-offs. The most I had ever made managing in the minor leagues was $22,000, and here in one check after the play-offs is more money than I had made managing over a full season in the minor leagues. And since then, there has been a lot more. And then there is all the licensing revenue available to you. I mean, it is amazing. And after my long tenure in the minor leagues, it's nice. But it's still a fantasy world.

֎

Most managers hate having to release players. Being released often means the end of a player's career, his dream, big money, and his identity as a professional athlete. Leyland talks about his approach.

֎

The general manager usually comes in, but I am the one to tell the player. It's hard, but the decision has been made. It's what the organization feels is in the best interest of the organization, and I'm part of the organization. I never put the responsibility on anyone else. I don't bring the player in and say, "I don't really want to release you but I don't have any choice." To me, that's chicken shit. I say, "Hey, we're releasing you. We made a decision."

I'll never forget that in Tigertown [Detroit Tigers' spring-training complex] the coaches didn't release players. Instead, management called them up to the office and the farm director released them. One time, during my first year managing, this kid had been released and came over to the manager's locker room and said, "I feel terrible. I've been released and if I could ever play for anyone, I'd want to play for you." This kid had the biggest tears in his eyes, and I was looking down on the ground, hurt and not knowing what to say. All I remember thinking was, "Good Lord, let me look this kid in the eye and tell him exactly the way it is." And I did. I told him he's got a new chance on life. We may have been wrong, but now he should go back to school, find himself something to do. And I felt so good about myself afterward that I forgot momentarily about the fact that he was hurt. But I felt good about myself for having told him straight and from that day on I never had any problem. You tell the truth. It's our opinion; we may be wrong, but this is the way it is.

Releasing someone has never been easy. And it's certainly never been something you look forward to. But a lot of those guys that I've released send me Christmas cards. They tell me what they're doing, what their life is about—and that makes me feel good. If you tell him the truth, he's pissed off for two or three days, but not forever. But if you lie to him, you've lost him forever.

A lot of getting to the major leagues is chance, getting the hit at the right time, taking advantage of your opportunities. That is one thing I always told my players in the minor leagues: that opportunity comes to some people many times, over and over; but for most people it comes maybe once or twice. When it does come, you want to make sure that you are prepared. When your opportunity comes, take advantage of it. There have been some very unfortunate players. You and I have both seen players that have been released down there that should have been big league players. Sometimes you feel that if you'd done a better job coaching them in the minor leagues, maybe they would have put a little more effort into what you said and they would be here today. There are guys we played with who you thought couldn't miss making it, but for some reason they did. It's sad. That's just the way it is and always will be.

When I get a new player who has been called up, I tell him, "You've listened to everybody in the minor leagues. You've had some success. And now you've been called up to the big leagues, so keep doing what got you here." You want the kid to be himself. You don't want him to go up there and have everybody filling his head with suggestions. I've always thought overcoaching was worse than undercoaching.

After the game, I find myself sitting around the clubhouse for two or three hours. I don't sit around drinking beer. I sit in my coaches' room with my coaches and talk. And when we're playing at home, I stay around to face the media for a while. As soon as that is over, I like to get home to my family, to see my son and spend some time with my wife. The guys [players] like to hang around and talk after the game, although I think they talk about different things from our generation of players. Today there's less baseball talk, less talk about the game itself and more about outside interests. I don't mean that there is bad talk going on. I'm not talking about broads and all of that shit.

Managing is not an easy job. It's tough. Yes, we are well compensated, but it is a tough job—the travel, the media, the slumps, the losses, and everything that goes with that. It's not easy. But it's very gratifying because at 7:30 [game time] I can put all this stuff behind me and go out there and try my best to win a ball game—just like we all did when we played in the sandlots. That's the fun part.

I am not sure what I will do when I am no longer managing—maybe some broadcasting. I'd like to be a color man. I have a lot of interest in that and I think it's something I could do. I think I could bring something to the party. I would go somewhere where they're looking for a local guy to do color, someplace where I might not have to travel. I'm an older father who wants to spend time with his son, so I don't want to be going to spring training every year when he's growing up like a lot of guys have to. I'll take all that into consideration before I decide what I do.

But I know I'd miss this a lot. I'd miss the players and the coaches. And beyond that, the number one thing I'd miss is the competition. That's the thing that motivates me—the competition. To think that I was not a good player and to be going in and managing against Joe Torre, one of the great players, I mean that is motivation for me. As long as the competition is there, I want to continue. But the day that fire is gone—and it will blow out eventually—is the day I'll get out. Right now I love my job. I love to come to work. I am happy. But, if that competitive spirit is gone, it will be time to leave.

Durwood Merrill

UMPIRE, AMERICAN LEAGUE

Each year several hundred individuals enroll into one of America's three umpire-development schools. After five weeks of training, only a handful is offered contracts in professional baseball to begin umpiring at the lowest levels of the minor leagues. The odds of their eventually making it to the big leagues is no better than that of first-year ballplayers, about 5 percent. In the major leagues, at the top of the baseball pyramid, there are seven hundred players but only sixty umpires.

Durwood Merrill, age fifty-six, has been umpiring in the American League since 1977. He studied history and education at East Texas State University, and then became a high school football coach and athletic director. Nine years of pressure-cooker Texas high school football took its toll, and he started thinking about finding a different career. While watching the Saturday baseball "Game of the Week," he learned about a school for umpires in Florida. He took a leave of absence from the high school and went to Florida, not knowing what would come of his efforts.

Those five weeks in umpire school were probably the hardest five weeks of my life. It was like boot camp—everything that I did was wrong. I walked wrong, I talked wrong, I called outs wrong, I called safes wrong, I called strikes wrong. They break you down and remake you into their own mold. But right from the start, I discovered that the one thing I did have was good judgment. You can teach an umpire a lot of things—where to be positioned on all the plays, how to call balls and strikes, the rule book—but you can't teach him judgment. That's a god-given talent. It's just like with a sprinter; people are born to run only so fast. You can't take a guy who runs 12 seconds flat and coach him down to 9.5 if he doesn't have the ability. It's not in his genes. So it is the same with umpires. They have to have the God-given ability to judge a ball from a strike and an out from a safe, in a split second.

There were 105 guys in my class [1972]. Only a dozen of us were offered contracts at the end of training. And of those, six of us eventually made it to the majors, and that was after all of us spent four or five years in the minors.

My first assignment was to the Class A California League, which was a long way from my home in Texas. Later I learned that my supervisors wanted to see if I could take the loneliness of being away from home.

Umpiring in the low minors is a lot different from umpiring in big leagues. You have only one partner. It's just you and him. You travel by car, you work in dimly lit ballparks, and the money is small. In 1972 we made just $300 a month in salary and $300 more in expenses. That's it. We stayed in the cheapest hotel in town, with one room for two of us. You just try to exist from Denny's to Burger King to McDonalds. You take your clothes to the laundry when you can.

At first, every night you go out on the field there is the risk of a fight because you are still green and still learning the trade—so you make mistakes. And you have to deal with rookies that were superstars in college and still think they're the greatest in the world. There are only two umpires to cover the whole field—one behind the plate and the other calling the bases. It's a battle every night; but that's your training ground. Either you say, "Hey, this is too tough," and you quit, or you stay with it and hope that it will forge the mettle in you.

Being thirty-one when I started was probably an advantage. I was mature enough to handle most arguments, and having coached players myself, I could understand and deal with men a bit better than the younger guys. After a while, I could tell that the managers and players

Durwood Merrill posing.

appreciated my work. I could see that I was learning to call a professional strike zone.

Anyway, I survived that first season, and the next year I got moved
up to the Texas League. That jump from Single A to Double A was my
greatest thrill—even bigger than going to the big leagues. When you
get that first promotion up the ladder, you feel like you're on the way.

⚖

After a year umpiring in the Triple A American Association and in the Puerto Rican winter league, Durwood broke into the big leagues in 1976, at first as a fill-in and a year later as a full-time umpire.

Major league umpires work and travel in crews of four. Each crew has a chief who is allowed to pick one man; the other two are chosen by the league's supervisor of umpires. In putting together a crew, the supervisor considers the personalities and the strengths and weaknesses of the individual umpires, and tries to assemble a group that will be compatible and complement one another's skills. The umpires are able to request that they work with certain individuals and the league tries to honor their requests when possible. At the minor league Class A and AA levels, two umpires comprise a crew, while in Triple A crews consist of three umpires. In the minor leagues umpires share hotel rooms, while in the big leagues they each have their own room—which is no small luxury since they spend over half of the year in hotels.

⚖

In the big leagues we have our own privacy. If one guy wants to watch TV, listen to the radio, sleep, or whatever, he can do it. When you're always sharing a room it can get hard to do your own thing. We're a very close-knit group, but we don't do everything together. You give each other space. If you don't want to go out with the group, that's fine. No feelings are hurt. And we don't always pair off with the same person.

Every four or five days we move to a new city, to a new ballpark, and to a new hotel. Some towns are better than others, but you don't think much about it. If you're scheduled to go to New York, you've got to go. You're not a tourist there to see the sights. Just like cities, some ballparks are easier to work in than others, but you don't think much about that either because it's all part of the job. What determines my feelings about where I am on the road most is the hotel I am staying in. I like to be in a place where I can get out, walk around, and eat in some good restaurants nearby.

As an umpire, you've got a lot of free time on your hands. After a game I come back to the room and watch a little TV. I try to have a book with me. Right now I'm reading a book on Billy Martin. I might read until 2:30 in the morning, kind of winding down from the game. Then I'll sleep till nine or ten. There is no use getting up at seven if you're not going to work until five at night. I get up, shower, and go downstairs to have some fruit and cereal. Then I come back and put on my gym clothes and go workout. After lunch I take a nap, get up around four, shower again, and begin getting ready to go to the ballpark.

We try to get to the ballpark several hours before the game. The plate man, the umpire who will call balls and strikes, is especially in his own world. He'll rub up the baseballs. Before the game, the home plate umpire has to get sixty of the game's baseballs and rub the gloss off them with the famous Delaware River Mud. [Manufacturers sell baseballs with a gloss on them that makes gripping the ball difficult for pitchers. It has long been the plate umpire's job to rub the balls with a dry mud, which comes from the bottom of the Delaware River and is packed in coffee cans to be shipped by the league to ballparks.] We sit around and talk—maybe about last night's ball game—or we watch the news or *SportsCenter* on television. Until about thirty minutes before the game, the mood is pretty casual. But then everyone starts getting on their game faces. It'll get quiet. The plate man usually sets the tone in the locker room. You kind of work around him. If you feel he wants to talk, then you talk. But if he wants to be by himself and be quiet, you let him alone. When I'm working the plate, I like it when they leave me alone. I like to be by myself. I might watch television with the other guys for ten or fifteen minutes, but then I'll back off. We know each other's little habits.

When I'm the plate man, I take time to review in my mind the pitchers. I keep a little diary, my personal scouting reports on the pitchers. During the day I will thumb through it and make mental notes. I want to know the characteristics of each starting pitcher. I want to know what's his out pitch—fastball, slider, curve, or what? I want to get a sense of what to expect: am I going to be looking at a lot of breaking pitches or what? A Roger Clemens and a Randy Johnson are very different pitchers, and each gives you a different look from a guy who has a controlled, soft, location, sinker ball. I also think about who might be in relief, and when he comes in I watch him warm-up. I get behind him and watch what he is throwing, what pitch he's going to throw to get the guy out.

I also want to know what kind of control the pitchers have. When they put a pitcher's stats up on the scoreboard, I'll look at two things—innings pitched and bases on balls. If he's pitched twenty-three innings and given up forty walks, I have an idea of what to expect. I know he's probably going to be behind the hitter. We're going to have a lot of three-and-two counts. We're going to have the bases full and he's going to be scraping for a strike. Those are the things I think about going into the game. By playing them over in my mind, I get myself emotionally focused.

In the big leagues, unlike the minors, there is the extra pressure caused by being on TV. Every call you make is on film and could wind up on ESPN. Everything that you do during the day is aimed at getting yourself ready for that three-hour battle that night.

There are three judgments in baseball: strike and ball, out and safe, and fair and foul. Every big league umpire can handle all three to a high degree of perfection, but not everyone is the same. Some are a little stronger or a little weaker in one area or another. We all know the strengths and weaknesses of the guys we work with.

⚕

From a crouched position behind home plate, a plate umpire makes between 270 and 300 ball or strike calls per game. The pitches he watches move at 70 to 95 miles per hour. At such speeds, it's impossible to watch the pitch's entire movement, so the umpire tracks the pitch as best he can and makes his call on the basis of its afterimage—that is, the momentary picture one has of an object after it has completed its trajectory. Like hitting, calling balls and strikes requires a high level of concentration; it also requires good eyesight and being in the best position to the see the pitch.

⚕

When I entered the American League I was colorful and used lots of action in my calls. Ron Luciano [a flamboyant umpire] said I was going to become his heir apparent. But that wasn't the image most people wanted an umpire to have, and I think it hurt me. In 1977, when I came into the league, they didn't expect an umpire to talk. You were supposed to be seen and not heard, out of the steel mines, not able to think for yourself. That wasn't me. Today we're a pretty educated group. Most of us have gone to college. We have our own identity. I'd like to think I helped break the barrier, helped forge a better identity for umpires. When somebody calls me and says, "Hey, I'd like you to talk about the strike zone." Well, not only can I talk about the strike zone, but I can also talk about President Clinton's economic policy.

⚎

Before the game, the plate umpire inspects the condition of the field; he is the umpire in charge and has authority over everyone on the field and in the stadium, including his umpire partners, the home team, and stadium employees. He is the representative of the league, responsible for delaying, postponing, and canceling games in case of bad weather.

About five minutes before game time the umpires convene the managers of the two teams at home plate to discuss ground rules and exchange lineup cards. The plate umpire then commences play.

⚎

Ideally, you want the game to move along at a nice crisp pace. And of course you'd like there not to be any disputes or arguments. Umpires don't want to attract attention. You'd like to work the whole game without anyone even noticing you're out there—ideally.

When I'm behind the plate, I like a pitcher with good control. It's much easier to call balls and strikes if he can throw strikes and can throw around the plate. It's a lot tougher with a guy like Randy Johnson, who throws 100 miles per hour but never knows where the ball is going.

Every umpire has his own idiosyncrasies, his own style. Players who have been around a while know your characteristics. When they walk up to the plate they know your strike zone, whether it's liberal or pretty tight. With me, they're thinking, "Durwood is a pitcher's umpire. He's going to call them hall-of-fame strikes so we got to be hacking."

I've always been a pitcher's umpire. You get into less trouble calling close pitches strikes then you do calling them balls. My thinking is that a good plate umpire should never miss a strike. He should call strikes the eight to ten pitches that you get every game that could go either way. Calling them strikes makes hitters hit. They're paid to hit. Fans come out to see them hit. People don't pay to see these guys walk.

When you're going good you get into what we call a "groove." Some players use the word "zone." You can go for weeks where you feel like they can't throw anything to the plate that you can't call and get right. But then one day it's not there. You've lost it. It may be due to being tired, being mentally stale, or whatever. You go out there and nothing is looking good to you. Your experience tells you that you need to back up a little bit and look at the pitch a little longer, or that you need to get a little higher. If it still ain't looking right you say, "Well, I'm gonna call strikes. The more strikes I call, the more I'm gonna get them hitters swinging that bat and we'll get through this." That's what you have to do. There are times when you must call on all your knowledge and experience to help you pull through it and to help you get back into the groove.

Even when you're not in the groove, you must show confidence. Players and managers respect confidence; they want to see it. The other night one of them hollered out to me, "That was a balk." I looked at him and said, "I wrote the book on balks." They laughed, and then one of them said, "I bet it wasn't very thick." Instead of just hollering, "No it wasn't a balk," you have to say something back to them that shows that you're in charge. That's the smart way to handle them.

Baseball is a long season. You can't attack every game like the Dallas Cowboys playing once a week. When I coached football everything built up to that one game, and you gave it all you had, full bore. But in baseball you're out there every day, so you've got to have a real good grip on it. You don't want to get too high on your good days, and you don't want to get too low on your bad days. When I first got into the game, I approached it from a football-coaching standpoint. I would try to fire up every game to max. One day I had a partner who said, "Hey, you'll be in a straitjacket if you keep that up."

Even though you want to stay level, on an even keel, it's different when you umpire a big game like a World Series or an All-Star Game. If I'm looking at an All-Star Game, I know it's just one game. So you can pump up for peak performance. If it's the World Series, you know the max is seven games and the minimum is four, so you can still use everything you got in your body. But over the course of a 162-game schedule, you just can't maintain that kind of intensity.

In the big games, like in a World Series, every umpire has an innate fear that a game might be won or lost by a call he has to make. You don't want to have to make a call in a World Series where the media or the losing team will forever say that your call cost them the game, or maybe even cost the team the Series. I know a couple of umpires who have been in those situations and they've never gotten over it. They've never completely put it behind them. You hope it never happens to you. It's not the end of the world, but at the time you sure do think it is.

Every umpire misses a play once in a while—we're only human. Usually when you go to the locker room, you know whether you got it right or wrong. Either someone else in your crew has told you or, with them putting replays up on the screen [Diamond Vision], you saw it. In the locker room with the other guys you might discuss it when you discuss the game. I'll say, "Tim, did I get that play right in the fourth inning? What do you think?" He'll say, "I thought you missed." He's not going to help me by telling me what I want to hear.

We always try to help each other. If you see that a guy's timing is a little too quick or a little too slow, or you notice something he's doing that he normally doesn't do, you tell him so that he can correct it. One of my partners last night said he has been struggling at first base and didn't know why. The play was just collapsing on him. It was bang, bang—and he was having a hard time reading it. I told him to move further away from the bag: "You have to get to where your eyes work best for you. It's all in the angle and the eyes." He moved further away, made a little adjustment, and his problem cleared up. That's the way it is—you depend upon your partners to help you with that fine-tuning.

For me, having a bad night is blowing a call or having to deal with a brawl, a bench-clearing brawl. With brawls, it's often something you had nothing to do with. But you still have to get in there and sort it out. When I was younger, I used to love to get into the middle of it. I've been hit, had my shirt torn and everything. But now I think it's just crazy. I stay on the outskirts and try to break it up as best as I can without getting pummeled.

When there's a brawl, the first thing you've got to do is get the managers and coaches to start breaking up their players and getting their players separated. That's their job. Second, you try to get them paired up. If everybody grabs a guy and holds him back, then we've got everyone covered. Then, after peace has been restored, we discuss how it all got started: who were the troublemakers, and who were the guys who prolonged it? Then we decide what to do about it, what the penalties should be, and who to eject. Later we have to file a report to the league office. The league also gets a video of the brawl to study at their office in New York City. With brawls, there's always a lot of second-guessing about what you could have done to have prevented it, to have broken it up sooner, or to have kept it from escalating into a full-scale donnybrook. But you can't dwell on it just like you can't dwell on missing a call, because you got to go right back out there on that field tomorrow.

People think there is a lot more fighting in baseball today, but I think it's been magnified by television. If you check back to the old days, you'll find there were a lot of fights back then too. Ty Cobb started more dang fights than you can shake a stick at. I can name a lot of other players that were brawlers too. Maybe guys charge the mound more often today, but otherwise I don't think it's much different. The league could stop them if they'd fine the players like they do in the NBA and in hockey, where if you leave the bench, you're done for three days.

Baseball is the only sport that lets the managers or coaches go out onto the field and rant and rave. You can't do that in basketball or you get a technical foul. You can't do that in football or you get a flag. The rule book in baseball says you can't do it here either, but over the years the higher echelon has said, "The fans like it; it's good for the game. So let them go out and assault the umpire."

With any dispute, the first thing you do when the coach or manager is in your face is to try to level him down. I usually say, "I'm listening. I'm here. Why are you screaming? I'm right here." If you can't gear him down, then you're going to have to eject him. As long as he doesn't call me any direct names, I'll let him go on for a bit. But when he starts saying you this and you that and starts attacking my character or manhood, then you have to run the guy. But as long as he's arguing the play, I'm going to listen. When he starts repeating himself, I'll say, "Now Skip, I've listened. You've made your point. I can't take the call back, and we've got to get going with the game. I'm going to walk on over there, and you go on back to the dugout." If he follows me, there's a good chance I'll run him.

When dealing with a dispute, you try to keep it one-on-one. You don't want the players and coaches to gang up on you or your partner. If you find yourself overwhelmed, you stand back, hold up your hands, and announce that you can only talk to one person at a time. You listen to the argument—especially if the play in question was close. Don't say too much. Let the upset parties do the talking. You want to let the aggrieved party speak his mind and then get the game going again. If the manager is arguing a rule interpretation, don't hesitate to call your partner over for a private conference. Take out the rule book and figure out exactly how to rule. Whatever you do, explain your final decision with specific references to the rule book.

If I know I've blown a play, made a bad call, there's no use lying about it. If I don't have any doubt that I blew it, and the coach comes charging out, I might say, "Skip, I just kicked it." There's no use in me pretending I got it right. I told Lou Pinella in Seattle recently, after he came rushing out, "Lou, I missed that."

He said, "Are you bowing down?"

I said, "Yes sir."

"Well then, I'll accept that. I'm out of here."

They'll have more respect for you when you're honest about it. But if in my heart I think I got it right, I'll stand there like a British bulldog.

⚖

Honesty has its limits. When umpire Ron Luciano first came to the American League, he startled managers and players by candidly admitting his mistakes. For a while, his honesty and humility took players and managers off guard. After a while, however, it irritated them more than it placated them, and it hurt his effectiveness, noted fellow umpire and author Joe Brinkman, and Charlie Euchner, in The Umpire's Handbook. *In the annual assessment of umpires by the American League's general managers, Luciano was rated the league's best in 1977. The next year, he was rated the worst. Brinkman advises against making a habit of telling players you made a mistake. Only admit the most obvious mistakes, he says, and never make a show of your contrition.*

⚖

To be an umpire, you've got to be able to take criticism. You've got to have a tough mental disposition. You've got to be a gentle personality at times but at other times be the baddest ass going. You've got to remember that everything you do is being watched and analyzed, right or wrong. Even President Clinton doesn't work under the scrutiny that we do. For us, the TV cameras are always there. There is no tolerance for error. A great baseball player will fail seven out of ten times and he is still called great. If I miss seven plays out of ten, I wouldn't be permitted to umpire Little League. So there is a lot of pressure. But I think it brings the best out of you—either that or it will make you a coward and make you want to get out of the game. It all comes down to how you cope with pressure. It's the same with great players. Some can't wait to get the bat in their hand in that key situation, while others would quake.

The thing to remember about umpiring is that there are two sides, two teams. They are both watching everything you do. If one guy is going to holler at you and get away with it, then the other guy is going to try the same. If you got to deal harshly with this side—maybe run somebody—you want the other side to see it and to remember. If one bunch gets to you, the other bunch is gonna get to you too.

Some people think we give the superstar the benefit of the doubt on a close pitch. That's pure bunk. That's television commentators filling in time. It might seem like the superstar gets the benefit, but maybe that's because he's got a better eye. The good hitters don't ask for anything different and don't expect to be treated differently. There was a critical situation the night before last when I knocked out [called out on strikes] Cal Ripken on a close pitch in a key situation. It was a pitch that I could have called a ball, but that's not my nature. He didn't say anything.

Sometimes you might make an example of a rookie who doesn't know his place. "Hey son, you don't have enough dirt in your cleats to be here." But normally the older players or the manager will call him aside and tell him to knock it off. Or if he continues on that pattern, they'll send him home with a bad report card. Players don't want to get a reputation, so most of them wise up pretty quickly. I remember when Pete Incaviglia came in to the league right out of college, never even spending a day in the minor leagues. He thought that he was going to eat everyone up. It didn't take Pete long to get the message. There's a dozen or so pitches every game that you could call either way. If this kid's jawboning me, turning around and questioning my calls, well I'm not going to give him a break, am I? That's just human nature.

There's no such thing as the home team having an edge with the umpires, like they sometimes do in basketball. In basketball you sometimes get homers and maybe in football too, but not in baseball. When the Cleveland Indians come into Yankee Stadium, they don't have to worry about the umpire giving the Yankees an edge. It just doesn't happen.

Spectators, like players and managers, can give umpires a hard time. There is a famous line in the Broadway musical Damn Yankees *that goes, "You're blind! You're blind ump! You must be out of your mind ump . . ." Durwood talks about how he reacts to the jeers and boos.*

⚖

I'd be lying to you if I said we don't hear them [jeers and boos], especially in the American League parks where the fans are often closer to you. I think showing instant replays gets some people fired up—particularly when they've had too much to drink. The jeers aren't something you dwell on, but you are concerned about safety. I worry about one of us getting hurt one of these days. I think it will probably happen. Baseball is supposed to be a game. The fans are there to be entertained by the game. But there's too much focus on the players, and people get all worked up over these darn guys. Some fans get obsessed to the point that they want to tear off an umpire's head or take somebody out when a call goes against their idol.

It's a long season—162 games plus another 30 in spring training—so there are times when you're tired. Everybody gets run-down. You don't always have 100 percent to give. Your body might only have 80 percent to give today. But if you can give 100 percent of that 80 percent, then you're going to be okay. That's what makes a person great in his field—giving all that he has.

By the end of the year there isn't anyone who isn't looking for a break, looking to get away from the game for a while, to do something different. I have a little ranch in eastern Texas called Field of Dreams. At home I take care of the cattle, paint the corral, work on the fences, mow the grass, work the hay—whatever has to be done. It's therapy for me.

⚖

Durwood also works part-time for a local Oldsmobile dealership and substitutes as a history and science teacher at Hooks High School. He also has a radio show, "Talking Sports with Durwood Merrill."

⚖

I really think umpires have split personalities—one personality during the season and another during the winter months. In the off-season most of us are the most laid-back people you ever saw, and most anything you want is fine with us because all summer we've been battling, banging it out night after night. At home we pretty much let mamma [Merrill's wife] have what she wants. When I come home from the season, I might say, "We should do this or that." She'll say to me, "Look, I did it this way all summer and it worked out fine." Then you think, "Hey, she's right; let her have her way." Usually . . .

A lot of baseball wives become very independent and learn how to handle things in the household by themselves. If the plumbing breaks or the car breaks down, my wife will get it fixed. She knows how to handle those things, and she doesn't call me unless it's a real emergency. She knows that if I'm in Boston, there's nothing that I can do about it anyway, so she may as well take care of it. Occasionally she'll join me on the road, but not very often. When she comes, she thinks she interrupts my routine, that I'm there to work and don't have time to be a tourist. So she'd rather stay at home.

When the season ends, I am so tired that I feel like quitting, but by spring I'm ready to get back out there. It's funny. I'm like the old goose, I guess. When the sun comes out in January and February [in Texas], the old bones get to feeling better and before long I'm looking forward to March 1st, ready to start all over again. I mean, I can't wait. Then I'm off to spring training to get back into shape and get ready for a new season.

If there is a downside to the job, it's the travel—moving every four or five days, and being away from home so much of the year. I've missed a lot of my kids growing up. I've missed their birthdays, their graduation from high school, and all that. At least now they let us go home for special events like graduations. But they didn't when I started out. It was something we had to fight very hard for. I remember when I asked to go home for my son's high school graduation, the umpire supervisor said cynically, "Do you have to walk across the stage for him?" He was an old bachelor with no kids, and he had no understanding of those things. Now we get one week off every seven weeks and we all head straight for home.

The need to always be focused wears you down after awhile, but I almost always still enjoy the game. I'm like an old racehorse that's been trained to go out there and run the best it can and not think much about it. I've honestly never lost my zest for the game itself. I think it's the competition that I enjoy so much, and that it's just me and the play. It's my call and nothing else. It's not politics, and it's not who you know—none of that crap. And I suppose knowing that I've got the judgment it takes to do the job right is also part of the appeal for me. And ballparks are great places to work—it's always showtime and that picks you up, gets your juices flowing. But I'd like this work even more if we had more day games. Then we could be normal human beings, going to work and coming home at the proper hour. Sometimes it's hard going to the ballpark in the late afternoon and seeing people barbecuing in their backyards and everything, their day's work done, and here we are just starting.

THE PRESS BOX

Anyone who has been in a minor league ballpark has probably noticed the elongated, shoe-box shaped, wooden structure above or suspended from the stadium roof. This is the "press box." In major league stadiums the press box is usually located between the first and second decks in the loge level. In both leagues the press box is always behind and above home plate to give the press the best possible view.

The term "press box" is a holdover from pre-television and pre-radio days, when newspapers were the only medium covering professional baseball. Today television and radio broadcasters, public-address system announcers, print journalists, scoreboard operators, the music man, and others work there. As radio and later television began to cover baseball, the press box expanded in size and then became internally divided into separate areas or rooms. Those who perform live and require a quiet environment—notably broadcasters and the public-address announcer—work in "booths." The booth with the best view of the game is usually given to the television broadcasters. When scoreboards became electronic in the 1950s, their operators moved from the outfield into a booth in the press box, adding to the crowd. The press box is governed by the home team's director of media relations, who with his staff determines who will be issued a pass, or "credential," and to what areas outside the press box, such as field and clubhouse, these individuals can have access.

The number of people in the press box can vary from a dozen or fewer in the low minors to about seventy in the major leagues. In the small, single-newspaper towns of the Class A leagues, there is often only one writer and one radio broadcaster. In Double A, where towns become cities with several newspapers, there are often three or four writers and both home and visiting team radio broadcasters.

In the major leagues there can be several dozen beat writers covering the game for different city and suburban papers, wire services, and national papers like *USA Today*, as well as correspondents and free-lancers for a variety of other publications, such as *Baseball America*, *Sporting News*, and *Baseball Digest*. The front-row seats are reserved for the regulars. Nameplates—The *New York Times*, The *Daily News*, and so on—are fixed to the counter top. Often at one end of the front row is the home team's media relations staff. Open seating in the back rows is taken by writers from the suburban papers and other irregulars.

As one enters the press box in big league ballparks, there is usually a table stacked with handouts of statistics on the home and visiting teams and players. These "media notes," which often run five pages of small type, are compiled by the home team's media relations staff for distribution to writers and broadcasters. They contain every imaginable statistic and trend, plus odd bits of information and reports from the club's minor league teams.

A convenient way to think about the media people who work in the press box is to divide them into two groups: those who cover the game live—TV and radio broadcasters—and those who don't—print journalists. For the latter, the press box is a pretty relaxed work environment. They need only to observe and to make occasional notes when something significant happens in the game. Should they be absent for a few minutes while going to the bathroom or getting a hot dog when a key play was made, they can watch the replay on the television monitors suspended from the ceiling. The work of writing an account of the game for the next day's newspaper readers is mostly done after the game is over. Broadcasters, on the other hand, report plays as they happen. There is no room for mistakes. Mangled syntax, mispronunciations, or stupid observations cannot be retrieved. The sportswriter, however, can always delete an awkward passage from the computer screen.[1] Broadcasters, like the players on the field, must focus; in fact, like players, some broadcasters say that they get mentally prepared for the game by "putting on their game face."

In the press box one can also distinguish the writers from the broadcasters by their dress. In television, appearances are important; the field cameras sometimes scan the broadcast booth and broadcasters often do on-air pre- and postgame interviews. Hence, broadcasters are usually well-groomed. Radio announcers, who are less concerned about their appearance than are television broadcasters, are generally neater than most writers. Writers, who sportswriter Leonard Koppett suggests are more inclined to see themselves as having intellectual qualities, tend to be less conservative and less careful about dress and appearance.

NOTE

1. Leonard Koppett, *The New Thinking Fan's Guide to Baseball* (New York: Simon and Schuster, 1991), 194.

Sherry Davis

ANNOUNCER, SAN FRANCISCO GIANTS

Sherry Davis did not see a professional baseball game until she was nearly thirty. As a youth on the Tidewater Peninsula in Virginia, her obsessions were ballet and theater. She took dance classes during her childhood, majored in theater in college, and later acted in a repertory company until a girlfriend talked her into moving to California. She moved to the mountains near Santa Cruz and, in her words, became a "belated hippie," working in a natural-foods bakery and joining a theater group. In 1980 the group moved to San Francisco; it was there that Sherry discovered Giants baseball.

※

In 1980 I was with a comedy troop, performing five nights a week and working as a secretary during the day. I went to a few baseball games because I wanted to be outdoors and it was just something to do that was available. I had never been to a game before, and I really liked it. The next year was Chili Davis's rookie year with the Giants. I loved his name and enjoyed going out there yelling, "Chili, Chili!" I started listening to Hank Greenwald, the Giants broadcaster, on the radio; and I started reading the *Sporting Green* the first thing in the morning and every baseball book imaginable—and there were a lot. I got very,

very hooked on baseball. It wasn't too long before I started going to spring training. It's been nine years in a row now. People who know my background in ballet and theater ask, "How can you go so far from that to baseball?" Well, I don't see a whole lot of difference. A baseball game is very dramatic and the movements are very graceful and beautiful. As a matter of fact, I have seen several ballets trying to capture its beauty and I haven't seen one yet that has really succeeded.

In 1992 the Giants public-address announcer left, and the team announced an open audition for a new announcer. I thought what a perfect job—baseball and performing, my two loves. But I didn't really go to the audition expecting to get the job. I really went because I thought it would be a once in a lifetime thrill to hear my voice over the PA system at Candlestick, and also to see the changes the new ownership was making to the park: new bleachers and a green outfield fence. It was just a chance to go sit in the ballpark before anyone else got to see it.

Five hundred other people showed up; and only eight of them were women. That's what really lit the fire under me. The first woman did this wimpy kind of deal: "Now batting, Barry 'Sweetbuns' Bonds." Everybody groaned, and I groaned too, annoyed that with so few women there, she would do something stupid. There were guys who didn't take it seriously either, but with so few women there, "Sweetbuns Bonds" wasn't something you wanted to hear.

It took me about three hours to get my turn on the microphone, and I did what I thought was a good audition. You never know what your voice is going to sound like—whether it is going to be too breathy or reedy—but from what I could tell, it sounded pretty good. I got applause from the three hundred or so guys that were left. I was very surprised because that was not standard for the day. As I was going back to my section in the stands to say good-bye to the group I had been sitting with for the past three hours, I passed guys who said: "Was that you? Great voice." When I left, the guys in my section started to chant my number, 161. So I left very encouraged.

Then I thought: "What am I going to do if I have a chance to get this job? How am I going to live? How am I going to keep my other job? How am I going to make enough money?" But my overriding thought was how could I *not* do it. I'd sleep in the gutter to do it. In about a week, I got a message on my machine from the Giants to call them. I was very nervous. I called, and the woman said I was one of ten callbacks. Nine of us showed up. Of the nine, I think seven of us

Sherry Davis announcing a Giants game. (Courtesy of the San Francisco Giants/Stanton)

had professional voice training of some sort. The Giants didn't know that beforehand. They had asked us back strictly on our vocal qualities. That really showed me the benefit of voice training.

At the callback we each had a long audition. They gave us the basic information, and we had to format it and then perform it. For the visiting lineup, they included every trick and hard name they could think, like—Andres Gallaraga. Then we did a home-team lineup, the first pitch, the national anthem—"Ladies and Gentlemen, please rise"— and the disclaimer, "Be alert at all times . . . Don't touch any ball in play." They then narrowed it down to three, and I was one of them. Then they had us just do a home-team lineup again. After a while the front-office people came back, and Pat Gallagher proclaimed that they had decided on an announcer: "We've picked someone who was natural, wasn't forced, and yet had a lot of authority. The winner is number nine, Sherry Davis." Then all the cameras turned to me and all the microphones were shoved into my face. My life changed tremendously at that point.

I was too excited to go straight back to work, so I called a girlfriend and we went to lunch nearby to celebrate. When I got back to the office an hour later, there had been so many calls for me coming in that they had to take a secretary off another desk just to pull messages off my voice mail. I had a legal pad full of messages at the office. When I called my home machine, there were another thirty-seven messages there. For the next two days I spent all my time either at a studio or on the phone talking to radio stations and reporters from all over the country. I was going crazy trying to respond to all these requests for interviews. Finally, I talked to the head of the Giants PR and told him that I was being overwhelmed: "I can't do this. I'm drowning." They then had a press conference. No one had anticipated how much publicity hiring a woman announcer would generate.

⚂

Sherry was the first woman announcer in any of the major American professional sports. The national print, radio, and television media all requested interviews. Six months later the NHL's Dallas Stars hired a woman announcer, and the following year the Boston Red Sox did the same.

⚂

I already had plans to go to spring training on my own, as I did every year. So a few days later I took a late flight to Arizona and got there around 11:30 at night. I was standing in line to get my rental car when people in line—mostly other Bay Areans who had come down for spring training—recognized me. They started asking for my autograph. It was surreal to be standing at a car-rental place in the middle of the night signing autographs. I checked into my hotel around midnight, and at four o'clock *Good Morning America* sent a car over to take me to the stadium for my first live national TV interview.

I announced three innings at spring training, and later I did two exhibition games—the Bay Bridge series between the Giants and the A's. The spring-training stint was a disaster from my point of view. I was just kind of plunked up there for the middle three innings. You know how many substitutions there are in spring training, and I didn't know where to find the names and numbers. I also didn't know how to use the equipment. I didn't think I did very well. I knew that I could have been a whole lot better. Everybody said I did fine, but I wanted to be perfect. I made a few mistakes. They were little things (a wrong first name, a wrong number), but when people are listening to your every word, they notice any little mistake. People don't normally listen that closely to a PA announcement, but since I was the first woman, they had more interest than usual.

I learned something about the media right away. After the game, they took me to a press conference and I sat there and delineated everything I had done wrong and everybody studiously wrote it all down. All my errors got printed all over the country. Pretty dumb of me, but I just was not very wise about that sort of thing. I was very naive. If I hadn't told, no one would have known. The writers wrote about them as though they themselves had detected them.

☯

At Candlestick Park (also known as 3Com Park), Sherry's workplace is a small booth next to the press box, only wide enough for two chairs. She shares that booth with a scoreboard operator. Behind them sits the music person, who is responsible for the sound in the stadium. The sound engineer is often in the booth as well. Sherry's equipment consists of a microphone activated by a foot pedal; binoculars to identify players who are entering the game; and a score book. She sits in a built-in desk from which she has a panoramic view of the ballpark. A large window may be closed to keep out the cold and the wind, which are frequent at Candlestick. Except on the chilliest nights, Sherry prefers to keep the window open to feel closer to the game. "Even though you can see fine, the glass is a separation that distances you from the action. The wind does have an effect though. All summer long, people see me 'Oh, you've been out in the sun.' I say, 'No, windburn. Candlestick.'"

☯

The most important attribute of any announcer is voice quality. The microphone is just a tool to assist you in using your voice. You have to know how to use your voice, how to modify your delivery as the circumstance requires. If it is a very exciting moment in the game, you must know how much to change your voice when announcing the next batter. You don't want to go over the top, but you do need to add a little something to the delivery. I'm not a cheerleader. I'm not there to whip up the crowd, but I do need to reflect what is happening on the field. If the crowd is screaming and yelling as the batter comes to bat, I need to reflect that and give the appropriate emphasis.

Announcing is performing and it takes a lot of energy. I didn't realize how much when I started out, and I used to berate myself during the middle of a home stand when I didn't have enough energy to do my laundry. Now I realize that during home stands I need to take it easy on game days.

The music man and I work very closely together. We decide when to come in with music. We will listen to the music together and then set cues. We work together. If a Giants player is coming up with the bases loaded, we will time the announcement and a flourish together—bugle/announcement, or chord progression/announcement over the chord/string. We also tell very bad jokes and kid around a lot. Early on there was one very embarrassing moment. It was when I was working two jobs. I had gotten up at five o'clock in the morning and worked from seven to four at the law office, then had gone to Candlestick for the night game. It was Jeff Conine's rookie year and his first visit to Candlestick. The whole game, the guys in the booth were doing Conan the Barbarian jokes in their Arnold Schwarzenegar voices— "Conan, the Left Fielder." So late in the game, when I was very tired, it happened. "Now batting, left fielder, Jeff Conan." I knew it the minute I said it, but it was too late. I thought, "Oh well, maybe nobody heard it." Of course everybody heard it.

Just like any job, there were a lot of things about announcing that I didn't know. No one trained me. I had no idea how closely you work with the plate umpire. I can't announce any batter until the umpire signals me. I learned that the hard way during my second game. There was a pinch hitter, and I wanted everyone in the stadium to know that I was on top of things by announcing him as he walked to the plate. The umpire turned around and stared up at me, and I thought, "What is his problem?" I found out the next day when I got a call from the umpire asking me please never do that again. He explained that he has to admit the player into the game, note the player into his lineup card, and point to me before I can announce him. I know a lot of people in the stands are thinking, "Why doesn't she announce the pinch hitter, or a relief pitcher. Dumb woman." Little do they know, I have my foot just hovering over the pedal [to activate my microphone] and I am literally saying, "Point at me, point at me, point at me." But until the umpire does, I can't say a thing.

Also, I think people have the idea that someone telephones or radios me with changes. Not so. I get all my changes [defensive changes in the field or pinch hitters] with only my binoculars and the umpire to help me. Sometimes the umpires forget to signal, so I check every position as they take the field to make sure there are no changes—especially in late innings. The changes do come across the speaker in the press box, but usually not until the inning is underway, past the time when I need to announce them.

Another thing a good announcer does is help to make the game flow smoothly for the fans. I have a stopwatch, and if I notice that a pitcher is taking an inordinate amount of time between innings warming up, I may announce the start of the inning before he throws the ball down to give him a little nudge. The commissioner's office has directed us to announce the next batter a minute and forty-five seconds after the final out is made. Of course, the announcer doesn't have any real authority over the pitcher, but there are subtle ways that you can nudge people along, speed up the tempo. These are the things the fans never realize.

Here's another example of what a good announcer does. Let's say it's late in the game, the pitcher is struggling, somebody is warming up in the bullpen, and Matt Williams is walking toward the batter's box. You know there is a chance that there may be a pitching change. So in that situation, I will not announce Matt Williams batting until the absolute last second, because if I do announce him and the opposing manager then comes out, it breaks the flow of the game. Then when Matt comes back to bat, after the manager returns to the dugout, he comes back to silence, no announcement or cheers, he just walks back. If that does happen, I'll turn to the music guy and ask him to give Matt a flourish, and he will do one of those music build-ups. But it's better if I never announce him in the first place.

Also, if a pitcher has gone eight solid innings, done a good job, and now is being relieved, I wait until he gets all the way off the field before I announce the reliever. But if the pitcher has not done well and I think he is going to get booed, I can avert that by announcing the reliever sooner. People usually won't boo then because they don't want the reliever to think the boos are for him. These are things that you just learn by doing the job; no one teaches you. You learn to watch the game differently, to ignore the high foul balls that the fans watch, and to keep your attention focused on the home-plate area, the on-deck circle, and the umpire who keeps you informed.

I try to treat the players on both teams the same. I will try to avoid boos for opposing pitchers and to hold off announcing opposing hitters if a pitching change is likely. I also try not to vary the volume in announcing visiting and home players. I will have a little more color in my voice for my own team, but I don't want there to be a noticeable difference.

Being a perfectionist, I have a hard time dealing with errors. They really upset me, and being a woman only makes them worse. When I make an error, the reaction of some fans is, "Oh, it's that stupid woman who doesn't know baseball." They will overlook an error made by a man and then jump all over me for something no different. One of the first interviews I had was with a radio station in Toronto. The interviewer happened to have been the Blue Jays' first announcer. I asked him if he had any tips for me. He said, "Yeah, you are going to make errors." I thought, "What kind of tip is that?" But it is the best tip he could have given me. Everybody makes errors, but they still upset me to no end. I suppose mainly because there are many people out there who want me to make an error to justify their idea that a woman shouldn't be doing this job.

When I took this job, I figured there would be some opposition to me, probably from old traditional, conservative men. But being in San Francisco, I thought it would be mild and brief. I had no idea how rabid and persistent it would be. For a long time I couldn't listen to talk radio because of it. It was especially upsetting because there is nothing you can do to change people's opinion. I'm not going to call a perfect game every day. Nobody can. But I don't think I make more errors than other announcers.

Oddly, I haven't gotten a lot of criticism from older men. I have met quite a few older fans who confess that they didn't like the idea of a woman announcer in the beginning, but that I've won them over. I think over time they have come to recognize that I love baseball and that my love of the game shows through my voice. It is mainly young boys and guys in their twenties who still complain about me. When the strike started, I was listening to talk radio and this young guy comes on saying how bad the strike was and that he was going to miss baseball. Then he said that there was one good thing about the strike. The host asked, "What's that?" He said, "No more Sherry Davis." I think young guys feel more threatened by a woman.

One comment that I heard more than once that really used to upset me was, "I go to the ballpark to get away from women." That really irritated me, in part because 40 percent of the attendees at Giants games are women. If you watched any of the Ken Burns baseball series, every picture of the stands, from the beginning of baseball on, had women there. Women have been wonderful fans. A lot of women have come up to me and said: "I learned baseball from my mother (or from my aunt). It wasn't my father but my mother who was a baseball fan." So when I hear their sexist comments, I get upset. They deny women a place in baseball. What those men really mean by their sexist comments is that they go to the ballpark to get away from women with any prominence or authority in the game.

I only need to get to the stadium an hour before the game, but I am usually there a couple of hours before because I love the ballpark. I like getting to the stadium before it opens to the crowd. That's one of the perks of the job. I even like watching the pitchers take batting practice. To enjoy the setting, I get there early, go into my booth, read my mail, and look through my copy from community relations or group sales or whoever has announcements during the game. Later, I sit down with the Jumbotron coordinator and the music guy, as a lot of my announcements are done in conjunction with them. [Jumbotron and Diamond Vision are trade names for the large screens that show replays, video bits, and stills. In most stadiums the director of the Jumbotron or Diamond Vision sits next to the PA announcer, enabling better coordination between the visuals on the screen and the PA announcements.] If I have two announcements during an inning break, we may "donut" them, which means they will bring up music for a few seconds, then I'll come in, then they will bring up music again between announcements. We script all the stuff out so that we pretty much know where everything is going to go before the game starts.

I usually take some hot tea with me into the booth. It's good to have some warm liquids around to keep your vocal chords supple in case your voice needs it. Cold fluids constrict the vocal chords, so you really don't want to drink anything cold. If I have a cold, I bring lozenges and hot tea with lemon and honey in it. I'm not sick very often, although I once had to announce a game with a migraine. That was one of the worst experiences of my career, really awful. But that's when I can fall back on my theater training. I can still sound happy and enthused while my head is killing me. I don't want to rely on technique—but just like in theater, if you really have to, you can.

When the visiting team arrives for a new series, I check on the pronunciations of all the names. As soon as I get the lineup, I try to find one of their beat writers in the press box to go over the names and write them out phonetically. Sometimes a player will change the pronunciation of his name between visits. Archie "See-en-*frac*-o" became Archie "Sin-*frac*-o." Hector "Vill-a-na-wav-a," who had been called that for years, switched to the real Spanish pronunciation "Vee-ya-na-wa-va," and Ricky "Goo-tee-*air*-es" became Ricky "Goo-*tear*-es."

I have to rewrite a lot of the announcements. The copy comes in from different departments and outside organizations. Some are either poorly written or do not flow well when read aloud. Some are well-written but have major typos. One of the funniest was from the American Legion for a pregame awards ceremony. Part of the copy read, "Some of the prior winners of this award were Ted Williams and Stan *Musical*." You have to have a good command of English and knowledge of baseball, or you can sound pretty foolish.

I do want to emphasize how supportive the Giants were—players and organization alike. And the umpires were very nice to me—especially that first year. They made a point of giving me clear signals and making sure I understood them. And so many baseball fans across the country wrote charming notes congratulating me. I am very, very lucky. I never dreamed that I would be a part of baseball. The nicest thing anyone said to me that first year was when I saw Orlando Cepeda after getting the job—"You're family now." To be part of the baseball family is the biggest thrill of all.

Rob Euans

BROADCASTER, NORFOLK TIDES

The broadcaster's primary "tool" is a microphone, which is hooked up to a telephone unit that carries his voice and the noise from the stands down the telephone line to a radio station. The sound is scrambled by an electronic unit as it leaves the broadcast booth. It is then unscrambled at the radio station by a decoder, which also makes the sound clearer. Also standard equipment for most broadcasters is a score book; assorted notes and media guides to provide information during the broadcast; a tape recorder, for later review of the broadcast; and binoculars, to get a better look at a dispute or an injured player, to see who is warming up in the bullpen, and to lipread conversations that a manager or a coach is having with his pitcher.

Rob Evans has been broadcasting minor league baseball since 1980, when the Tulsa Drillers of the Texas League offered him a position selling advertising during the day and broadcasting their games at night. At the time it seemed like the job he had always wanted to do.

When I was growing up, I, like a lot of kids, would dream of being a baseball player. My friend and I would get the bats and balls out and we would draw batter's boxes in the backyard and have the fence all lined out and everything. At night I would listen to the Cardinals games in my bedroom at my grandmother's house in Rolla, Missouri, where I went every summer. I would get the desk out and fix up a little microphone stand, set up pictures of all the players, and get out pieces of paper and act like I was writing down notes. Then, as the game was being played on the radio, or if I was watching it on TV, I would announce the game. My grandparents said that they could hear me chattering away up in my room late at night.

I think that's how I got started. I was never that good of a ballplayer. I recognized early that I was not going to be a player, although I loved the game. Announcing just clicked. But as a kid I was never sure I had a good enough voice. In fact, for a long time I never thought I could get into radio because I didn't have a great voice growing up.

⚈

Evans majored in history and took broadcasting courses at Southwest Missouri State University. He dropped out after his junior year and volunteered to announce high school baseball and basketball games for a local radio station. He says he pestered the director to let him do a game. His first assignment was to cover a game between two teams that had not won a game all year. He performed well enough to be asked back. For the next three years he worked the graveyard shift as a janitor in a restaurant, worked odd hours in a car wash, and broadcasted high school and college basketball and baseball. Meanwhile, he sent scores of letters to professional baseball teams in order to secure a full-time broadcasting position. He finally got a call from the Tulsa Drillers.

⚈

It was an entry-level position, $500 a month plus commission from the sales I made of season tickets and ads for the outfield fences and the program. Selling baseball is like selling anything else, you have to make contacts. I would do it over the phone or make appointments to go see potential sponsors. Most businesspeople know in advance whether they want to support the baseball team by buying a program ad or season tickets. So you don't have to convince them that they need this like you do with life insurance. But I would try to get them to buy a larger ad than they had planned.

Once the season started, I had the type of job where you went in late in the morning and stayed until the game was over late at night. Not only was I devoting all my time to baseball but I was traveling with the club as well and calling in reports on the road games. I was not getting any time off. During home stands, I would work with the clean-up crew as well, helping them pick up garbage under the stands.

It was a little bit ridiculous doing all that for only $500 a month. So I got out of baseball at the end of the season and took a job with a radio station in Bolivar, Missouri. A few years later some of my friends who were still in the game mentioned that there was an opening for a broadcaster in Beaumont [Texas League], and I applied for it. I spent three years in Beaumont, from '84 to '86, again, working long hours, 8:30 A.M. until after the ball game late at night, and traveling on the road as well. I had my hand in a little bit of everything, from public relations to pulling the tarp. After a few years, it wore me out. When I left Beaumont, I made a decision that if I ever went back to baseball, it was going to be as broadcaster only. No more was I going to put in a full day of selling tickets and things and then have to broadcast. After working a whole day, you are dead and you cannot do a good job in the booth. I moved back to Springfield [Missouri], and my wife and I decided that we weren't going to move again. But then the folks in Tidewater [Triple A International League] called and offered me a job. They had a reputation of hiring good broadcasters, some of them went to the major leagues. It was too good of an opportunity to pass up.

The difference between the Texas League and the International League was like night and day. The cities and the ballparks were so much bigger and better in Triple A. In the International League, you are in eastern cities and the teams draw nine to ten thousand fans per game instead of the two thousand that you would get in El Paso, Beaumont, or Tulsa. But oddly, in a lot of ways, the travel was tougher. Instead of getting on the bus and riding all night like you do in Double A, in Triple A you go back to your hotel room, sleep for four hours, and fly out early in the morning. In Triple A you fly commercial, not charters like in the big leagues, and you take the first flight out in the morning. By the time you get to your destination, it's midday. And then you have to be at the ballpark by 3:30. You don't get much rest. Sometimes you get in so late for a day game that you don't even have time to go to the hotel. You just go straight to the ballpark. That's a lot tougher than riding the bus all night.

⚏

While at Tidewater Evans had the unusual experience of influencing the promotion of a player, Jeff Ennis, to the major leagues.

⚏

I was in the hotel room with the manager, Mike Cubbage, and the newspaper man who covered the team on a daily basis, George Mc-Clelland. We were just going out to eat when Cubby got a phone call in his room. He called back over his shoulder to me and said, "We are going to lose a pitcher." Someone on the big club had gone down with an injury and they were going to call up one of ours. Cubby told me to get my notebook. So I ran back to my room and got my stat sheets. We were talking about the pitchers. The pitching coach and manager were going to send somebody else to New York [Mets] when I said, "What about Jeff Ennis? This guy really deserves to go." After some more talk, the manager agreed. I was in a daze, because that was the first time that I was ever involved in something like that. I just happened to be in the right place at the right time. Pretty heady stuff for a country boy from Missouri.

Later that night, after we got back from dinner, Jeff was still wandering the halls of the hotel with a grin on his face. That's one of the things I will always remember—the first time you see a kid's face when he finds out that he is going to the big leagues.

At the end of the '87 season in Tidewater, I was out of a job. The general manager told me that I had not made as much progress as he had hoped and that he wasn't going to hire me back. That was a load of crap and I had the tapes to prove it. The guy who was going to replace me was the general manager's friend and longtime assistant. What happened was that the GM's friend wanted to go back to being a broadcaster, and he did his best to make sure that I came out looking as bad as I could. The news came too late to find a job for the next season, so I sat out 1988.

⚏

Rob was looking for work outside baseball when a friend told him that the Birmingham Barons were looking for a broadcaster. Going back to Double A would be a step down from Tidewater, but the Barons had a new state-of-the-art ballpark, and he if he got the job, he *would be broadcasting in one of the country's top fifty media markets. He sent the organization a sample of his broadcast tapes and was offered the job. The salary was less than he had hoped for, but the GM promised that he could make an additional $300 a month from newspapers by phoning in game reports, and another $200 a month doing some part- time work for another radio station. I first observed Rob at work in the Birmingham broadcast booth, where I conducted the first of his two interviews.*

Being a radio play-by-play man is sort of like being an artist sitting in front of a blank canvas. But instead of paints and brushes, you have your microphone, your vocabulary, and your knowledge of the game, all of which are used to paint a picture for the people who can not see the game but are listening to it on the radio. You create pictures for the fans so that they can see the game in their mind's eye. When you are going good, you are giving them vivid descriptions. But on a bad night, you draw stick figures, just giving the listeners the basic, bare necessities. If you say, "A ground ball to short, the throw to first, the side's retired"—well, that's the bare bones. That might sound fine, but that's not what I want to do. I want to say, "There is a ground ball to short, and he made a backhanded stop and a strong throw across his body to first base, which gets there just in time." Instead of verbally drawing stick figures, you want to put uniforms and caps on them and give good detail that will make the action come to life.

Broadcasting baseball is very different from broadcasting football or basketball. Football is more of a hit-them-on-every-play, get-them-excited approach. It's four quarters of high-intensity broadcasting. Football and basketball are like a sprint, where baseball is a marathon. Football and basketball are clock sports, where baseball is kind of timeless. Football and basketball, to me as a broadcaster, is coat-and-tie: you get all dressed up; there's high intensity. You have to be really focused for four quarters and then sit back and you are done. Baseball is more of a put on your three-button golf shirt, get out your lounge chair, settle back, and hey, let's just talk. The slow pace of baseball is ideal for radio.

A baseball game is also easier to describe on the radio. It's linear. Everything is laid out for you. If you close your eyes, you can see where everybody is on the field. If I tell you that the ball is hit to short, you can pretty much see it in your mind's eye. Whereas in basketball, if I tell you that there's "a 15-foot jump shot," you can't see where the player is shooting it from. Or if I say, "left corner, left wing," it's still hard to see since these aren't fixed positions like in baseball. In baseball, when there is a ground ball to short, you know where everybody on the field is. You can see it. For me, baseball is the only game made truly for radio. It comes equipped with everybody in position.

What I envision when I talk on the radio is a guy driving down the road in his car or a family sitting around the house with a radio on and me basically sitting down, pulling up a chair, and having a talk with them. That's the way I try to approach the listeners.

※

Every few innings during the game, Evans is handed a copy of the latest news to come over the Sports Ticker, which is much like an AP or UPI wire service except that it's devoted entirely to sports. It supplies the scores of all major league games and highlights every half inning. Like all announcers, Rob works this material into his broadcast. The amount of "filler" used during the broadcast depends on how the game goes. If it's an "ugly," slow game, he may use a lot of filler. While watching Evans work, I became interested in what affects a broadcaster's performance. Like players, broadcasters have good nights and bad nights. But what causes them?

※

Everybody has days where anything you attempt seems to turn out wrong. Some of it is lack of concentration. There are days when after traveling and being on the bus all night, you are physically fatigued. Those are my toughest days. You really have to fight it to stay focused. After a travel day, you sometimes see players go through the motions because they are tired. Well, announcers get tired too. Once in a while it may even be a physical problem like having a cold sore on the inside of your mouth that makes it hard to talk. Everybody will have bad days, but the important thing is to keep them to a minimum; to be successful, you have to be consistent.

The size of the crowd in the stands can have an affect on your work too. Two nights ago, in Jacksonville, there was hardly a soul in the ballpark. No matter how loud I turned up the crowd mike [a microphone that is lowered from the broadcast booth down into the stands], I felt like I was in a studio because there was no crowd noise around me. Every time I was quiet, all I'd get was silence because there was nothing down there. I felt like I had to talk more to cover up the silence. A good crowd is important to a broadcaster because he can let the crowd noise fill in to give the listeners the feeling they are in the stands watching the game.

The pace of the game can also affect how well you do. Long games are tough because it means you are getting a lot of walks and errors. Long games are usually sloppily played and begin to drag, especially if the score is lopsided. It's hard to sustain interest in your listeners. Last night we had a nice snappy ball game and I was focused the whole time. I felt the broadcast went fairly well. The night before there was nothing about the ball game to help me gain my focus. I found myself staring out at the interstate watching the cars go by between pitches.

Like I said earlier, when I am having a bad night, I don't describe things as well as I would like. I make verbal stick figures as opposed to putting uniforms and caps on the guys. And I know right then and there when you could have said something better. Two or three seconds after I call the play, I am thinking, "Boy, that was stupid." I am having a mental conversation with myself saying, "I could have done that better." But then it's time to announce the next batter and you can't go back and fix it because it's live radio. If you make too many of those mistakes, it begins to steamroll and you don't talk at all because you are afraid that what you say is going to come out wrong.

ⓙ

One of the surprises for me in getting to know several broadcasters while traveling with teams was how much time they spend collecting, organizing, and reviewing information in preparation for the broadcast. The process is not unlike what professors do in preparing notes for a lecture. This is especially true in the minor leagues, where teams do not have large media staffs to prepare material for the broadcasters.

ⓙ

Doing prep work for your broadcast is kind of like the ballplayers going out on the field doing their stretching, running, wind sprints, and all that. Ballplayers don't like to run, but they do it because they know if they don't they won't perform well. That's the way I look at preparation. My normal routine is to get up and grab the local papers and

USA Today. I read the papers—especially *USA Today,* which has notes on every team—because often there is something I can use in the broadcast. I take the box scores from the local paper and fill in my notebook on how our hitters and pitchers did the night before, fill out the numbers, then I type up my notes. I try to list all the hitting and hitless streaks and things like that, plus I make a brief bio on the starting pitcher for the night's game, describing what he did in his last start and anything else that might be interesting. I type about five or six pages of notes onto the computer every night, but I rarely refer to them during the game. By compiling them and typing them into the computer, I learn them. I think minor league announcers know their material better because they have to compile it themselves. In the big leagues they have a staff to do that stuff. But in the big leagues, announcers have more free time to spend talking to players, managers, and other broadcasters and to learn about the teams.

You have to have a good knowledge of the game to do your job right. It's very tough to go out and talk knowledgeably about a subject for three hours a night for 144 nights a year if you don't know it well. Your knowledge of the game is your foundation. It's kind of like the undercoating of a car—before you paint the car, you put on a good primer. It's the same with broadcasting baseball, and that's where some people fail. They might have great voices and be able to do decent play-by-play, but they really aren't fans of the game.

You also have to develop a relationship with the manager. Some people treat the team broadcaster like "the media," like we are a pain in the ass. You have to convince them—players and managers—that you're on their side. If they do something off the field that doesn't need to be reported, you are not going to say anything about it. I am only up there to report what they do between the white lines. In Birmingham, I got along great with Tony [the manager]. After a while he treated me just like one of the coaches in terms of what he would say in front of me—for example, he might be critical of a player who was not doing well. He knew that I wouldn't use that material unwisely. When I moved to the Mets organization, the manager wasn't comfortable with me. It takes a while before they can completely trust you not to say something that you overheard that could be embarrassing to the club. It takes a while before they fully understand that, hey, I am the team broadcaster, I am the house man, and I am not going to use anything that makes them look bad.

In the major leagues, the play-by-play announcer is teamed with a color commentator, often a former player with inside knowledge of the game and its personalities. In the minor leagues the broadcaster has no help. Evans talks about going nine innings without relief.

A ball game is a lot like a boxing match, with each inning being a round. You basically have a nine-inning fight with you as the announcer who has to go the distance. Usually, somewhere in the middle of the game, you coast a few rounds. You loose your focus a bit. When we are playing at home the public relations director comes in sometimes and does a couple of innings of play-by-play to relieve me. Being able to take two innings off really makes a big difference. When I come back it's much easier to keep my focus and intensity, and I sound a lot better in the later stages of the game.

In a lot of ballparks there are no rest-room facilities in the press box, so I have to run down into the stands to go to the bathroom and get back there before the next inning starts. I have ninety seconds to get down those stairs and get back up to the press box. One night in Midland, Texas, where the water is undrinkable—looks bad and smells bad—I got a bad case of Montezuma's revenge. I told the engineer at the radio station to just play commercials until I got back because I had to go downstairs to the bathroom. But when you get the runs that bad, you can't run very well anyway. When I got back, there were two outs in the inning. For the folks listening to the broadcast, that was the fastest inning in baseball. I gave them a first pitch ground ball to short and then a first pitch fly ball to center. Most of the time, you just hold it. And I can remember sometimes when I had to go so badly that I could barely walk down the stairs at the end of the game. Basically, you train yourself, condition yourself not to use the rest room. I know some guys who keep large jars up in the booth to relieve themselves during the game. It sounds crude, but that's what you have to do when you are the only man up there who can do the job.

Perhaps more than other professional sports, baseball has a large specialized vocabulary or jargon, which insiders often refer to simply as "baseball talk." Several books have been devoted exclusively to it, such as How to Talk Baseball, *by Mike Whiteford. In all fields, vocabulary changes over time, and baseball is no exception. In returning to baseball after a twenty-five-year absence, I found that much of the jargon that had been current in the 1960s was no longer used—such as "pill" for a fast fastball or "Texas Leaguer" for a bloop single. I wanted to know if Rob kept up with the jargon and whether he used it in his broadcast.*

⚾

There are a lot of colorful expressions that help you avoid having to use the same terms—strikes, ball, single, ground ball, fly ball—over and over again. Your broadcast would be pretty boring if you didn't vary the words and phrases. When you are describing, say, a pitch to the plate, which is going to happen a minimum of 225 times per game, you don't want to describe it the same way every time. I don't sit back and consciously come up with different ways of describing the pitch, but I do try to vary my descriptions. When I listen to the tapes of the previous night's broadcast, I often pay attention to how I say what I say. One time I might say, "Here's the pitch." Then I might tell what kind of pitch it was. Next I might say, "Kennedy goes into the windup, comes to the plate with the ball, and the delivery is low." Or I might say, "Here's the throw to the plate." Lately the pitching coach has been reminding me that I shouldn't say "throw" because pitchers don't throw, they pitch.

There are a few things I try to describe the same way throughout the game so that my listeners, who might be doing other things while listening to the ball game, will pay attention. If there is a home run, I will say, "It's a swing and a drive, deep . . ." So the folks at home who listen to me enough will know that the ball has a chance to go out. If it's hit by one of our guys, I will try to build it up a little bit. If it's the opposition, I will play it down and maybe talk about something else right away, like scores from the majors. I don't want to talk too much about their home runs because that's not good for our side and our listeners are not going to be happy to hear about it.

I try to know the jargon as best as I can. I learn a lot of it from the players and coaches on the team. When I was in Tidewater there were some guys who always referred to a home run as a "big fly." They would sound like an old Indian chief who drops his words, like "Jones hit big fly." Some of the guys on this club describe a pitcher who is throwing a good fastball as "throwing serious gas." That's one I have used.

Sometimes you'll hear another broadcaster use a phrase that you like, and it will creep into your vocabulary. When a guy strikes out, Ken Harrelson, who announces for the White Sox, says, "He will go grab some bench." I like that and have heard myself saying it. Overall, I try to never to overuse anything and I try not to use cliches.

☙

During the baseball season Rob's wife, a nurse, and his ten-year-old daughter remain at home in Springfield, Missouri. Rob talks about the effects of working in baseball on his family.

☙

At one time my wife wanted me to quit baseball because I was gone so much. She had a hard time understanding my choice of work. In her mind it was like, "If you love us as much as you say you do, then why do you want to be gone five or six months of the year?" I told her that that's not the point: "The reason that I am doing this is because I *do* love you, and because I want to provide a better life for all of us. The best way I can further my career, given the talents I have, is in broadcasting." I think she understands and accepts that now. She knows that I love baseball and that baseball makes me happy. But my leaving is still tough on her. It has made her become very independent. We laugh about the time when I was in Texas on my first road trip, and she was at home. The radiator hose broke on the car and antifreeze went all over the garage. She called me and said that the car blew up and that there was oil everywhere. I got her to calm down and asked her about the color of the fluid on the floor. She said, "It's green, and it's everywhere." I started laughing and told her what the problem was, and she got it fixed. She has done so many things on her own during the times I have been away, things that she wouldn't have had the courage or wouldn't have been able to do before. It's made her realize that she can do a lot of things without a man around.

☙

EPILOGUE

Rob has spent the past five seasons with the New York Mets Triple A team in Norfolk, Virginia. At age forty-one, his ambition is still to make the big leagues. He is only one step away, but it's the most difficult step of all—especially, he says, "if you don't have friends in major league front offices who will push for you." He is discouraged when announcers less qualified than he are offered big league positions because of who they know or because they once were ballplayers. But for now, Rob finds satisfaction in the knowledge that as a Triple A broadcaster he is one of the top one hundred in his chosen profession. "That's pretty select company," he says. Another reason Rob stays in the game, despite five months separation from his family every year, is the satisfaction he takes from being a "baseball man." With pride, he tells a story about how, when considering a job offer he had outside of baseball, the Birmingham Barons field manager told him, "Face it, Rob. You are a baseball man just like the rest of us. You are not just a broadcaster looking in from the outside, you are a baseball guy who happens to be a broadcaster."

Sally O'Leary

ASSISTANT DIRECTOR OF MEDIA RELATIONS,
PITTSBURGH PIRATES

Sally O'Leary became interested in baseball through her mother. At home in Sheffield, Pennsylvania, 140 miles north of Pittsburgh, they would listen to Rosey Rowswell's radio broadcasts of Pirate games. After high school, Sally went to business college in Buffalo, New York, and then took a job with an advertising agency.

O'Leary did not see a major league game in person until 1956, at age twenty-two, when she traveled to Pittsburgh to visit her sister. She moved to Pittsburgh in 1957, and in 1964 she was hired by the Pittsburgh Pirates, becoming one of the first women to work in baseball media relations. In three decades with the Pirates, she has been part of great changes in her work and the game.

⚾

Baseball has ruled my life for thirty-two years. I have missed a lot of weddings, reunions, and family get-togethers because I had to be at the ballpark. Sometimes it bothered me and sometimes it didn't. I have a position that a lot of other people could never have and I am very proud of that.

When I moved to Pittsburgh I took full advantage of going to the games regularly. Working for an ad agency, I was able to get complimentary tickets through the media, but I also bought my share of tickets. There was an organization in the city called the "Gus Fan Club." One of the officers was Frank Gustine, a former Pirate player. During the season they held luncheons attended by a few Pirate players and the visiting team. Since I always went to those luncheons, I made a lot of my baseball and media friends there. Frank owned a restaurant, so it was difficult for him to come to a lot of the meetings. When he couldn't make it, I started taking the money at the door. He made me the honorary treasurer of the Gus Fan Club.

At the ad agency I mainly did the secretarial work for account executives, but I also scheduled commercials and typed copy. That's really how I got into baseball. One of the clients was Mellon Bank, a sponsor for the Pirate radio and TV broadcasts. My name was on the commercial as a contact in case there were any problems. Bob Prince, who was the play-by-play announcer for the Pirates, called me one night about the copy, and that started a great friendship. He became aware of my interest in baseball. And he knew that I had applied for a job at the club a couple times, but there were never any openings. I always got the form letter back saying that they would keep my name on file. Of course I never thought that it would happen, but he kept telling me that someday there would be an opening and that he would help me get a job there.

The woman who was in my position had been with the club for about eleven years, and it was generally thought that she, a Philadelphia native, would stay forever. But when she got an opportunity to go back to work at Temple University, the job opened up. Prince arranged for me to have an interview, but he warned me that they would never be able to pay me enough money to leave the ad agency. So he said that if I got the job I could be his baseball secretary and that he would supplement my salary year round! That was the only way that I could afford to take the job, because front office baseball positions do not pay. The job paid only half of what I was making at the ad agency.

I had my interview with the PR director during a Saturday afternoon ball game at Forbes Field. He more or less told me that I had the position but that he would have to check a couple things and would call me on Monday to see if I still wanted it. When he called me back, he said there was one major question he forgot to ask me. Could I type? Of course that was no problem. My first day with the Pirates was on May 24, 1964.

Sally O'Leary at work at Three Rivers Stadium. (Courtesy of the Pittsburgh Pirates)

The ad agency had been glamorous—downtown Pittsburgh, nice modern offices and equipment, and windows. Forbes Field was built in 1909 and was located in Oakland, near the University of Pittsburgh. We had no windows, the offices were odd sizes with low ceilings, and the office equipment was not modern at all. The excuse was that we were going to have everything new when we moved to a new ballpark. In 1964 plans were already in the works to build Three Rivers Stadium, but we didn't open that until 1970, so there were six years of putting up with what we had. That didn't bother me at all. Working right at the ballpark and being able to walk out my office door and down the steps right to my seat gave me a special feeling. I didn't miss the ad agency one bit because I was doing something that I really liked.

The club was owned by the Galbreaths and it was run like a family business. There were no more than twenty-five people in the front office and we were very close. I am still friends with those people I worked with back in the sixties.

Today baseball is a big business. I would have to get a calculator to figure out how many people work for the Pirates. Now we have separate departments for community relations, group sales, public relations, media relations, promotions, ticket sales, and so on. Every department has a head and a couple of assistants.

When I started working, I was the secretary to the public relations director, Jack Berger. It was just the two of us. We did everything from promotions to group sales to player appearances. The job required all kinds of secretarial work and statistics. I had to update the stats every day, and in those days we had no adding machines, calculators, or even electric typewriters. And there was no such thing as a computer. I had a manual typewriter and a mimeograph machine. My first day on the job, the club had been on the road and had played a double-header in San Francisco on Sunday. Monday was an off day and I had to update all the statistics and prepare the press notes for the first home game on Tuesday. I understood the game and box scores and I'd had a few days training with my predecessor before I started, but to do this on my own was a little scary.

My job required that I stay throughout every home game, mostly to keep the scores in order to update statistics for the next day. It also required that I work Saturdays, Sundays, and holidays.

Bob sort of made me famous in Pittsburgh. He called me his "Gal Friday." He'd pose a question during a broadcast, like if someone was approaching a record during a game, he would say, "I'm sure my Gal Friday is listening and if she can get the information to me, she knows how to find me." I had the phone numbers of the broadcast booths all over the country so I could call and give him the information. Today that's not necessary because someone who travels with the team handles that.

Our department received all the phone calls from fans and we handled all of the fan mail. We would get calls all the time about baseball questions going back in history. We had all kinds of books to refer to, but one of my biggest problems initially was learning which book to look in. You knew the basic questions, but you couldn't always find the right page in the right book. Eventually I learned the easiest way was to keep a log of the questions that came up and keep it handy. Then for the usual questions, I had the answer right at my fingertips.

One question we were asked a lot is who the first black player was on the Pirates' roster. Curt Roberts. Also, the right field stands at Forbes Field were very high and we are still asked today how many home runs were hit over those stands. Eighteen. Babe Ruth hit the first one in 1935. In 1972 Danny Murtaugh had an all black starting lineup. We are often asked who was in that lineup. People also ask about the lifetime batting average of a player, or who got the first hit at Three Rivers Stadium, or the last hit at Forbes Field—anything and everything! We are even asked to settle arguments. We get calls from the fantasy leagues, like why a certain player is on the disabled list, or who we called up from the minors to replace someone.

With complaint calls, I had been told from the very beginning to just listen politely and kill them with kindness. You simply have to thank them for calling, which sometimes is hard to do because there are some callers who think they know it all and wonder why they are not the general manager. When there is a major trade with your club, you naturally receive all kinds of phone calls—some people happy with the deal; other advising us that we've given away the team.

One of the busiest times with the phone was when Roberto Clemente was killed. That happened on New Year's Eve 1972. Of course we weren't in the office, but when we came back to work the phones rang constantly. That time people were calling to express their sympathy. They felt they had to say something to somebody; they had to talk to a person. Those calls were extremely hard to take because we were all feeling sad over that tragedy too.

In PR confidentiality is required—especially when the club is preparing for a trade or a major announcement. There are always rumors that such and such might happen and the media is always calling to get the story first. You just have to maintain your cool because you just can't leak that kind of information. Everything is timed for a news release or a press conference. I remember one firing that really was a surprise. We knew it at noon on the day it was going to happen, but everything was timed to when that person was going to come into the office to see the general manager and he wasn't going to be there until four o'clock. The person about to be fired was Bill Virdon, our manager. My boss got the word that morning that Bill was going to be fired. We had to prepare all the copy but we couldn't tell anybody until Bill arrived at the park. As he always did, he stopped in my office, sat down, and chatted a little bit. He got up and said, "I'll see you after the road trip." The team was leaving for Philadelphia around five o'clock. And my heart just dropped as he walked down the hall and got the word that he was gone. He came in the next day, looked at me, and said, "You knew all along didn't you?" Of course he knew there was no way I could tell him, but that was one of the hard times.

Another part of my job was keeping scrapbooks—clippings of everything that happened in Pirate baseball. I am also involved in the preparation of our publications. That means updating the biographical information on all of the players and a lot of proofreading. There are a lot of figures in there, but I love detail. So that's a job that I still really like today. We maintain files on every player who has come through our organization in the major leagues. We have 110 years of history here with the Pirates. Our files are full of clippings and photographs.

In 1987 the Pirates club was 100 years old, and the club decided to form a Pirate Alumni Association. It fell to me to try to get it organized. I tried to find all the living former Pirates in the country, anybody who played even one inning for us. I ended up compiling a mailing list of over five hundred names. We now do a newsletter twice a year called *The Black and Gold* to keep in touch with all of these former players. They are thrilled to learn that they haven't been forgotten. Most figured that once they were out of the game, that was it.

Today we don't have the closeness to the players that we had in early years. I used to know everybody on the team. They came through the office a lot and I saw them; I built friendships with them and with their families. Today I don't ever see them. I haven't met half of the players on the current team. I don't know their families. It's a strange feeling and I am sorry it's that way, but that is the nature of the game today, I guess.

When network television would come to Pittsburgh for the "Game of the Week," I often worked with the announcers as their eye in the booth. I helped with statistics and watched who was warming up in the bullpen and who might be pinch hitting. I also gave them any little tips that they could use in their broadcast. That gave me an opportunity to meet some really great people who are still my friends, like former Pirate Joe Garagiola, Jim Simpson, Tony Kubek (I worked in the booth on his very first game), Merle Harmon, Charlie Jones, and even Leo Durocher. People said to be careful of Leo because of his reputation as a womanizer, but he was a perfect gentleman.

In the early years I worked closely with the media. After we moved to Three Rivers Stadium in 1970 and all of the staffs were enlarged, I went strictly to public relations, which meant that I didn't have to work the games anymore because there was another assistant in public relations. He kept the stats and traveled part-time with the team, and I went back to mainly secretarial and research work. Some people might view it as unfair, but it really didn't bother me. At one time it would have been nice to travel with the team and see some of the country and the other clubs, but I don't know that I would have been at all comfortable with it. I would have been the only female on trips. I feel baseball on the road is certainly a man's world, even though many clubs today have women traveling in various capacities. I still haven't gone to spring training because most of my work is here and it is especially busy in the front office prior to the start of a season.

On opening night at Three Rivers Stadium I attended as a fan. The stadium had this grand scoreboard and management realized after one game that they needed another person in scoreboard operations. I was the logical person because I understood the game, could type messages, and keep track of scores of other games. At first I refused because there was no extra pay involved. I had never been paid for any of the extra work I'd done at Forbes Field, but now I had to travel all the way across town to get to work, which was more of a burden. So they offered me extra pay.

When I worked at Forbes Field I always had to buy my dinner, but at Three Rivers the Pirates said they would provide it because they had a press lounge where the media ate. However, women were not permitted to go in there! The press lounge and press box were run by the Baseball Writers Association (BBWA) and at that time (1970) there just were no females in those areas. An usher had to bring my evening meal to me in the scoreboard operations room. I felt like I was in a prison or something. That changed in the late seventies when one of the local TV stations hired a woman in their sports department to cover the Pirates. She was fully credentialed and there was no way they could keep her off the field or out of the press area. Finally, the baseball writers all over the league agreed to change and to permit women into restricted areas. So I was finally allowed to have my dinner in the press lounge like a normal person.

In 1987 the Pirates honored media people who had covered the ball club for an extensive period of time—Rosey Rowswell, Bob Prince, and a couple of other writers. I helped plan the event. We had plaques made and a big media luncheon. Unknown to me, the organization also had a plaque made for me. Now I'm on the Media Wall of Fame in that same press lounge where I once was forbidden to eat.

In my early days there was really no big issue made about a woman being in the job because I guess I was considered more as a secretary. Many people assume that women want to work for a sports team because they will be able to get close to the players. I have made it clear that is not why I am here. Naturally I was always pleased to meet the athletes, but I have never been one to seek autographs or to be seen with them. I felt I knew my place and I stayed in it.

Once the season is over there is kind of a letdown in the office. Things wind down for a couple of months and it's a time when most people take vacations. But in December you start preparing again for the next season. We begin preparing the media guide, which involves a lot of writing and editing. After the first of the year things really pick up. Season credential requests start arriving, and we work on getting the schedules out to the public. In February the front office people who go to spring training head south in the middle of the month and are gone until opening day.

As we get close to the season, we also work on the scorecard magazine, which is available for the first game of the season, and the yearbook. So there is a lot of print work to be done. By this time the fans are getting interested in the upcoming season. The phone calls and mail start again.

As spring approaches there is a general excitement about the season getting underway. Of course opening day is always a huge event. It used to be that opening day was an afternoon game, but now with the game being geared toward television, most clubs have an opening night. Everybody wants to be at opening night. Most of the local stations want to come and do their live news from the stadium that night, and we have to credential all of these people and find a working area for them.

Then after opening day is out of the way, you settle into a regular routine with your home and road schedule. When the team is at home, my work includes handling requests for media credentials, complimentary press ticket requests, and answering mail and phones.

I look forward to the team going on the road because things quiet down for a few days and I can catch up on my other responsibilities. We don't do scrapbooks anymore, but we still collect everything that is written about the Pirates and put it on microfilm. I have to update rosters for the scorecard, so I have to keep on top of any transactions that are made by all the teams. You are always updating bio information so that if something happens with a player, you have the latest information on them that is available. We do that with computers now, which makes everything easier.

I liked baseball so much I just thought working in the game was a lifestyle that would be fun. Certainly it was different. My job was one of only twenty such jobs in baseball at that time. Landing that job was a pretty big deal for someone like me who came from a small town. Sure the days got long at times. Even though the games lasted until to eleven o'clock at night, we still had to be back the next morning at nine. When I was younger, that didn't bother me one bit. Another thing, I could have tickets to every ball game, and I thought, "Boy, I'll never get tired of going to a ball game." But after thirty-two years I have.

I really got tired of it maybe ten years ago. I worked overtime on the scoreboard through the 1982 season, when they were installing a new one, and I felt that that was enough. By that time my two sisters were living with me and we were sharing expenses. I was weary of working those long, long hours. It was strange after working all those years to be able to walk out at five o'clock. I had a guilt complex to tell you the truth, but I got over it pretty fast.

I still watch most of our games on television. I feel if I don't watch or listen to the games that I am missing something and I won't be able to properly handle phone calls I might get the next day. I have to know what is going on in order to do some of my job.

I enjoy the work during the season the most because that's when I'm busiest. It's exciting to go through a season. But coming into the office is much more fun when you win and you can talk about what might be happening in October. Everybody seems to be up when we win a few games in a row. We think that we're on our way and then we lose four, five, or six in a row and wonder if we will ever get out of the slump again. Our people seem to take losses to heart. I guess we take it personally because it's our livelihood—if the team wins, you share in the benefits, and if they lose, you know the club is going to continue to lose money and that there probably won't be any raises or any postseason games. In losing years, you can't wait until the end of the season.

There were years when we had good teams, like the ones we had in 1990, 1991, and 1992. We got to the postseason those three years, but we didn't make it to the World Series. Those were very disappointing seasons—especially the '92 season. We were down to the last out of the game and we lost it. We had really built ourselves up to go to the World Series, so it was very depressing. The next day many people just didn't bother to show up for work and those that did were not in a good mood. There had been so much preparation done for the World

Series—we had worked many long days and nights to get ready—and now it wasn't going to happen. The depression lasted for several weeks, but then we had to get started on plans for 1993.

Looking back, I am very fortunate to have worked with the Pirates for two World Championship seasons as well as several Eastern Division Championships. I have two World Series rings because of that and many players never even get one. I've been here for two All-Star Games, for the creation of the Roberto Clemente Statue, and for the opening of Three Rivers Stadium. I've had the opportunity to work with some great people and to meet so many others who have become friends. There is nothing like being affiliated with a sports team and sharing in that excitement—nothing like it at all.

⚓

EPILOGUE

Sally has just retired but is still actively involved with the Pirate Alumni Association. She produces their newsletter, The Black and Gold. *In need of space for a home-office and for all the memorabilia she collected over thirty-two years in baseball, she has moved into a new house.*

Jim Riggs

SPORTSWRITER AND SCORER, JAMESTOWN EXPOS

Jim Riggs has been covering minor league baseball and other sports for the Jamestown Post Journal *in western New York since 1975. Working at a small paper, he has a wider range of responsibilities than his counterparts at larger newspapers. Besides writing about the Jamestown Expos of the New York–Penn League, he sometimes fills in as photographer, and is the team's official scorer.*

⚾

I was born in East Liverpool, Pennsylvania, about 40 miles from Pittsburgh. As a young child, I hated baseball until the Pirates won the World Series in 1960. I was then ten years old and became a baseball nut. For the next ten years, I lived and died with the Pirates. I took pride in the fact that I either heard on the radio, watched on TV, or was at every Pirate game, including spring training games. To keep that streak going, I often had to use the old radio-headphone-cord-up-the-sleeve trick in school. I even managed to keep track of a couple games during weddings.

In the mid-1960s I discovered Strat-O-Matic Baseball, the board game with cards for each major league player based on their previous season's statistics. I would play the Pirates' current season schedule with the game. In 1972 I took the plunge and began to replay the entire 1971 National League season. I kept score and the stats for every National League game for 1970. I quit doing it early in September, mainly because I couldn't get the Pirates into first place.

I was always fascinated with statistics. I kept score of all the Pirates games I watched on TV or attended. It was a perfect background to someday becoming an official scorer.

We had a summer home at Chautauqua, which is how I got to the Jamestown area. After I graduated from Jamestown Community College, I went to a four-year college in Pittsburgh, where I could fulfill my dream of living in Pittsburgh and attending as many Penguin and Pirate games as possible. For three years there I had a Penguins season ticket. Fortunately, the Pirates won the World Series in 1971 and I could get on with life, like beginning to date a girl who later became my wife. If the Pirates hadn't won the Series, I might still be living and dying with them. After I finished my degree in journalism at Park Point College, I came back to Jamestown for a job with the *Post Journal,* and I've been here ever since.

I like my job here in town. Everything fits in just right. The [New York–Penn League] is great because it starts in June and ends in September. I cover a football team in the fall, and I cover the basketball team at the junior college in the winter. In the spring, I don't cover anything as a beat until the baseball season starts up again. Everything just fits together into a nice little niche.

The guys at this level [short season Class A] are easy to work with. There are probably a lot of people who think, "Why do you want to go down there and waste your time covering an A team?" Well, I really enjoy it. Years ago, I thought it would be nice to do a Triple A team. I never really thought that it would be fun to do the majors because of all the hassles.

I go into the newspaper at four in the morning to do the layout. I am usually out by about 11 A.M. and then I go play golf. I come down to the stadium at about 5 P.M. to cover the game at night. I am also the official scorer, so I don't usually get home until eleven or twelve at night. Then I get up at three in the morning to do the whole thing again. During the summer, I get by just fine on three or four hours of sleep. During winter, though, I take naps.

During the game, I write all the scoring into my computer. After the game, I go down and get some quotes from the manager and players.

Jim Riggs scoring a Jamestown Expos game. (Photo by Joe R. Liuzzo)

Then, when I go into work in the morning, I already have the boring part—the play-by-play—done and I mainly have to write the lead and plug in the quotes. Like anything, you're always looking for a good lead. Tonight's game is a laugher so I guess I'll talk to Jim Austin [Expos' outfielder] because he has had a heck of a night. Maybe I'll talk to the other manager, since our team has the best record in the league; I'd like to ask him if the Expos are the best team that he's seen so far this year. But usually, I try to single out a player or write about some trend. You always want to find a catchy little lead, but sometimes you feel like, "Let's just get this written."

When I first started, I used a tape recorder for the interviews. It was the trend then. Half of the time, you don't need it. Boy, have I learned that. If a guy talks for twenty minutes, you may use only two minutes of it. Last night I interviewed the relief pitcher that saved the game and got quotes from the manager and the pitching coach. I bet I talked to the pitcher for two or three minutes, the manager and the coach for another two, and that was it. It was enough. Friday though, we had a wild game and the manager was just spouting off great little quotes. He was really describing the game. So instead of me having to write about it, he described it for me.

Today most players and coaches are pretty cooperative. A few years ago, we had one hard-ass manager here who could be a real pain in the ass. Otherwise, I can't think of a manager that wouldn't talk after a game. Although I had a visiting manager about a month ago who sulked and wouldn't talk. He lost a tough game and I wanted to ask him about it. He gave me the snub and said that I should go over and talk to the Expos. But I've never had the home manager do that. You can tell when they—even the visiting ones—have been told by somebody higher up to cooperate with the media. When you ask, "Hey, have you got a minute?"—and you know that it's not the perfect time for them—they still stop and talk. They were told to cooperate with us, because the media is publicity. And the minor leagues need all the publicity they can get—even though their popularity is booming now.

Once I've written down all the scoring plays and plugged in the quotes, I can do the story pretty quickly—in anywhere from ten minutes to a half hour. The average time I spend on an article is probably about twenty minutes. Of course, when I first started doing this it took longer because I wanted to write the Pulitzer Prize winning lead and all that bullshit. Now I've learned that there are other things that you have to get done. Besides, I find that if I rattle one out quick after the game, it's usually better than the one where I have been able to go home, think about it, and then write it the next morning at my leisure.

I never read my stories. I don't even look at the sports page. There are too many times that we will have a 48-point headline that was incorrect and has been sitting out in the composing room the whole morning and nobody saw it. So, you pick up the paper and it looks as if it has printed red. It's probably a defeatist attitude, but I never look at the sports section. I do have to clip out my story to keep it in my files, but I don't read it. If I did and I saw a mistake, it would bother me. So I just prefer not to see it.

But I do like to look at my pictures and see how they turned out. People from big papers say, "Gee, you have to take your own pictures?" I tell them that it isn't that we don't have someone to do it. It's merely that I like to do it. On some nights if I don't take the pictures, it feels like I am not doing anything. I got into photography late and got bit by the bug, and now I think that it's just a lot of fun.

After the game, I also have to send in a report to the other team's newspaper. We do it as a trade-off, so that we'll get reports from them when our team is on the road. Things have changed and now everybody is giving their team good coverage. I think it's all part of the boom in minor league baseball.

The other hat I wear is being the official scorer. Most people think the big deal about being the official scorer is simply calling the hits and errors. That's all they think of. Well, that's about 1 percent of the job. The main thing is that you have to prepare a stat sheet for each game and then fax it in [to Howe Sportsdata in Boston]. It's an $8\frac{1}{2} \times 12$ sheet with every single statistic of the game. So your main duty is to keep all the stats straight. If one kid's hit doesn't appear in the stats, it will drop his batting average; and that means a great deal to the kid. It can even affect him in a borderline case of who moves up and who doesn't.

Scoring a play, a hit, or an error is no small thing either. Sometimes I'll sit up there [in the press box] with the guy that runs the scoreboard and with the announcer and we'll debate it, discuss the play. But, in the end, it's got to be my decision. I read last night that when Randy Johnson of the Seattle Mariners, who began his career in Jamestown, lost his no-hitter, the official scorer looked at the replay of the ground ball hit five times. We can't do that down here [minor leagues] because we don't have replay.

Usually, before the season begins, I tell the manager to tell his coaches and players that if there is a serious doubt about a call, they can ask me after the game. I might not see that the ball took a bad hop or that a guy took his foot off the base. Just because I called it a hit or an error during the game doesn't mean that it's etched in stone.

It's not too often that a player questions your call. Years ago, we had some guys in Jamestown that would get all upset about an error. Let's face it, unless you made a ton of errors, they weren't going to keep you from making it to the majors. One of the worst fielders that we ever had here was Delino Deshields, who is now with the Dodgers. I once had him for two errors in one inning. And later in the same inning he made a third, but I didn't have the guts to call it. And here was a guy who went to the majors really quickly.

Once, in a famous game, our guys were playing Auburn at the end of the season. Both teams stunk, so the game didn't mean anything. There was a pop fly to right field and the Auburn second baseman had to go far to the right to get to it and the ball went off his glove. It was one time in my life when I had no doubt, and I said to the guy on the scoreboard, that's a hit. Pretty soon, out of the dugout, I heard the manager say in front of the crowd, "What the fuck game are you watching?" I looked at the guy beside me, who was on the radio, and he said, "What's his problem?" There wasn't any doubt about the call. And here is this guy ranting and raving, yelling at me from down below in front of the fans, and swearing like crazy. The only thing that I could think of was that neither team was going anywhere and that he must have been looking out for his pitcher. So after the game, while I was in the Jamestown locker room, the manager came charging in and started to ream me out again. "How could you call that a hit?"

I said, "How could I rule that an error? The guy did all he could and it glanced off his glove."

He went on and on and on before he finally admitted it and said, "Look, I don't have a good team. I don't have any guys on this team that are prospects but the pitcher."

I said, "Listen. I am not going to screw your second baseman to help your pitcher." He finally admitted that it came down to the same old thing—that he always looks out for the pitcher. When I get flak, it's usually because someone is looking out for his pitcher.

But the other night, after the game, one of the coaches asked me about an error I had ruled on. "Well," I said, "The second baseman had plenty of time to get his body in front of the ball, but instead he took the easy route and tried to backhand it and it bounced up on his shoulder, so I ruled it an error." The guy made a mental error and it ended up being a physical error. The coach claimed the ball took a bad hop and should be ruled a hit. We went back and forth. Finally he said to me, "Oh well. Mike has had a hard time, been in a slump and a hit would have really done him some good." Later I checked the score sheets and saw that Mike had gotten two hits that night anyway.

But that kind of thing doesn't happen too often. Most managers don't get involved. A few players this year have questioned their stolen-base stats. It can be easy to miss a steal once in a while. If it's here at home, then I can correct it. If it's on the road somewhere I have to get the official scorer there to do it—and that is a real hassle. But other than that, we haven't had any guys that were ready to pound the hell out of me over a call.

After the game, I get interviews from the manager and a few of the players and then come back up to the press box to add the stats. It doesn't take too long if I've kept up-to-date, mainly filling in the names and all of the numbers. But I have to have all of my put-outs and everything ready. Like I said, that is your chore as the official scorer, not just calling all the hits and errors.

Before I leave the ballpark, I fax the stats to Howe Sportsdata. These faxes are great. Years ago, we filled out a long form by hand. We had to mail it within twenty-four hours. I tried to be pretty strict about doing it, but because I had my own stuff to do, I didn't always get them off right away. Some guys wouldn't send them in for days at a time. Everything now is done so quickly. And you get so much more information—stats for every player and every team in the country. Like today, when I went into the office the stats were right there for the whole league, updated from last night's game.

You don't make much being a scorer. In fact, sometimes they [Montreal Expos] can be so damn cheap. Before, when Bill Stoneman was vice president of the Expos and was placed in charge of the minor leagues, I had gotten paid a flat rate per game for scoring. I told Tom O'Reilly [Jamestown's new general manager] at the beginning of the year what rate I was getting, fifteen dollars per game, and he said okay. Then I got my first check and it didn't add up right. So I went down to the office. Well, they were paying me less for doubleheaders because the games were only seven innings. I said, "Wait a minute. What if the games goes to twelve innings? Am I going to get more? What if the home team doesn't bat in the bottom of the ninth inning? Am I going to get less?" Give me a break. Tom said that it wasn't his decision and that he was following instructions from Montreal. I said, "You mean when they are paying all those guys a million bucks a year up there, they are concerned about saving pennies on my paycheck?" I heard the pitching coach talking about some equipment that he couldn't get for his guys, saying, "They'll spend millions in the majors, but they nickel and dime us down here." I couldn't believe that they wanted to pay me less for a seven-inning game. It's amazing.

I don't have to make the road trips with the team, except for the first game of the season and if they make the play-offs. Let me tell you about last year's play-off with Pittsfield. It was the trip to hell. Pittsfield was the Mets' team and they were sort of cocky because they had the best record and everything. The first play-off game was here. Pittsfield flew to the game, so when they got to the ballpark, they were really cocky. They had flown and all that shit. After the game, everyone had to go to Pittsfield. That is about 400 miles, and the Mets were going to fly back while we, the Expos, were going by bus. Anyway, Pittsfield was leading the game in the bottom of the ninth and it looked like the game was over. With two outs, one of our guys hit a triple and we won the game. The Pittsfield guys were totally in shock.

They got on their airplane and flew back to Pittsfield and we got on the bus. We left here around 1:00 A.M. I had to write my story on the bus and call it in later. I was concerned about the time, so I figured if we left Jamestown at 1:00 A.M. we should be in Pittsfield by eight in the morning at the latest. We were supposed to go to the southern tier, straight across [New York state], up to Albany, and then to Pittsfield. Simple, right? I am typing my story when I look out the window and I see a sign for Geneseo 20 miles. The driver is way the hell and gone off course. He had gotten off at Corning and turned up the thruway on 390. I was a nervous wreck and wanted to get there as quick as I could. We backtracked a bit on the thruway and got over to Albany. I was keeping an eye on what was going on, but I dozed off. Then it was like dawn, and one of the players in the back of the bus yells, "We're going to New York City." The dumb-ass driver was heading south. He'd made another wrong turn and had gone another 20 miles out of our way. We got to Pittsfield at ten in the morning and the play-off game was that night. We should have been there three hours ago, easily. The Expos lost the game that night, but won the next game to win the championship. We left Pittsfield at about 11:00 P.M. Of course, they stopped for beer on the way back, so the whole trip was wild. I have the whole thing on tape. The guys got up and each did a little speech. And one guy had written an entire poem. I was sitting there typing my story with the tape recorder on. We were driving, the beer was flowing, and everyone was getting happy. I was typing away and listening to all of this and laughing at everybody. And once again, I took a look out of the window. We had been on the road at least an hour. I looked out the window and saw a sign, Pittsfield 10 miles. The driver started going to the east and had started to come back. When the players noticed, some of them were half-tanked and they were ready to strangle the driver. The pitching coach still talks about that trip.

THE FRONT OFFICE

The term "front office," which first appeared around the turn of the century, was used in the New York City underworld to refer to police headquarters.[1] Today it is a synonym for the main office of any company. Many people use it when talking specifically about the business operations of professional sports teams. In baseball the front office is almost always housed in the ballpark itself, although in the low minors the lack of space sometimes results in the front office spilling over into an outside trailer or two.

As one ascends from the low minors to the big leagues the number of front office employees rises markedly. Major league teams in big media markets like New York, Los Angeles, Chicago, and Boston have staffs in excess of one hundred full-time, year-round employees, while their affiliates in the small towns of the low minors may have only a half dozen year-round staff. The Cleveland Indians, for example, have as many different departments (eleven) as their farm team in Kinston, North Carolina, has staff.

In the minor leagues front office staffs routinely have contact with the fans. Some team owners and general managers even greet arriving fans at the gate. The location of minor league front offices reflect this greater accessibility to the public: as most are at ground level and open onto the main concourse. Major league offices, in contrast, are high above on the mezzanine level near the press area and skyboxes. Their entrances are guarded by security so that only those with credentials may enter. Major league front office staff rarely venture into the stands to mingle with fans. As will become evident in the narratives that follow, at all levels of professional baseball the pay is usually low, the days are long, and the work is varied. And office morale is influenced by how well the team plays, especially in the big leagues.

NOTE

1. Richard H. Thornton, *An American Glossary: Being an Attempt to Illustrate Certain Americanisms upon Historical Principles* (New York: F. Unger Publishing Company, 1962), 3:155.

Dennis Bastien

OWNER AND GENERAL MANAGER,
CHARLESTON WHEELERS

*Dennis Bastien and his wife Lisa are the last full-time owners and op-
erators of a minor league team in professional baseball. A graduate of
Southern Illinois University, Dennis became the general manager for the
Class A Gastonia Cardinals (Western Carolina League) at age twenty-
five. After three years there, the South Atlantic League asked him to
resurrect their Macon, Georgia, franchise. He had to raise $85,000 in
back taxes before the IRS would take the padlocks off the gates. He
turned that venture into a success.*

*The Bastiens later bought the Winston-Salem Spirits, and Dennis
served as the general manager. They have also owned Appalachian
League franchises in Martinsville, Virginia, and Huntington, West Virginia. Dennis was named Minor League Executive of the Year in 1988
by* Sporting News. *At the time of this interview, he was the owner and
general manager of the Charleston Wheelers. He uses the pronoun
"we," referring to him and his wife, because they are a team. Their
five-year-old son Wyatt has been raised at the ballpark.*

⚉

In college, when I hurt my shoulder and realized I wasn't good enough
to play professionally, I decided to pursue the business end of sports.

Southern Illinois had just hired Gale Sayers as their athletic director and I went to him for advice. We designed a program where I could get a graduate degree in athletic administration. That was before all these colleges had these asinine sports administration programs that serve zero purpose. My roommate was the son of Cotton Fitzsimmons, the coach of the old Kansas City Kings and the Atlanta Hawks. I did a couple of summer internships with him running basketball camps.

Gale Sayers told me he could get me a job in the sales and marketing department for the Tampa Bay Buccaneers. So I interviewed and explained that I wanted to be a general manager of a sports team someday. They told me flat out that I could never be a general manager starting out in a department of an NFL team, an NBA team, or a major league baseball team. They told me that you've got to start down in the minor leagues of baseball and do it all.

They suggested that I go across the bay to St. Petersburg to the office of the National Association of Professional Baseball and talk to them. So I did. Coincidentally, the winter meetings were in Orlando the following week, and they told me that would be the best place to find a job in minor league baseball. At the meetings I was very fortunate to get a job as the general manager of the Single A Cardinals in Gastonia, North Carolina. I couldn't even find the town on the map, but I was told that the team needed me to start working the next week. I had already put everything I owned in my beat-up old car in case the Buccaneers hired me, so I drove straight to Gastonia. Then I ran back to my southern Illinois home, picked up a few more things, and ran back to Gastonia. That was December of 1978, and I've been doing this ever since.

Back then, when franchises weren't what they are now, there was only a general manager. I was the groundskeeper and the stadium clean-up person. I also ran concessions, did the PA, and was the secretary. I worked twenty hours a day. I was still blowing down the stadium when the sun came up, then I'd mow the field between six and eight in the morning, make the bank deposits, set up the concession stand—everything. I did that for three years.

⚾

After a season in Macon, the South Atlantic League asked Dennis to take over the Spartansburg, South Carolina, franchise. That too be-

*came profitable. There he met his wife, Lisa, whom he had hired to do
phone sales for tickets.*

⚘

During my time in Spartansburg my dad realized that I knew my job,
that I knew the baseball business. He thought it was silly for me to go
in and resurrect franchises for someone else and make a minimal salary.
So he mortgaged our family's small seed-cleaning business and we
bought the Winston-Salem Red Sox of the Carolina League in October
of 1983. We got in when the getting was fair—not good but fair. I
would not have been able to do it without the help of my dad. We paid
the highest price ever for a Class A franchise at that point and we've
done okay. Had I just continued as a GM, I wouldn't have been able
to buy even a rookie team today. Baseball people cannot buy baseball
teams. They don't have the money. Baseball people work for these New
York City limited partnerships who want to be small-town George
Steinbrenners and say they own 5 percent of a minor league team.

I chose to own a Class A team for job security. When you're a general manager you are hired to be fired. Anytime one of these new big
conglomerates buys a minor league franchise, they bring in their director of marketing to operate it, and most of these guys don't know
that much about the game. Too many of my friends who went on to be
GMs in Double A or Triple A have been fired. It's usually not because
they were doing a bad job. It's just that when the franchise is sold, the
new owner wants to bring in his own person. I'm not going to fire myself here. By the same token, I am not guaranteed a paycheck. There
have been many months when my wife and I went without one. But
we've watched the equity in the franchise go up twenty-fold. I guess
I'm a millionaire on paper, but I couldn't buy this team lunch.

The first thing we did at Winston-Salem was change the name. We
were one of the original innovators of using your own team colors and
your own team name. We built a stadium club, an office complex, and
new concession stands. In 1983 the Winston-Salem Red Sox had the
best record in all of professional baseball, though they were beaten in
the play-offs by the Lynchburg Mets. They only drew 42,000 people
that year. In 1984 as the Winston-Salem Spirits, the first team to wear
blue and green as team colors, and with a new logo, new marketing,
more sales, more promotions, and the worst team in baseball, we drew
98,000 fans.

Even though we borrowed to get that club, everybody on the staff still got paid those first two years. So there were a lot of times when my wife and I didn't get a penny and had to borrow to get groceries. The day we were married we moved into the home locker room because we couldn't afford to pay rent. We did that for three months. It really wasn't that bad though. We had a whirlpool, six showers, unlimited hanging space, cable television, and refrigerators. And we set up the manager's office like a little kitchen. If the players hadn't arrived from spring training, we'd have still been there.

After four years we paid off our loan. We decided to get a second club. The only way that would be possible was to buy an expansion team in the South Atlantic League. We wanted to find a city that hadn't had baseball in a long time, so we chose Charleston, West Virginia.

The team name "Wheelers" is short for stern-wheelers. Charleston has an international stern-wheel regatta every year on the Kanawha river. When we were first testing the market we talked to some of the old guys in the barbershop. I asked what the area was known for, and they said, "Well, there's those damn wheelers out on the river every fall." We thought that was pretty catchy. We were an independent co-op team our first year, then a Cubs team, now we're a Reds affiliate. It doesn't matter, we're still the Wheelers.

The first year Lisa and I ran the clubs [Winston-Salem and Charleston] simultaneously out of the trunks of our cars. Both of us were at every home game of one of the teams. We met passing on the road between four and seven in the morning. That got old pretty quickly. We thought that the long-term prognosis was a lot better in Charleston than it was in Winston-Salem. We had won three straight championships in Winston-Salem but still never made the front page of the paper. Down there, we were a distant third behind NASCAR and ACC sports. Here in Charleston we're number two in the state, behind West Virginia University football. So we sold the Winston-Salem franchise and moved here.

Actually, there's more money made at the rookie level than at the major league level. The lower the level, the higher the percentage of net profits. In other words, if you took a ratio of what your revenues are for the entire season over what your expenses are, that percentage is highest at the rookie league level. One reason is that rookie ball doesn't start until June. In Charleston, we start playing in April, when often it's 35 degrees and drizzling. You only have 150 people in the stands, and why they're here is beyond us. Here we draw approximately 80 percent of our attendance in 50 percent of the season. That same 50 percent is the entire rookie season. We would love to have just 36 home games, take the biggest promotions, and do one per game. We could take in 75 percent of our total gross revenues, but only have 25 percent of the expenses we have now.

People think that this is a glamorous job. A lot of people think we go in and put up our feet, sign player contracts, and scout prospects. It's not like that. I've been in situations where I didn't even know the major league GM. There's seldom any interaction or any discussions between him and us. Most of our conversations are with the minor league director, and even those are rare. People ask, "Why did you send that guy up to Double A?" Well, we got a phone call from the Minor League Director who said, "Send him to Double A. Put him on a plane." Fans ask, "Why did you get that rookie kid to play right field?" Well, they told us to. We really have nothing to do with that. As far as our relationship with the players and managers here, we really have none. The team is handled by the manager and the coaches, we do the business and the operation end of things. When the players get off the plane from spring training, that's when we know who will be playing for us.

Sitting down to do this interview [which was begun in the stands during a game] is probably the most I've seen of a game in twelve years. I never have any idea what the score is. The people who think it's glamorous should come watch us after a series when the visiting team has left and we have to clean the toilets in their clubhouse and jump-start their broken-down bus. We're probably the only people in the world who have callouses on the first knuckle of their fingers. You only get those from pulling tarps. This job is eighteen hours a day of hard work and dealing with people's problems. When fans pay to come in, they're our guests and we have to act as though we're throwing the biggest party in town every night.

The off-season is our toughest work. Anybody can do what we do during the season because we're mostly executing the stuff that you prepared in the off-season. If I had a dollar for every time somebody asked me, "Well, what do you do in the off-season," I could retire. From September 15th to April 1st, from 7:30 A.M. to 7:00 P.M., we're out knocking on doors, marketing, promoting, setting up appointments, speaking to civic clubs, selling group nights, and selling advertising packages. We have to have our program to the printer by late February so we can have them ready for opening day and we have to have our pocket schedules to the printer by late January so we can have them distributed in late March.

The day starts with a one-hour sales meeting where we post our sales on charts. We keep team charts, staff charts, individual charts, category charts for full pages sold, half pages sold, full-color pages sold, season tickets sold, outfield signs sold—everything. After the meeting we hit the streets.

During the eight months of preseason, there's a tense mental strain that people have to put on themselves to hit certain sales figures. If people can't bring in seven times what they're being paid, they can't justify their own existence.

I hadn't had any sales experience before my first job in Gastonia, but the beauty of it was selling the greatest product in the world. If you can't get somebody excited about being involved with a business where you come out on a summer evening, water the infield, lay down the white lines, and somebody sings the national anthem—if that doesn't raise a lump in your throat, I don't know what will. If you can't get somebody fired up about professional baseball, then you've got no business being in the business world in the first place.

We're very creative in our sales technique. We hand everybody we call on a business card attached to bag of peanuts. As we're talking, we're waving around a bat-shaped pen. That's the official contract signing pen of the Wheelers. We don't sell those. They're only for people who sign contracts. Every person we call on, we follow up with a thank-you card the next day. We cold call, we go to every business within a 30-mile radius, and we pitch them on being a part of a success story and being a part of championship Wheelers baseball. We do our homework and we prove that an outfield sign at our ballpark is more cost-effective than a three-year lease on a highway billboard. We do have an advantage here, though, in that over three hundred games are played here in a year. When we're on the road, there are three or four amateur games played here a night and on weekends. In our sales pitch we bring up some of the hidden costs in baseball, like our insurance policies, which run us over $100,000 a year, and that we spend $30,000 a year on bats and $20,000 a year on balls. When we say we spent over $3,000 on detergent and over $2,000 on toilet paper, that brings it down to every man's level. And we say, "Well, that's why you need to be a part of Wheelers baseball and here's several ways you can do it."

There's a big advertisers' night at the end of the season with free food here at the ballpark. We also have a Christmas party and a Wheelers Winter Banquet in February. The banquet is a black-tie affair in a giant ballroom. We bring in former Wheelers players who are now in the big leagues. And just by being a part of Wheelers baseball, advertisers get an invitation—whether they have a small ad in the program or a big promotional package.

We probably spend more money on sales presentation materials than most folks in baseball. We have a video tape, a highlight film, and a sixteen-page, four-color, high-gloss sales brochure. We leave them sample pictures and two tickets to any game during the season. We stress that we are more than just a baseball team: we're a corporation. We're not a DuPont and we're not a Union Carbide, but the Wheelers are larger than 70 percent of the businesses in the Kanawha River Valley. Studies have shown that minor league baseball is a phenomenal boost for an area. If nothing else, it promotes civic pride.

We're also heavily involved with the community. We're on the boards of several fund-raising groups. I've spoken at over four hundred civic clubs, fraternal organizations, Boy Scout troops, and Little League banquets in our seven years here. People know us. They like us.

We bring dollars into the community that wouldn't exist if we weren't here. Everybody feeds off that. When the players rent an apartment, the apartment owner then pays his power bill and the power guy pays his workers and they pay their rent, buy gasoline, and buy clothes. The players' salary and meal money is provided from the major league team. That money is sent in from out of state. Very few businesses in this area can say that.

If you use an economic multiplier equation, we are somewhere between an eight and ten million dollar a year corporation, as far as new dollars brought into the community. On paper, we have to bring in about $750,000 to break even. We show them that we're not just somebody that opens the doors and hope people come. We need substantial preseason sales to justify our existence. That's part of our sales presentation.

In the off-season, after a full day of sales, we often change clothes and from 8:00 P.M. until midnight we work inside the ballpark. We paint, build, plumb, and wire. I was born and raised out in the country, and if you needed a new shed for a piece of equipment, you didn't pay to have someone else do it; you built it yourself. Anything that has been built, any concrete that has been poured, or any seat that has been painted, we did it ourselves. Until we put in plastic blue and gold seats, every seat in this house was painted. Every year we painted 4,384 wood seats. We started in the back row and worked our way down. January was a green month, February was a blue month, and March was a gold month. People couldn't believe we did it. But, rather than pay somebody $30,000 to do it, we did it ourselves. We won't hire an assistant or a staff member that doesn't know which end of a hammer to hold.

If a person doesn't know how to do that stuff, there is no use getting into baseball. Every year at the winter meetings there are between six hundred and a thousand people looking for jobs in baseball. Most are clueless about what we do. That's because of those sports administration programs they come out of. They teach the theory of athletic philosophies and things like that, which don't have any application here. Right now, the perfect candidate to become a Class A assistant GM is single, celibate, has done a little bit of everything from plumbing to building, has a little bit of sales experience, and has a pickup truck. I'll hire that person tomorrow. Many young people have these little sports cars now. If you send somebody to pick up twenty bags of Diamond Dry [crushed corn husks used to absorb moisture on infields], what are they supposed to pick them up in? But nobody tells them that because these professors in sports administration programs don't know that themselves.

My advice to people who want to work in baseball is to work in baseball. I have a new son. He'll be raised in the game. I don't care if he goes to college. In fact, I'd almost discourage it. For me personally and for anybody else I've talked to in baseball, it was a total waste. In most cases, the young interns that we hire ought to pay us. Most of them came out of four years of college and didn't learn a darn thing about what they wanted to get into. You're better off going into a minor league city when you're young and bugging the GM, saying, "I'm willing to do anything. I'll help you clean the stadium, I'll help you work on the field, and I'll help you pull the tarps. Get me started. Show me things. Let me be your gopher. I'll tie a 10-foot rope around my waist and follow you wherever you go the next three years." That's the way you get started and learn. It's also one of the reasons the salaries are so low. Why pay somebody big money when there are a thousand people who will do it for almost nothing?

Ideally, the guy to hire right now is our batboy. He's been here two years. He's sixteen years old and knows more about what we do and how to do it than 99 percent of those college graduates with sports administration degrees who go to the winter meetings looking for jobs. I've had people waiting outside my door at six in the morning at the winter meetings just to hand me a résumé. You can't blame them. They have to be aggressive because there are so many people looking to get into baseball.

We take eight days off after the season is over in September. We need three days to put the stadium to bed—box up inventory, winterize, take the picnic tent down, take the net down. Then we take five days off to go kick into gear. On September 15th, the next year begins for us.

When the season starts, then we're talking about being here from daylight to take the tarps off the field, straighten up, set up for the promotion that night, stuff programs, run inserts, stat packs, fill out the promotion boards, and get tickets, which were sold the previous November, to the company that has company night. During the season it's simple. It's just long physical hours. There's no mental strain.

Bill Veeck did things back in the thirties and forties that right now people copy and just give different names to. There's always a new innovation and then everybody copies it. That's what this game is about. That's why we have the winter meeting seminars to share ideas. I saw an ad for a cap in *Baseball America* saying this was the first team to have a Sunday cap. We did that in 1988. We had the Wheelers White Weekend Wear. We had a separate uniform just for Saturdays and Sundays. As far as I knew, that was original. Now almost every team has a white cap. I don't know if they copied us, but if they did more power to them.

Today, to draw a crowd you need promotions. We'd love to think that this was 1925 and that we could just open our gates on a Tuesday afternoon and have a packed a house. Those days are over—even in the major leagues. Now you can only pack Wrigley Field on Tuesday afternoon if it's Cap Day. We have a base of about 400 baseball purists—people who will be here if there is a tornado under the grand stand. We don't need to market to them. When we have Cap Night and draw 3,000 people, most of them are here for the cap. My opinion is that if you get them here for the cap, The Chicken, or the fireworks, they'll probably have a good time and come back.

We do a lot of discounts, but we don't do free nights. In most minor league cities there's usually a business that's giving away free tickets for at least one game a week. There's is no reason to go to tonight's game if you can go for free tomorrow. It's like a service station selling gasoline for twenty-five cents a gallon on Tuesdays. What day would you buy gasoline? Some clubs have the philosophy that if they let everybody in for free, they'll make it up in concessions. Some owners do that to build their attendance numbers in order to inflate the value of the franchise, knowing that they're going to sell the ball club. They have inflated numbers that make their bottom line look good, and the new owner may be unaware of how they accomplished that.

We don't do that. But we do have fifteen to twenty discount-coupon nights over the course of the year. We sell a sponsor a block of 5,000 coupons, and each coupon lets the entire family in for somewhere between two and five dollars. There's still a value to the ticket, and we get more money from the sponsor for doing that than if we sold the same amount of tickets at full price. That gets more people here and more sponsors involved.

Tonight we have a decent crowd for a Thursday—somewhere between 1,400 and 1,700 people. Tonight we've got to pay off some bills that we didn't pay off last night because it was cold and it rained. Baseball is one of the few businesses that is highly dependent on the weather. You can spend $20,000 promoting a big night—put posters all over town, issue discount coupons, run television and radio commercials, buy newspaper ads, promote it here at the ballpark for two weeks in advance—and God can open up the skies from 6:00 P.M. until midnight and you're out all that.

On a typical night with no promotion you see a big cross-section of the community—especially a lot of young couples with children because frankly there's not that much else to do around here. Movie theaters now are $7.50, and you've got to use a credit card for popcorn. We love it when major league baseball raises its prices each year and when movie theaters go up another fifty cents. It only proves our point that nobody else can offer what we do—three G-rated hours, out on a breezy summer evening, under a beautiful sky, at a ballpark watching future major league players. Where else can a family go for three hours of G-rated entertainment—this includes parking, a ticket, a hot dog, and a soda each—for under ten dollars?

Sam Kennedy

INTERN, NEW YORK YANKEES

Many front-office employees of baseball organizations began as interns. In the last fifteen years internships have become the primary entry into the "business" side of professional baseball. Major league clubs typically have between six and nine interns, while minor league teams have two to four. Interns do much of the grunt work involved in operating a professional baseball organization, such as running errands, compiling statistics, and filing papers. In the minor leagues, interns may even help the grounds crew pull the tarp. As an intern with the Birmingham Barons, J. J. Weiner once played the team's mascot, an oversized dog named Babe Ruff. Interns may work for just a summer or for a calendar year; some are paid, while others get only the experience. Either way, the jobs are highly competitive.

Sam Kennedy was a junior and an American Studies major at Trinity College in Hartford, Connecticut, when he was hired as an intern with the New York Yankees.

〽

My last exam was May 12 and I started here with the Yankees on May 15. I showed up at 8:30 in the morning, and the two security guards at the front desk thought I was crazy because people don't usually come in until 9:30 or 10:00. So I sat by myself out in the stands for an hour until somebody came.

I had never been in an empty baseball stadium before. It was an overwhelming feeling to be in this enormous place all by myself with no fans, just me. Then, when the front office people started coming in, I went upstairs, and as I walked into the office, I saw the Yankees World Championship trophy shining in a glass case in the front lobby. Being from Boston, I was amazed, thinking that the Yankee's had twenty-one other trophies just like that one! Then, Mr. Lawn, Yankees' vice president, took me on a tour of the stadium, down to the dugout and into the clubhouse. It was a dream come true. From that day on I was allowed to go wherever I wanted, wherever I was needed.

The first day I just listened a lot, to get the gist of what I was expected to do. Some interns are assigned to specific departments, like public relations or ticket sales; others, like me, are considered "floaters." We go where ever we are needed. Because I float around, I've gotten to know lots of people and have worked in every different department. I've done work for people in accounting and in media and community relations, and I've spent a lot of time in the ticket office.

I've had other internships before, but they weren't anything like working in a baseball stadium. I interned for a law firm in Boston, Dean Witter in Hartford, and even the American Embassy in London. People are impressed that I worked in the American Embassy. It was neat, but being at Yankee Stadium is more exciting. When I take my lunch hour, I go out in the stands and sit in the sun. Sometimes I work out and jog around the upper deck or go down on the field and jog around the warning track. I might go to the weight room. I mean you are in a baseball park, not any old office building. After being here I can't think of anyplace I would rather work than in a ballpark.

Working at the baseball stadium is far more intense than working in anyplace I've ever been. I worked for a hockey team—the Hartford Whalers—for a while and it wasn't anything like this. The Whalers only drew about 5,000 fans a game; a lot of the public relations was taking ten or fifteen hockey sticks to the locker room before the game for the players to sign. That's an exaggeration, but it wasn't anything like here. At times, the stadium is very busy, even hectic—especially when Mr. Steinbrenner is in town. Then people are really uptight, wanting to make sure that everything is perfect. One busy night this summer—it was Phil Rizzuto Night and Mr. Steinbrenner had Joe

DiMaggio sitting with him in his box—Mr. Steinbrenner wanted some glossy photos of Joe DiMaggio for him to sign for his grandsons. Since DiMaggio hadn't been with the club for forty-five years, it took seven of us a little too long to find those pictures in the media archives. We learned the lesson that when baseball owners want something done, they mean quickly!

A lot of people here put in incredibly long hours at the stadium. Rain delays make the day even longer. But no fan ever writes a letter saying how much they enjoyed coming to the game on Saturday— "Thanks for having me, thanks for putting on a great show." Instead, we get lots of letters filled with complaints. Maybe New Yorkers demand a lot because they pay a lot of money for everything. But we get people complaining that a vendor was rude to them, and they now want free tickets because of that. I remember going to Red Sox games as a kid and being upset that I didn't get someone's autograph, but I would never think to call up the Red Sox and complain. But you get that kind of thing here.

People pay seventeen dollars for a ticket and expect something more than just watching a ball game. There are all kinds of fans calling up looking for free promotional items, free tickets, or even a meeting with Bernie Williams. Those demands are pretty hard to take when you have staff working so hard for twelve or fifteen hours a day, every day. A common line around here among the staff is, "I'm gonna go out and get a real job in the real world someday."

Four or five times last summer I slept in the clubhouse because I was still here at one or two o'clock in the morning. I had to be back by 9:00 A.M. so there was no point in going all the way into Manhattan and then coming back six hours later. The batboys sleep here in the clubhouse on game nights because they need to work a few hours after the game doing laundry and cleaning out players' lockers. I slept on Buck Showalter's couch. I woke up in the morning, took a shower, and was right back at work. At the time I didn't think anything of it, but when I got back to school and told people that sometimes I would sleep in Yankee Stadium on Buck Showalter's couch, they'd say "You slept in Yankee Stadium. Wow!" I suppose that is pretty neat, but after you've been here for a while you take it for granted.

Anyway, I have seen a lot of people put in incredible hours. Frank Swain, the ticket director has been working for thirty or forty years in the ticket office, which is probably the most high-pressure job in this organization. He sounds like he is going to have a heart attack any day. He is always trying to get every last fan into the ballpark. One day when I walked into the office he was asleep on the floor at nine in the morning with his coat on. He hadn't been home. I said, "Frank, go home and get some sleep." He said, "I can't sleep, I don't have time to sleep." He wasn't kidding; he really didn't have time to sleep! During the season there is tremendous pressure on him to fill the ballpark, to make sure that attendance numbers are as good as they can be. He is a fan who loves baseball. Why else would anyone work fifteen hours a day?

People outside baseball often ask if I get to know the players. The staff in baseball operations and media relations have frequent contact with the players, but they are the exception. I think the players like to keep some distance between themselves and everyone else. The players have fame and fortune and sometimes have trouble relating to us mere mortals. Sometimes I think it's hard for them to separate the people in the front office from the fans. On the other hand, I think it's hard for a lot of us to relate to what players do, to how hard players work, and to how much pressure there is on them from all those guys in the minor leagues or on the bench trying to take their jobs.

⚓

EPILOGUE

After finishing his third summer as an intern with the Yankees, Sam took a job in radio, first selling Yankees baseball on WABC, and then selling sports sponsorships on a sports network, WFAN Sports Radio in New York. Although he had daily contact with professional sports in New York, he was dissatisfied: "Each day it became more evident that I did not belong working at a radio station, and I wished I could be back in baseball." He got his big break on the field at Shea Stadium, where he met a former high school teammate, Theo Epstein, now the media relations manager for the San Diego Padres. "As we talked about his job, I knew I would do whatever it took to get back into baseball, and then Theo mentioned that the Padres might have an opening." Four months later, Sam landed the Padres job—account executive, coporate development. He now sells in-stadium signage, promotional days, and television sponsorships at Jack Murphy Stadium. "I feel so fortunate to have made it back into baseball. This is where I want to be. One day I will look back to my days as a new intern in the Yankees ticket office and remember it as the place where it all started."

Jack Boehmer

DIRECTOR OF STADIUM OPERATIONS, BOWIE BAYSOX

When the town of Bowie, Maryland, received a Double A Eastern League franchise, it did not yet have its own stadium. So they played their first season in Memorial Stadium, the old home of the Baltimore Orioles. No other major league city also had a minor league team, and no minor league team has had a major league ballpark as their home. This occurrence coincided with Jack Boehmer's first season in baseball as director of stadium operations.

Before baseball, Jack had worked as an advertising salesman for a radio station and as the supervisor of a warehouse. He speaks in a low register with a Baltimore accent and goes by the nickname "Fat Jack."

⚾

I can't think of a better way to spend an evening in the summer than sitting at the ballpark, beer in one hand, hot dog in the other, watching these kids try their damndest to make it to the major leagues.

When the Keys, a Single A franchise, came to Frederick [Maryland] in 1989, my wife and I started to attend their games. In the first three seasons, I only missed two or three games. I sat in the same seat right behind home plate every game. Once in a while, if I had a few extra beers in me, I might get up and try to spell out K-E-Y-S with the fans or lead the clap cheer. I was just very loud and I'd always be razzing the umpires.

One time, a sponsor wanted the mascot to chase a fan around the bases, like they do in many ballparks. But Frederick didn't have a mascot. They explained that the closest thing they had was Fat Jack. So, I was selected to chase this fan around the bases. I was the most noticeable fan in the ballpark.

Eventually, the front office staff got to know me because they wanted to find out who this loudmouthed guy was. They wanted to make sure that I came back to the games because I had become part of the attraction for the first couple of years. I gave the front office a few ideas for promotions and they seemed to like them. I put the song "The Earl of Baltimore" on cassette and gave it to them to play over the PA system. It became a big hit. There were about nine athletes from the metropolitan area who participated in the Summer Olympics, and I thought it would be nice to honor them before a game. They did that too.

When the Baysox became a reality, they offered me a job. At that point in time, the luster had not worn off of the idea of a job in baseball. I accepted in a millisecond. I think I was offered the job because of, one, my ability to get along with just about anybody, and two, I think they realized that I knew the game. Another reason was my work ethic, which the GM, Keith Lupton, told a writer from my hometown newspaper was one of the things that made me a good candidate. Keith knew that I was at the ballpark late every night and that I got up and drove 30 miles to be at work at seven in the morning.

When I started in February, we had our offices down in Laurel because it wasn't certain where we were going to play the 1993 season since the new stadium was not ready. Then, after it became evident that we were going to play in Memorial Stadium [in Baltimore], we moved the offices up here and started to go out and sell the advertising in Baltimore. I had some sales experience when I was in newspaper and radio, and this wasn't much different. In minor league baseball, everybody has to sell. The team is not going to survive if it depends on the money you get from attendance. We had some signs in the outfield, program ads, radio ads, and some promotional nights. In many cases, we ran into the problem where people had already committed their entire budget to the Orioles; we came into Baltimore as the weak step-sister, and we were perceived that way by a lot of people. We had to fight and scramble to establish ourselves.

When the second week of March rolled around, I switched from selling to putting together the ballpark staff. I can describe that process in one word—nightmare. We knew enough not to advertise in the newspaper that we were going to be hiring ushers, ticket takers, and ticket sellers. Had we done that, I had visions of four thousand people standing outside wanting to work in minor league baseball—especially in Memorial Stadium. Still, we had an awful lot of people calling to inquire about the jobs, so I interviewed everybody that made any contact with us.

The best attributes you can have to be an usher, a ticket taker, or a ticket seller is to have a smile and to know how to get along with people. The first person you make contact with as you enter the stadium is the ticket taker. We wanted to have people who could be cheerful even on hot days when they're on their feet for a couple of hours and may not really want to be here.

In minor league baseball, there is a rule prohibiting fans from bringing food or drink into the ballpark, but there is always that one person who thinks the rule shouldn't apply to him. Ticket takers have to be able to handle that diplomatically. With ushers, you look for someone who you think is alert and has good interpersonal skills. If they're seating somebody and another person walks down to a better seat when their backs are turned, they have to politely but forcefully tell that person to move.

It's very hard to hire good people for what you pay them in minor league baseball. My ushers and ticket takers get twenty dollars a night. The ticket takers work from the time the gates open, an hour before the game, until the middle of the fourth inning. My ushers work from an hour before the game until the end of the game. If we have an extra-inning game, that means my ushers are putting in over five hours for a flat rate of twenty dollars. You can make more flipping hamburgers. Most of the people I have here—especially the ushers—do it because they would be here anyway. This way, they don't have to pay for tickets.

I thought that the things that happened in my life at Memorial Stadium would always be as a fan. The first day that we came here to look over these offices and walked out onto the concourse, it finally hit me that, "Damn it, I'm going to be working at Memorial Stadium every day." I got a few goose bumps and said to the other people, "You know, there are a few chunks of my heart down there on that field." By the same token, because of what I've had to do here, Memorial Stadium has lost a little bit of its charm.

You get downstairs and this glorious old stadium that you picture in your mind takes on a whole different character. When you walk into the bowels of this place and see every closet and every nook and cranny, you realize that this place is forty years old and is starting to show it. Sometimes you wonder what the builder was thinking when you find a triangular shaped closet with 6 square feet of floor space.

I have the keys to everything that the Baysox have access to. One of the good things that has come out of this experience at Memorial Stadium is that I've lost 40 pounds. I would love to get one of those pedometers to see how many miles I walk in the course of a day. It's very unusual for a Double A team to play their games in a stadium that holds fifty thousand.

THE DAILY ROUTINE

Since I live in Frederick and work in Baltimore, a typical day for me begins around 4:30 in the morning, when I go through my daily hygiene routine. Then I try to relax with a cup of coffee, get in the car, and drive to Baltimore, which takes me an hour to an hour and a half, depending on the traffic. I get to the stadium, make a pot of coffee, and try to sit down and relax for a while before anyone else gets here. If it's a game day, we have a normal ten o'clock meeting, which gets the day in order. We discuss promotions, the first-ball ceremony, the national anthem, who is working where, and what the interns are scheduled to do. We also review what went good and bad the day before. The meeting is over by about 10:30. I then check out the stadium to make sure that it looks clean or at least that the crew is making progress toward getting it clean. I check in with the concessionaire to make sure that he is not having any problems. I check with the city superintendent to see if he has any complaints or questions, because the stadium is part of the Department of Parks and Recreation. Finally, I check with our clubhouse manager, to make sure everything is still going smoothly down there, and to see if he has everything he needs.

After lunch I make one more round through the stadium to make sure that the cleaning crew didn't miss anything. I drop off anything that's going to be given out at the gates that night, get the turnstile counts so we know where we start, and make sure that my staff show up and arrive at their stations at the assigned time.

When 6:30 rolls around, I open the gates and hope that nothing goes wrong. As the game goes on, I continue to make my rounds. I might get a chance to watch an inning or two, but seldom more than that. During the game, I'm hoping that I don't hear my name over the walkie-talkie a lot, but that's inevitable: "Jack, I have somebody at gate W2 who wants to know why they can't bring in their peanuts." "Jack, I have somebody who says they are on a special diet." "Jack, can you help me? I've got a complaint in section 20." Another thing you hate to hear, and you know that if there are dark clouds in the sky, you could hear it at any moment, "Jack, this is Jimmy [grounds-keeper]. Get ready to put the tarp on."

We get complaints about almost anything. For example, somebody's cigarette or cigar smoke is irritating the person near him. And we get complaints about the personnel sometimes: "Boy that usher was rude to me," or "Who does that security person think he is talking to me like that?" We get complaints about the quality of the food: "My hot dog roll was soggy," "I got too much ice in my soda pop," or "The fountain water is warm." If you cook the best steak in town but have to make two thousand of them, there is always going to be one person who thinks his is too rare or too well done. You listen to all the complaints and try to handle them as tactfully as you can.

I wait till the game is over, hope our team won, and give the fans an ample amount of time to get out of the stadium. Then I go back out and make sure that the stadium is clear of fans, lock up, go back to the police command center, report that the stadium is secure, except for the last gate which I will lock after they leave. I go down to the gate with them, say good night, lock the gate, and come up to get a cup of coffee for my ride home to Frederick.

I get back to Frederick between 11:30 and 1:00. I have a few beers to relax before going to bed. The next morning it starts all over again. The long home stands are killers—and that's not just for me, that's for anybody involved with this organization. I can guarantee you that I will not go through another year of commuting. Not only do I spend over two and a half hours a day in the car, but it's nerve-racking and gas is not cheap.

It's funny, I have less access to the players now as a member of the staff than I had as a fan. In Frederick, the first year, there wasn't a kid on that team who wasn't at my house for either a crab feed or a barbecue or something. I got to know them all. There are many females who want to work in the front office because they think it's a good way to get to know the players. They don't realize that the girl standing outside the gate asking players for autographs is probably getting to know the players better than she is.

⚭

EPILOGUE

The next year, Jack became the director of food services for the Baysox. Jack and his wife did not move to the Bowie area as he had hoped, and eventually the commute became too much. Close to home, he took a job with the Frederick Keys [Carolina League] overseeing their food services. But he eventually quit over a dispute about concession prices, which he thought were already too high. "If there is one thing that can kill minor league baseball, it's greed. No team is going to be a positive part of the community by gouging its fans." Jack is now a sales representative for an automotive parts store.

Billy Johnson

ASSISTANT GENERAL MANAGER, KINSTON INDIANS

*Billy Johnson began his career in baseball as the mascot of the Louis-
ville Redbirds, while he was studying journalism and communications
at the University of Kentucky. He has had several front office jobs in
baseball since then.*

※

My playing career began and ended in the sixth grade. Johnny Bench
was my hero, and I had always wanted to be a catcher. I was warming
up a pitcher without a mask on and I didn't get my glove up. The ball
hit me right in the forehead and knocked me straight back. I've been
scared of a baseball ever since. As much as I would have loved to be
able to play, that was the end of it.

Louisville is about a hundred miles from Cincinnati. I remember listening to Joe Mecksaw and Marty Brenneman call the Reds games on
the radio. My family used to get together at my grandmother's or
aunt's house to listen to the Reds games. We were big Reds fans; we'd
go to two or three games a year, which was a big deal. Then in 1982, my
junior year in high school, the Redbirds [Triple A, American Associa-
tion] came to town. The first year I probably went to forty-five or fifty

games. The Redbirds games were *the* place to be in Louisville at that time. And I was a big fan.

A. Ray Smith, the man responsible for bringing the Redbirds in, was a hero to Louisville. That first year the team drew 848,000 people, which was just unheard of and shattered an all-time minor league record for attendance. They had an average of 20,000 people a game. A. Ray Smith was bigger than the mayor; he was bigger than the governor. He signed more autographs after the games than our players did. He really knew how to make something big.

Going to the Redbirds games, I saw The Chicken, and I thought I could probably put on a show like that. So that's what I did. After I graduated high school in 1983, I went to A. Ray Smith and told him that I could be a good mascot if he gave me the chance. He paid me $15 a game to dress up as a bird. We called him Billy Bird. I guess my act got to be pretty popular because it ended up paying for my college tuition.

My intention then was not to get into baseball. I did it for fun. I was in college and I just wanted to be involved and to be goofy. During my first few months as Billy Bird, I didn't really know what to do out there. My thinking was that if no one could see your face, then you could pretty much do anything you wanted. And that's what happened. I got kind of brave, and the braver I got the more popular the character became.

⚉

By his fourth year, Billy was doing choreographed skits on the field and had become a Louisville favorite. Perhaps the height of Billy Bird came during a prolonged drought. Billy announced that he would camp out in the ballpark until it rained. He was there for fourteen days and nights, and his stunt received national media attention.

⚉

Where most people in college join fraternities or go to parties and have friends from that, I was making all my friends at the ballpark. I think being around baseball everyday is what made me want to get into the front office. When an internship became available, I took it. I was working under the public relations director when he quit. One day I had to run an errand to a newspaper to deliver an ad. When I came back, I was the new public relations director—on a trial basis at least.

I guess if it's possible to fall into a job, I did. Two years later I was still in the job, but the added responsibilities meant I could no longer perform as Billy Bird. The toughest thing I ever had to do was to hire my own replacement.

I had worked my way into a front-office situation where I was learning something, and I took what I could from it. You reach a point in an operation that big where you are keyed in on just one aspect of the business. In Louisville we had twelve separate departments. I couldn't see what happened with promotions or concessions or souvenirs. There was no way I was going to learn what it took to run a ball club staying in Louisville. A lot of things pointed to where I should leave and learn some things.

⚾

During the following season, Billy became the marketing manager for Sports Promotions in West Palm Beach, Florida. His job was to interest large corporations in putting advertising dollars into spring training and Florida State League baseball.

⚾

I was going to a lot of games, but didn't feel right sitting in the stands being just a fan. I had spent six years with the Redbirds, and now here I was mostly sitting around watching baseball. Being in baseball is something you don't realize you miss until it's gone. When I worked in baseball, I got in a habit of taking notes on things that needed to be changed and improved. And here I was in West Palm Beach sitting and looking, thinking to myself, "This needs to be different and that needs to be different." But it wasn't my place to say anything and that was frustrating. I needed to be back in it.

⚾

The following season, Billy returned to baseball as the assistant general manager of the Kinston Indians in the Carolina League.

⚾

Some people say why go from Triple A down to Class A. Well, you don't become the managing editor of the *Philadelphia Inquirer* without having first worked someplace where you had to run the presses yourself. Baseball is very similar to that. Compared to what I did in

Louisville, there are so many new aspects to what I do here. The years that you spend down here allow you to be creative—to plan solutions to problems, to fix things, and to exercise your brain in a way that you have never before. Here I have a variety of responsibilities.

During the season, when the team is in town, I come to the ballpark at about 9:30 or so. Usually, I'll go to the concession stand and make sure we have hot dogs and buns and all the other stuff we have to sell, and I do a quick check of inventory to see if there is anything I need to order. Then I spend an hour or two on advertising. We do all of ours right here using desktop publishing software. I do all our print ads in one sitting. It might take an hour or two, unless it's a big event—then it could take three or four hours. That brings me into the early afternoon. If I don't have ads coming up, I'll work on our newsletter or do something with the media, like get the team in a paper where we're not getting coverage. By 4:00 P.M., I start getting ready for the game. I run through the concession stand one last time. Once in a while I go down to the clubhouse and spend fifteen or twenty minutes with the manager talking and joking around a little bit. We have to make sure that they have fruit, that there are sodas in the machine, and that they're generally taken care of. During the game I help run the concession stand, take care of any large group that is having a picnic, organize our on-field promotions, and answer any questions or complaints our fans might have. After the game, I help close up the concession stand and lock up the ballpark. I usually don't get out of here until very late at night. That makes for a long and tiring day.

I deal with the long hours by knowing when enough is enough. I take a long lunch once in a while and enjoy myself. I have to know how to relax and I must have a sense of humor. I can't complain and moan about the long hours, not if I'm going to stay in baseball. I look back to the time I wasn't in baseball and I look at all the people who want to be in it, and that's how I deal with the long hours. There are lots of folks out there who'd like to have my job.

When the season ends, we relax for a few weeks, reorganize the files, get the office straightened back up and take it easy for a while. Then we'll kick right back into it in mid-October. It takes all five months of the off-season to sell the advertising space in the program, on the fence signs, and on the radio. You never really stop selling. You're always trying to get that last ad or that last gimmick in. The printer is always mad at you. You could have the space in your program sold out two weeks before you have to get it to the printer, and you're still going to add pages.

I love selling. I wouldn't sell encyclopedias or cars. But baseball I can sell because I believe in baseball. I believe that it brings people together. That's corny, but it's true. Thousands of people come to the park and everybody is enjoying the same thing. For those few hours, there is nothing else in the world going on. Those people aren't mad at each other anymore—the blacks with whites, Native Americans with Latinos. Everybody is together. The issues that divide people aren't raised in a ballpark. I believe in that. Just look at the diversity of the team: you have African Americans, whites, Venezuelans, and Dominicans; and they play as a team. It's an example to everyone. As the James Earl Jones character said in *Field of Dreams,* "Baseball is a symbol of everything that once was good and could once be good again."

Kinston is a town of just 25,000, one of the smallest minor league towns in the country. But 30 miles in each direction there is another town of a similar size—in between there's just corn and tobacco—and there are three military bases, Seymour Johnson Air Force Base, Camp LeJeune, and Cherry Point, all within 40 miles of Kinston. We've targeted those people with free military admissions on Wednesdays and "Thirsty Thursdays," when beer is only seventy-five cents. That blows attendance through the roof. We've made this the Eastern Carolina Indians instead of the Kinston Indians. You got to think regional, not just local, and the beauty is that it's all true. I can get an advertiser excited about half a state instead of one town.

We try to portray ourselves as a big league club. With our printed materials, everything is multi-colored. Our advertising and sales brochures have four colors and they look like they came out of an ad agency. The program is not a program anymore. It's a magazine. We probably have the best newsletter in baseball because we take an extra week to put it out and make sure that it's top notch. It's on marble paper and printed in two colors. We work a lot on our image. We want people to perceive us as their big league team. That's something you learn to do as you go.

If being a mascot taught me anything about baseball, it was that the first priority is entertainment. When I become a general manager, it's going to be a very entertaining atmosphere at the ballpark. There's going to be a lot of goofy stuff going on. The dumbest ideas are often the ones that entertain the most. It seems to be opposite of the way it is, but that's what I've learned. For example, our right fielder looks exactly like Jerry Seinfeld. I wrote a letter to Seinfeld and offered him a player's contract for one dollar to play right field for one pitched ball, the promise being that we have a right fielder that looks just like him and no one would know the difference at first glance. I followed it up with a press release and before you knew it, this town was going crazy. The story was in *USA Today* and *USA Today International.* We were on live radio all week—in Los Angeles, Boston, Minneapolis/St. Paul—I mean the thing was out of control. I thought maybe we'd get a nice thank-you note from Jerry Seinfeld and three inches in *Baseball America,* but we never expected it to go that far. It was even scheduled to be on "Entertainment Tonight." If we had planned this, I doubt it would have worked. It was just a whim.

We've put a lot of emphasis on the quality of the entertainment—whether it's the kind of contest we run on the field or the kind of ads we run in the paper. When the Durham Bulls were in town, we ran ads in the paper that had a picture of a cow and the headline read, "That's No Bull." It's silly, but it worked. People liked it. During the games we have a "Dirtiest Car in the Parking Lot" contest. We announce a license-plate number, and that person wins a free "SuperWash" at the local car wash. Our general manager, North Johnson, and a woman named Beth Smith came up with that about three years ago. To this day, it still gets laughs and now it's all around minor league baseball.

On our big give-away nights, where we'll draw 5,000, the appeal is fun. And we're trying to appeal to a younger crowd now. If you listen to our public address, you're going to hear rock 'n' roll and you'll hear it loud. That makes the older folks a little bit angry, but we have to diversify ourselves. We have to make sure that we're bringing in a new generation of baseball fans, because college kids aren't going to come unless we do something to get them here. We've got East Carolina University 30 miles away, and then we've got the military all around. It would be foolish for us not to have rock 'n' roll baseball out here. We couldn't draw 60,000 people in a season by just trying to appeal to baseball diehards. We can draw 130,000 if we make it fun for the people who are under thirty. So that's what we're doing.

Baseball is also for families. A four- or five-year-old kid is not going to get into the hit and run. A four- or five-year-old kid is only going to have a great time at the ballpark if something goofy happens. Whether it's fireworks, a guy falling off a bicycle, or the Phillie Phanatic soaking the visiting team with a water gun, that's what entertains children. A great example of that is our Andy's Cheese Steak promotion. A fan has forty-five seconds to put on a jersey, stirrup pants, and a hat. To make it fun, if it's a big kid, we give him pants that are too small; and if it's a small kid, we give him pants that keep falling down every time he tries to put something else on.

I bet if every minor league operator wrote down an idea they had right before they went to sleep, there would be a lot more Mike Veecks [known for his outrageous promotions, such as Disco Demolition Night at Comiskey Park]. It just takes that leap of faith to do it. And if it flops, it flops. If it flops miserably, you're embarrassed for a couple of days, but it passes and you try again. If it succeeds, the feeling you get is incredible. Anybody who has been doing their stuff in the minor leagues for a while will blow away the guys in the big leagues, because up there they really don't have to market baseball the way we do. Down here I've have had to do the bizarre to get attention—like dress a player up in a girl's bikini top. I would love to get my hands on a big league marketing position that would give me a free reign to do these absolutely wacky and bizarre things that are fun and entertaining. Unless it's tasteless, nothing is beneath the dignity of baseball.

⚘

EPILOGUE

Billy Johnson left Kinston to become the assistant general manager of the Chattanooga Lookouts, a Double A team. He later moved to Lansing, Michigan, to help in the development of a new franchise in the Midwest League. However, he was let go without explanation after three months. Today he works as a graphic designer for Sportsprint *in Atlanta, Georgia, and is considering a return to baseball.*

Dean Taylor

ASSISTANT GENERAL MANAGER, ATLANTA BRAVES

The general manager's office oversees the acquisition, development, and evaluation of both minor and major league players. In this narrative, Dean Taylor describes the work of an assistant general manager and what it takes to build a ball club that can win a World Series. The job requires the skills of a scout, attorney, and, at times, psychologist.

When I was a freshman at Claremont Men's College, I was a premed major. I had just finished my first semester and at the time I was not all together convinced that that was what I wanted to do. One day I read a column in the *Los Angeles Times* about the sports administration program that Walter O'Malley had helped start at Ohio University. As soon as I finished reading the column, I said to myself, "That's what I want to do."

That very afternoon, I went across the street to the registrar's office and changed my major to economics. That was the closest thing to a business major that I could pursue at Claremont. I didn't tell my parents immediately. I called them after the fact and told them my decision. That's how certain I was about going to Ohio University. Reading that column changed my whole perspective on a career choice.

My first memories of baseball are from when I was growing up as a child listening to the Dodgers games. I became a student of baseball because of Vin Scully. We could pick up the Dodgers games on KFI in Roseburg, Oregon, where I grew up. Of course I also played—in Little League, high school, and even in college. What really got me interested in the professional part of the game was, like most kids, the hope of someday playing in the major leagues. Unfortunately, my ability, wasn't quite up to it.

As planned, I went to Ohio University, along with one of my friends. Our desire was to get into baseball at the minor league level. The program at Ohio combines course work with an internship. We had an opportunity to intern with some major league clubs, but primarily as ticket sellers. That didn't interest us much. We wanted to try to learn everything we could about a professional operation, rather than channel ourselves into one small area.

Eventually, we decided to actually start our own minor league club for the internship. In those days you could start a minor league club for an initial investment of about $12,000. We found a financial backer during Christmas vacation of 1973. Then I made a blind phone call to Bob Richmond, president of the Class A Northwest League. I told him that we wanted to start a minor league franchise and that we had a potential owner but didn't have a town to operate in. As it turned out, the Northwest League was holding a league meeting in Walla Walla, Washington, about three weeks later. The league was planning on expanding from six to eight clubs. Four other prospective ownership groups were scheduled to make presentations, but Mr. Richmond told us that we were also welcome to make one.

He put us in touch with the western field representative for the National Association of Professional Baseball Leagues who was familiar with all the available cities in the northwest that had adequate ballparks. He recommended New Westminster, British Columbia. So we went there to speak to the city fathers and to look at their stadium. We wondered how well Canadians were going to accept Class A baseball. At that time, there were no minor league clubs in that area of Canada. Although we had some questions about the financial viability of a franchise in New Westminster, it had a ready-made ballpark.

We went to the league meeting and made our presentation. We were fortunate to be one of the two groups that were awarded expansion franchises. Here we were, at the end of January, two twenty-one-year-

Dean Taylor at the start of the 1996 World Series. (Photo by J. Stoll)

old kids in graduate school with a minor league baseball franchise on our hands. I went back to school for a couple of weeks with the good intention of finishing the term, but simply found there was too much to do in preparation for the upcoming season. So I went back to New Westminster and started the operation of the club.

We didn't begin play until mid-June. With no major league affiliation yet, we had tryout camps in Washington, Oregon, and California, and had to sign all of our own players. We knew it was going to be a tough road because we were looking primarily at players who had been released from other organizations and at guys who had never been drafted. The truth of the matter was that there was a good reason that they weren't drafted.

As things turned out—and I don't want to use the word "disastrous"—but we had a very difficult year. We went 34 and 50 and drew about 11,000 fans for the entire season. With thirty-five dates, that averaged out to about 300 fans a game. We lost a lot of money, but we learned a lot.

⚉

The next year, Taylor moved the team to Boise, Idaho, where the team was affiliated with the Oakland A's. The franchise prospered, but Taylor had to leave to fulfill a two-year ROTC obligation with the U.S. Army. He taught in the field artillery school at Fort Sill, Oklahoma. Anxious to get back into baseball when he left the army, he was hired as general manager for the Cincinnati Reds' Northwest League franchise in Eugene, Oregon.

⚉

I had always had major league aspirations. I thought the best thing was to start at the bottom rung and work up the ladder from there. I wanted to learn about tickets, management, public relations, marketing, player contracts, concessions, sales, and so on. My feeling was that a broad-based background would help me land a job with a major league organization.

While in Eugene my thrust became player development. The Reds' philosophy was to get their minor league general managers involved in the process. We received critique sheets every year asking us which players on our club we thought were prospects and which were not. The other major league teams did their own assignment papers, payrolls, contracts, and most other player-related administrative tasks. The Reds asked their minor league GMs to handle these duties.

My career break came on Election Day 1980. The phone rang and on the other end of the line was John Schuerholz from the Kansas City Royals. He had just received a promotion and was looking to hire someone as an assistant in the scouting and player-development department. Someone from the Cincinnati Reds had given him my name. I flew to Kansas City for an interview and was fortunate enough to get the job. My title was administrative assistant. I handled much of the paperwork related to scouting and player development. I got involved in negotiating the contracts of some of the Rookie League and Class A players. I also handled the medical insurance and injury reports for our minor league players. We had lots of injuries, and along with them went insurance forms, medical claims, hospital bills, doctor's bills, and things of that nature. I also served as the contact for the minor league general managers. If they had a question about some policy or procedure, I handled their calls. If we were moving a player, I handled the travel arrangements and notified the general managers.

After I had been there for one year, John was named the general manager and I was promoted to assistant director of scouting and player development. Now I became much more involved in scouting. I talked to our scouts on a daily basis about players they were seeing and made assignments for them to see other prospects. More importantly, I became involved in the amateur draft. After the Royals' World Series win in 1985, I became assistant general manager.

⚉

In 1990 Dean moved to the commissioner's office in New York City, where he was manager of baseball operations under Fay Vincent. He was there less than a year when John Schuerholz became the general manager of the Atlanta Braves and recruited Dean to be his assistant.

⚉

At the commissioner's office I missed the competitive environment that you see every day at the club level. The winning and losing, the process of trying to create a winning organization, signing good players and developing them, and basically trying to beat the pants off everyone else in the industry.

When John called me about the Atlanta job, I didn't say a word at first because I had just been to their ballpark. It had been a hot July evening with only 6,000 people there to watch the Braves and the Astros. The field was in absolutely terrible shape and I couldn't believe I was watching a major league game.

I knew Atlanta was going to be a great challenge. That was another reason I decided to accept his offer. The organization had only one way to go, and that was up. I knew that we were very rich in talent at the minor league level and that some of the young pitchers who had been in the major leagues for a short period of time were hopefully about to get over the hump. Our timetable was to make this a championship organization in three years. We were fortunate to do that somewhat sooner.

My responsibilities here vary depending on the time of year. In the off-season, from December until we go to spring training, I am totally involved in the contract negotiations for our players who are not free agents. It's a tremendously long and difficult process. I did over twenty contracts last year. It is not unusual for me to spend virtually all day on the telephone. I do statistical and salary comparisons of comparable players using the Player Management System, which is a database I helped design when I was at the commissioner's office.

Learning technical contract language the first time around can be difficult, but after you've done a few you get the hang of it. In many cases, language is transferred from one contract to another. If we really get stuck, we get help from the Player Relations Committee in New York.

Every major league player has an agent. Occasionally a player will come in and talk to you about his contract face-to-face, but for the most part the negotiating is done with the agents. Almost half of the players in the minors also have agents, and as they move up the line, they all get them. I've learned to accept dealing with agents. This is a business. Sometimes it's difficult to accept what a utility infielder makes today, but that's what the market bears. Salaries are obviously important, but sometimes egos also become involved. I guess that's human nature.

In some cases, I am glad the players have agents because it keeps them out of the dirty work. A lot of times the players may not even be aware of the nuts and bolts of the negotiation process. When the contract is completed, the agent says, "Okay, here is your contract. Sign it." Unless you go through an arbitration hearing where the player actually hears the case that is being presented against him, you don't get involved in the contractual process with the player.

It's good to keep it at an arm's length because it allows us to develop a personal relationship with the players. I like to think we have a good relationship with most players on our club. I could ask for a favor from anybody in our clubhouse and have a good feeling that they'll do it. It's important for somebody in my position to cultivate those relationships, even though we're management and they may see us as being on the other side of the table.

The fans probably don't realize how frustrating it can be dealing with the business aspects of the game and the cold reality of the agents and the players. They don't appreciate some of the things that we go through in order to put a ball club on a field. You just can't throw out the bats and balls and let the players play. Day in and day out, we make tremendously difficult decisions. It's not easy to trade, demote, or release a player, because it can change his life and his livelihood.

After contract negotiations, we're into spring training. We go through an important evaluation process with the players at that time. We watch the workouts and the games every day and decide who we're going to keep on the club. There are also a lot administrative details to attend to in regard to running the camp, some of which are my responsibility. Early in spring training is also when we negotiate our minor league contracts.

Once the season starts in April, most of my time is spent in the office attending to administrative matters and reading scouting reports for the amateur draft in June. We start the meeting process for the draft in mid-May. Sitting through the preparation for the draft is similar to being sequestered on a jury. In essence, we lock ourselves into a hotel suite for about three weeks and discuss all the players we are considering for the draft. There are absolutely no distractions.

The organization must be totally committed to the draft process, because it is the single most important function that the Braves or any organization goes through in a year. No matter how great your ticket sales, public relations, marketing, or stadium operations staff, unless you have quality players to put on the field, and unless you have that continuous pipeline of talent coming through the organization, you're never going to succeed.

We go through the entire scouting process carefully. Our scouts prepare written reports throughout the fall and spring on all potential prospects. We might receive three or four reports on a typical prospect and sometimes as many as eight or ten on a potential first-round pick. We may have as many as 2,000 reports coming into our office and we read every one of them.

At the draft meeting, we invite all the area scouts in. Each has an hour to discuss the players he has seen in his geographic territory [see Hep Cronin]. The players who are highly touted by the area scouts have also been seen by our regional and national cross-checkers. They listen to the analysis that the area scouts give and add their input. When you read a report on a player, you are able to form a picture of him in your mind. When the scout comes to the meeting and starts talking about him, you may get a completely different picture. Then, when you see the player in the flesh for the first time, you may get a third totally different picture.

After three days of listening to the area scouts, we—our director of scouting and player development, our assistant director of scouting, our five regional and national scouting supervisors, two special as-

signment scouts, John Schuerholz, and myself—sit down and put together the draft list for the Braves. We rank the players in the country
from top to bottom. Obviously, the most crucial part of this process is
getting the players ranked in the proper order. We talk about it for
hours on end.

I remember my first draft in 1981. We had a lot of debate around
the table about two players who were high on our draft list. We had
the first eleven guys ranked in order and then we debated for hours
about the two players being considered for the twelfth spot. One was
a high school outfielder named Charles Pennigar, the other was Mark
Gubicza. Finally, the GM went around the table and said, "Enough,
you've all heard the pluses and minuses, tell me who's the next player
on the list. Gubicza or Penningar?" Most people chose Gubicza. We
picked him in the second round and Gubicza ended up being a solid
major league pitcher until he hurt his arm. I don't think Pennigar ever
made it out of Double A.

We try to take as much chance out of the draft as possible. We feel
that we can outscout, outevaluate, and outproject any other organization in the industry. We feel we have hired the best scouts, and we
know that their productivity is the lifeblood of this organization.
Without them you don't win championships.

By the time that the draft ends in June, I start making some some
road trips with the club. If we have any slack time in the office, it's
probably in July and August. We might make a trade, sending a few
players up and down, but these types of things are not terribly time-
consuming. It's a good time to do special projects.

One project that I'm working on now is our schedule. I'm our representative in the National League scheduling process. The majority of
the schedule is developed by a computer consultant. I enjoy being involved because I was a scheduler for the Northwest League for twelve
years. There are a lot of things to consider in making a schedule. One
is to look at travel patterns. The mileage each club travels is a major
consideration. When we go to San Francisco, hopefully we'll play Los
Angeles and San Diego on the same trip. We don't want to go from
Los Angeles to Philadelphia and then back to St. Louis.

The league tries to be as equitable as possible in the distribution of
weekends and holiday dates. The schedule calls for each club to play
one weekend series in each of the other cities in the league. In a bal-
anced schedule, each opposing club comes to your city once on a

weekend and once during the week. Making all those pieces fit can be difficult. In instances where there are two clubs in one city, such as Chicago or New York, some consideration is given to minimizing the number of dates that both clubs play at home. Here in Atlanta, we also have television considerations because we're a division of Turner Broadcasting. In some cases, we take input from the television people in regard to starting times. In many ways the entire schedule is similar to a large puzzle. If you like to work on those sorts of things it can be very enjoyable.

Once the season is over, we start preparing for the following season. People ask me all the time what we do during the off-season. "Are you on vacation for three months?" Actually we go through a series of organizational and industry-level meetings. The general managers' meeting lasts a week, the winter meetings last a week, and so on.

Baseball can be very tough professionally, and in some cases it's difficult to develop a solid family life because of the time spent away from home. The time I have with my wife is precious to me because I don't have a lot of it. She comes to most of the home games and we sit together. I'm fortunate because she worked for the Royals and knows what to expect from someone involved in a baseball career. We do go to an occasional party in our neighborhood, invite our neighbors to come to games, and sometimes we might go out to dinner or a movie with them. But a lot of what we do socially involves other baseball people. With all the meetings throughout the year, whether it's the All-Star Game, postseason play, or spring training, you wind up spending your time with other people in the game.

Obviously, baseball has been very demanding of my personal life. If someone asked me right now, "Dean, what are your hobbies?" I'd probably scratch my head and say, "Working on schedules?"

The Nature of Baseball Work

As oral historians well know, it is difficult to generalize about a lifestyle from a small number of narratives, even when they represent a common experience. The diversity of baseball work in this volume makes the task even more tenuous. The twenty-one narratives represent not a single occupation but a range of jobs in a large industry—both the "business" and the "baseball" sides of the game. Nonetheless, some common threads are evident.

Here we attempt to arrive at some generalizations about baseball work. To this end, we draw upon the narratives as well as other data we gathered, including many in-depth interviews with baseball people who could not be profiled in the book. During our four seasons of conducting research in ballparks, we also spent countless hours talking informally with people and observing them at work. Much of this information was recorded in field notes. The following discussion is also informed by our own work experiences in baseball, as a player and anthropologist (Gmelch), and as an intern in the front office (Weiner).

In the narratives, we saw that most baseball people are not just employees of baseball organizations but also fans—especially of the team for which they work. Being a fan means that they identify strongly with their organization. It is commonplace in the front office, for example, for employees upon arriving at work in the morning to talk about their team's performance the night before. When the team is on the road, many employees watch the game on TV. A Yankee Stadium usher, for example, described going home after finishing his ushering duties in the third inning and watching the rest of the ball game on TV. The message on Sherry Davis's answering machine begins with, "Hello, fellow Giants fans . . ." Many employees wear polo shirts and blazers with their team's embroidered logo; some travel with carry-on bags emblazoned with the team insignia. Teams allot regular employees two free tickets per game, enabling them to bring their spouse, children, or friends to the ballpark. Not surprisingly, watching the games enhances their identification with the organization.

We found that many game-day staff—ushers, vendors, concession workers, and ticket takers—sought jobs at the ballpark because, above all else, they were fans and wanted to be at the games. Some also admitted that they enjoyed being able to say they worked at Fenway Park, Wrigley Field, or Camden Yards.

Unlike the corporate world, where profits are a measure of a company's success and are reported quarterly, in baseball a team's worth is measured by wins and loses. The mood in baseball organizations is influenced by that outcome. When the team is winning, the mood around the ballpark is upbeat. People are more talkative, there is more joking, and some respondents say they have more enthusiasm for their work; the day doesn't "drag" when the team is doing well. Some jobs are also made easier when the team is winning. "No matter what type of promotion you're trying to sell," said an employee in the Yankees marketing department, "you have a lot more success when the team is winning. People want to come out here when the Yankees are doing well. Besides, when we win, everything else ticks right along and management is happy, so they're not on your back." Sportswriters say their jobs are also easier when the home team wins because the players and the manager are more talkative and give better interviews.

Conversely, when the team loses, the offices are quieter—particularly in the morning. During a losing streak, many say that the workplace mood is "gloomy" or "somber." "You don't want to make a joke," said a Pirates front-office worker, "because you're afraid someone might overhear you and take it the wrong way—like you don't care." As Sally O'Leary noted about her media relations job with the

Pirates, "Losing makes it a lot tougher. You're always trying to get out positive things about the club, but when they're losing everything from media comes out negative."

Compared to most of the corporate world, office dress in baseball is more casual. The suit and tie of the downtown office building is less appropriate to such baseball departments as media relations, where employees are outside in the press box and moving from field to clubhouse to office much of the time in warm, humid summer weather. Also, the long hours of baseball work, requiring that they be at the ballpark for evening games and work weekends, also contributes to less formal attire.

SPECIALISTS VERSUS JACKS-OF-ALL-TRADES

When we compare work in the minors with the big leagues we find that the higher one ascends the professional baseball ladder, the larger the staff and the more complex the division of labor. Conversely, the range of tasks a single person performs increases as you go down the ladder. In Class A, for example, one individual, sometimes with the assistance of an intern, is responsible for all aspects of public relations, whereas in the big leagues an entire staff, divided into departments—public relations, media relations, community relations, and special projects—does the job. In the Class A New York–Penn League, we saw that Jim Riggs was not just a beat writer covering the Jamestown Expos games. He also served as the official scorer and sometimes took photographs of the game for the local newspaper as well. In the major leagues most beat writers only cover baseball. Likewise, minor league broadcaster Rob Evans prepared team and player statistics and then single-handedly did both the play-by-play and color commentary. In the big leagues broadcasters only do one—either color or play-by-play commentary—and the statistics and other data used during broadcasts are prepared by a staff of several employees and interns.

GENDER AND WORKPLACE AMBIANCE IN BASEBALL ORGANIZATIONS

Clearly, baseball, like other professional sports, is dominated by men to a degree not found in most business spheres. We wondered if baseball's male dominance had much influence on its work environment. Since the narratives themselves do not directly reveal much about gender in the office, we decided to go back to the network of baseball contacts we had developed over the previous four years and, mostly in telephone interviews, ask specifically about this issue. We spoke with baseball employees in ten major and minor league clubs, many of whom had once worked outside baseball and therefore could make some occupational comparisons. Nearly all agreed that working in baseball was indeed different from their previous work settings, but no one attributed the differences only to the preponderance of men. Some did believe that the office environment, especially those departments that work most closely with the players, was influenced by the masculine—some said "macho"—culture of the team.

In hindsight, we realized that the front-office environments that we came to know during the research did have a jockish ambiance. Teasing, joking, and repartee among employees, for example, was far more frequent than anything we have ever witnessed in the halls and offices of university campuses or in the varied business settings in which our relatives and friends work. Baseball offices are typically festooned with sports memorabilia—team pictures, baseballs, and trophies—that give them a masculine feel.

GETTING IN

Many of the narratives suggest that getting a job in baseball requires knowing someone in the game. According to one Yankee employee, "Contacts are everything. Baseball is a fraternity and you have to be invited in." With so many people wanting to work in baseball, there are many applicants for each opening. The absence of any specific work qualifications for many jobs makes it possible to hire friends or friends of friends. Unless you want to become an umpire, trainer, or a member of the new generation of groundskeepers, there is no formal education that prepares you specifically for work in baseball. Only trainer Mark Letendre and groundskeeper Paul Zwaska learned their discipline in a university classroom; Durwood Merrill attended a six-week umpire school.

Most people learn baseball work on the job through long apprenticeships in the minor leagues. Ten of the interviewees employed in the major leagues had worked their way up through the minors. It took Jim Leyland eighteen years to reach the big leagues as a third-base coach for the White Sox, while Mark Letendre and Bernie Williams made it in only four years. The average number of years in the minors for the interviewees was seven; those who remain in the minor leagues still hoping to reach the majors (such as Rob Evans and Scott Jaster) have already served an average of eight years in the minors.

Some interviewees talked about having a mentor who was essential to their success. For Jim Leyland, it was manager Tony La Russa; for Paul Zwaska it was the Orioles' head groundskeeper Pat Santarone; for Dean Taylor, it was the Braves general manager John Schuerholz; and for Mark Letendre, it was the head trainer Gene Monahan. These mentors were not only good teachers. Some were willing to use their positions and networks to get their protégés promotions or jobs with other baseball organizations.

THE DAILY ROUTINE

The narratives say much about the daily routines of baseball work. The day for many baseball workers is divided into the pregame, the game, and the postgame phases. For most, the pregame phase takes up the largest amount of time. Scott Jaster and Bernie Williams described the typical preparations players go through—stretching, throwing, batting practice, infield or outfield drill, and, beyond the view of fans, visualizing and reviewing video of past at bats against the upcoming game's opposing pitcher. Jim Leyland and QV Lowe, representing the workday of managers and coaches, describe getting to the ballpark early to begin their preparations. Leyland, for example, arrives before his players to read his mail, set the lineup, and give media interviews before pregame practice begins. As pitching coach for the Chicago Cubs, QV Lowe said he didn't see much of the cities in which the team played because he routinely, after getting up late, went to the ballpark around 1:30 to get things organized before his pitchers showed up. Likewise, trainer Mark Letendre and his staff spend hours getting players ready for the game. They tape ankles and go through other measures to deter injuries to limbs and joints before the players begin their warm-ups. They also direct the rehabilitation treatment of injuries. Evans described the hours he spends before broadcasts preparing and reviewing statistics, looking for trends or "tendencies." Paul Zwaska and his groundskeepers begin their preparations—mowing the grass, chalking the foul lines, cleaning the dugouts and bullpen— eight to ten hours before game time.

From the time the baseball season gets underway in early April until it ends in October, the routines of the players and those around them hardly vary. And it makes little difference whether the team is playing at home or away (although when they are on the road they can report an hour later for batting practice). Either way, they are still at the ballpark every day, and except for the occasional day game, they are there until eleven o'clock at night. Still "keyed up" after the game, player (Scott Jaster), coach (QV Lowe), writer (Riggs), and broadcaster (Rob Evans) all talked about the need to unwind before going home to bed. They usually go out—to eat and drink—and when they return to their hotel rooms or to their homes, they stay up watching TV (often late ball games from the West Coast or on ESPN sports).

The daily routine of workers in the front office and stands, in contrast, is determined by whether the team is at home or away. When the team is on the road, most office staff return to a normal nine-to-five day with weekends off, while game-day staff—ticket takers, ushers, vendors—do not work at all. When the team is at home, the typical workday is twelve to fourteen hours, ending when the ball game is over at night. Intern Sam Kennedy described how it was often so late when he finished his work that he would sleep at the stadium, sometimes on the manager's couch. Clubhouse manager Pat Young, whose responsibilities also kept him at the park into the wee hours, routinely slept in the clubhouse where he made a bed of two training tables pushed together.

Time and again we heard baseball people talk about the long hours they work. Clearly, the hours are a defining characteristic of the profession, in much the same way that road trips are a defining feature of life for players and team personnel. According to Birmingham Barons broadcaster Curt Bloom, eighty-hour workweeks are common during home stands:

I tell you there is no car salesman, no secretary, no doctor alive who puts in those hours. Our office people are in at ten in the morning and they'll be here until eleven at night when the game is over. That's baseball.

Jim Riggs described getting by on just four hours of sleep during the baseball season. And there are few days off. Major league teams average only two days off per month, and minor league teams average only one day off per month. Norfolk Tides media director Shon Sbarra, who barely sees his wife at all during home stands, said: "We always make a joke April 1st when the baseball season starts. It's like, 'Well, I'll see you in September.'"

In some baseball jobs there may be a lot of "down time"—time when employees are on the job but not working. Once employees—whether they be players, groundskeepers, sportswriters, or broadcasters—make preparations for the game, there is often little to be done until the game begins. Idle time is often spent talking, playing practical jokes, and telling stories that contribute not only to the oral tradition of baseball but also to the development of its distinctive subculture.

In spite of their long hours and the mandate that one work on weekends and holidays, most baseball jobs do not pay well. While the public hears much about the huge salaries of players, most other baseball employees earn less than they could make doing comparable work outside baseball. One public relations director, for example, determined that his $50,000 salary was probably $30,000 less than what his two decades of experience would command in a downtown setting. Clubhouse manager Pat Young said he earned less than half of what he had earned in his newspaper job, yet worked more than twice as many hours per week. Rob Evans quit his first baseball broadcasting job because the wages were so low. But, in general, most seemed to take low wages as a requirement of the profession, with the alternative being not working in baseball.

FAMILY LIFE

The unique demands of baseball work affects the lives of many employees outside the ballpark. Baseball games are played seven days a week; most of the year's major holidays—Easter, Memorial Day, the Fourth of July, and Labor Day—fall during the baseball season and are workdays for baseball people. Road trips plus working nights and weekends when the team is at home means that many baseball men are often away from home and their families.[1] "You don't get to do things normal people do in the summertime. When everyone else is home barbecuing in the backyard, you're at the ballpark," said one trainer. Many baseball men complained that they had missed a lot of their kids' growing up—the birthday parties, Little League games, high school graduation, and so on. "One of the ironies of baseball," said media director Tom Skibosh, "is that people think your kids have a big advantage when it comes to playing Little League. But the truth is you're hardly ever around to watch them play, much less coach them." Groundskeeper Paul Zwaska said that he only sees his children ten or fifteen minutes a day during home stands.

Partners and children who are at home also feel the loss. Lowe and Evans' wives wanted their husbands to quit baseball. Lowe's wife divorced him when he didn't. Following our interview, Waleska Williams wrote about her anguish as a baseball wife in Puerto Rico's leading newspaper, *El Nuevo Día:*

Believe me the separation [from husband] is painful no matter how full the bank account. How do you respond to your 5 year old boy when he asks why Dad doesn't go with him on field trips or baseball games while he sees other boys with their dads. How do you give comfort to a pregnant lady giving birth whose husband isn't there?

After her letter appeared in the paper, Waleska received phone calls from other baseball wives who thanked her for speaking out and telling the public what their glamorous lives were really like.

Presenting the perspective of a child whose parent works in baseball, Lyn Rigney, the daughter of a former player and manager Bill Rigney, talked about her upbringing:

We only had a normal family life a few months of the year. We didn't take family vacations together, for instance, because summer was baseball. The year Dad was fired [as manager] and we went up to our cabin in the Sierras was the only time that we were all somewhere together away from home on a holiday.

Typically, the spouses of the players, coaches, and others who travel with the team spend about half of the six-month baseball season alone. Fran Kalatatis, wife with nine minor leagues seasons behind her and twenty-three moves described the loneliness:

When the guys went on the road most of the time you stayed alone. So there you were in a strange town, in a strange apartment, and in the early years maybe without a phone because you couldn't afford one. Eventually you get used to being alone and not being afraid.

Some baseball spouses refer to themselves not as a "baseball wives" but as "baseball widows."

One result of being on their own so much is that many baseball wives become very independent. They learn to extend themselves and find companionship and activities in ways they might not have if their husbands were around. "You learn to make friends quickly, to seek out other wives, to find 'grandparents' for your kids so that on Grandparent's Day at school your kid has someone to bring in," recalls Sharon Hargrove in her memoir, *Safe at Home*.[2] When their husbands are traded or reassigned, it is the wives who pack up the household and move the family to the new town or city.[3] In the absence of husbands, many baseball households are run by women. "I am both father and mother for half of every year," said one wife. Lynn Rigney recalled how her father would tell her mother not to bother him with family problems while he was on the road, since there was nothing he could do about it.[4]

The high level of job mobility in baseball, especially for players, makes it difficult to put down roots. Baseball people, especially those moving up through the ranks, postpone buying houses. And as renters, without a certain future in any one town, there is little incentive to become involved in the community. Frequent moves requires that they postpone purchasing major possessions. After nine years of marriage, the only furniture Sharon and Mike Hargrove owned was a set of bunk beds, a TV, and a rocking chair.[5] Life in the minor leagues is such a nomadic and financially insecure existence that most players believe it is unwise to marry before they reach Double A.

Some wives spoke of not being able to get their own careers "started" as long as their husbands were still in baseball. Seasonal moves to new towns and cities make them poor candidates for white-collar work, professions, or going into business. "It's difficult to find a decent-paying job," explained Jan Butterfield, the wife of a Yankee coach. "You can't just show up in a new town and expect to get a good job. First off, you don't know anybody there, and secondly, nobody wants to hire someone who is only going to be there for five or six months."

The subordination of the wives' career aspirations to those of their husbands is evident in the language they use to talk about their husbands' work. Some use the plural, such as "my husband and I" or "we" when they discuss their husband's career transitions. Overall, baseball spouses are more involved in the careers of their mates than are wives of men in other professions. The wives of players, coaches, managers, and other baseball workers regularly come to the ballpark, often bringing their children along to watch the team play. Some wives score the games. In the modern world, watching one's spouse perform at work is a rarity in most occupations.

THE APPEAL OF BASEBALL WORK

Despite the long hours, low wages, and stunted family life, most baseball people like their jobs. Perhaps nowhere is the allure of baseball better seen than in the narratives of those who left the game and later yearned to return. QV Lowe thought he had retired from baseball for good when he took a job teaching elementary school. But when spring came around, being out of the game began to "gnaw" at him. He said he had an "itch" to be back on the ball field to such an extent that he quit his teaching position to become a pitching coach in the low minors. Scott Jaster, after injuries and failure forced him out of the game three times, tried to come back, even quitting college in mid-semester and leaving a decent-paying job. Every spring there are stories in the sports pages of retired players who have enjoyed major league careers, which were sometimes quite long, and are trying to come back.

But what about the press box and front office workers who don't enjoy large salaries, who are not directly involved in the game, and who are not in the limelight? Do they also feel the same about their jobs? All of the interviewees, except clubhouse manager Pat Young, liked their work. Some felt fortunate, or "lucky," to be in baseball. Billy Johnson left baseball to work for a sports-promotion firm in Florida. Although his new job took him to ballparks, he still felt "restless" not being in baseball itself. After a year on the outside, he returned to baseball as an assistant general manager of a Class A team. Jerry Collier turned down a better-paying Wall Street job to work at a Baltimore bank so that he could continue to vend beer at Camden Yards. We encountered more evidence of job satisfaction when we called major league organizations to get information about internships for students. Time after time we were told that job turnover in the front offices of baseball was very low because baseball people rarely quit their jobs—"Once you're in baseball, you stay in it."

What is it about baseball work, much of which is no different from the tasks done in other fields, that produces such satisfaction and commitment? Why in a society in which a majority of the workforce claims to be unhappy with their jobs are baseball workers an exception? The narratives give several clues. Having a lifelong interest in baseball and being a fan obviously contributes to the positive feelings many workers have about the jobs they do. "Typing a letter is typing a letter, answering a phone call is answering a phone call. But when the information that you are typing or giving out is something really dear to your heart, it's a lot more pleasant and fun," explained American League public relations director Phyllis Mehrige, comparing her job in baseball with her previous work for a sewing-machine company. The belief that they are promoting something of value—the country's national game, cherished by so many Americans—also contributes to rank-and-file baseball workers feeling good about the work they do. Owner Dennis Bastien's remarks about baseball are telling:

If you can't get somebody excited about being involved with a business where you come out on a summer evening, water the infield, lay down the white lines, and somebody sings the national anthem—if that doesn't raise a lump in your throat, I don't know what will. If you can't get somebody fired up about professional baseball, then you've got no business being in business in the first place.

Another factor in workers' enthusiasm is the ballpark itself. Ballparks are interesting and pleasant environments in which to work. As one broadcaster said, ballparks are "magical places"—the sweep of the grand stands, the rainbow of color in the different sections of seating, and the emerald-green field crisply outlined in chalk. Some, like Chicago's Wrigley Field, Boston's Fenway Park, and New York's Yankee Stadium are also historic places, rich in folklore and legend. For those who work in Yankee Stadium, the statuary in front of the stadium and the monuments in "Monument Park" behind the left-field wall remind them of the park's storied past—"The House That Ruth Built."

Admittedly, the look-alike multipurpose stadiums built in the 1960s (for example, Pittsburgh's Three Rivers Stadium and Cincinnati's

Riverfront Park) and the domed stadiums in Seattle, Minneapolis, Montreal, and Houston do not have the same charm as other ballparks. They are symmetrical ovals with uniform distances to right and left fields that lack the idiosyncracies and personality of the old-time ballparks. But even so, there is an aesthetic and an atmosphere at these stadiums that can't be found in office buildings. As announcer Sherry Davis, who only needs to arrive at her job at San Francisco's undistinguished Candlestick Park an hour before the game, said: "I am usually there a couple of hours before I need to be because I love being at the ballpark."

Although their facilities are smaller, minor league ballparks offer the same aesthetic qualities—and sometimes more. "Just a Little Bit of Heaven," was the title of a *Sports Illustrated* article by Daniel Okrent about Wahconah Park, the home of the Pittsfield, Massachusetts, team in the New York–Penn League. And Wahconah has no more charm than hundreds of other minor league ballparks, whose allure and uniqueness cause many fans to make summer pilgrimages to minor league ballparks around the country. Craig Wright and Tom House in *The Diamond Appraised* ask, "When was the last time you heard of a football fan making a pilgrimage to all the NFL stadiums or a basketball fan bragging about which NBA arenas he's been to?" Part of the appeal of journalist David Lamb's best-seller *The Stolen Season,* a chronicle of his 16,000-mile odyssey to minor league towns of America, are the ballparks he describes.[6]

Philip Lowry called his book on major and negro league ballparks *Green Cathedrals* because the more he studied ballparks the more he thought they resembled mosques, synagogues, churches, and similar places of reverent worship. He believes many Americans have a "spiritual reverence for ballparks, because they hold treasured memories and serve as a sanctuary for the spirit." Indeed, for many workers, ballparks hold a wealth of childhood memories of having watched ball games with a father or mother and of the famous games, players, and the heroics they observed there as youths, some of which have passed into folklore.

On a more tangible level, another attraction of ballparks as a workplace (domed stadiums excluded) is that many employees are outside in the fresh air. We asked eighteen ushers, concession workers, vendors, and an assortment of press-box employees at four ballparks (New York's Yankee Stadium, Albany–Colonie's Heritage Park, Birmingham's Hoover Met, and Pittsburgh's Three Rivers Stadium) what they liked about working there. Their most common response was that they liked "being outside." A female food vendor in her mid-twenties compared her daytime job as a salesclerk in a shopping mall to her evening job at the minor league ballpark in Albany: "Here you are out in the fresh air on summer nights, and you're dealing with people who are happy because they're here to watch a ball game and be entertained." When we asked Birmingham Barons broadcaster Curt Bloom if working in a ballpark had any influence on how he felt about his job, he said:

When I'm here in the open air looking down on that green grass and white chalk lines and that smooth brown dirt, I can't imagine anything in sports being better. The guy at hockey is looking down at frozen ice and it is cold; the guy in the basketball arena is inside and has to wear a tie.

Ballparks also offer their workers interesting and secure places to eat, relax, and even workout. Sam Kennedy compared working at Yankee Stadium to his previous workplace, the U.S. Embassy in London:

It was neat, but being at Yankee Stadium is far more exciting. When I take my lunch hour, I go out in the stands and sit in the sun; sometimes I workout and jog around the upper deck or go down on the field and jog around the warning track or I might go to the weight room. I mean you are in a baseball park, not any old office building. After being here I can't think of anyplace I would rather work than in a ballpark.

VARIED ROUTINES

The varied nature of most baseball work helps keep the work interesting. Very few ballpark employees do the same task all day. A day's work in the minor leagues may involve setting up a promotion, getting tickets to the business that has a "company night," preparing statistics for the media, overseeing the cleaning of the stadium, stuffing inserts into programs, and if rain threatens, helping to pull the tarp across the infield. "Baseball's not like working for Blue Cross/Blue Shield or the automotive industry, where the work is routinized," explained a Detroit Tigers secretary Audrey Zilinski. "Every day I come in here, there's something new. You don't find that in most jobs. It's never dull." The narratives of Dennis Bastien, Jack Boehmer, and Jim Riggs all describe in positive terms the wide range of work they do in the course of a single day. Only Rob Evans, who found his other responsibilities detracted from his broadcasting, viewed it negatively.

Most baseball jobs also change fundamentally during the course of the year. In other businesses work routines remain pretty much the same throughout the year. That is not so in professional sports. Minor league front-office workers have work responsibilities that change drastically according to the time of year. During the season, their jobs revolve around finding different ways to attract fans to the ballpark, entertain them, and ensure adequate coverage of the team by the media. During the off-season the work changes to marketing and selling the team. For example, they sell advertising packages, sell ads in the program and on the outfield fences, and place radio and TV ads. They also promote the team by speaking to civic groups. Their work during the off-season also entails designing the pocket schedule for the upcoming season and putting together the new program. And if you are an owner like Dennis Bastien you might even be repainting the seats in your ballpark.

Spring training contributes to the variety and, for many, the satisfaction of baseball work. Few other industries move their operations and staff twice each year. In February team personnel, media relations, and part of the front office relocate to Florida or Arizona for spring training, where the players get into shape, practice the fundamentals of their positions, and play a thirty game exhibition schedule. When spring training ends in April, club and front office personnel return to their home ballpark and city, while the organization's six minor league teams move to the towns and cities in which they will play. For most baseball people, especially northerners, spring training is also a welcome escape from the dreariness and cold of winter.[7] Moreover, the places where the teams train are mostly resort towns—Orlando, West Palm Beach, St. Petersburg, Sarasota, Daytona Beach, Scottsdale, Palm Springs, Mesa, and Phoenix. Such are the perks of baseball.

In closing, baseball organizations are in many ways no different from other modern American businesses. There is ever-increasing bureaucracy, commercialization, hierarchy, and quantification; and the bottom line remains the bottom line. But baseball is also significantly different in that its product is still a game—a game that continues to be the country's "national pastime," despite the growing competition from football and basketball. Because the product is a game, there is hoopla, excitement, and daily indeterminacy of wins and losses. This is infectious. It seeps into the front office, the press box, and even the changing rooms of the ushers, vendors, and game-day staff. Added to this mix is the enthusiasm of employees, who have had a serious interest in the game since they were kids. It is not surprising then that baseball people share the feeling of being part of a select group—a baseball fraternity; most baseball people love their jobs; and many who could make money elsewhere stay in baseball. Indeed, for some, baseball is sacred . . . and the ballpark is church.

NOTES

1. Women in baseball—being mostly game-day staff or in secretarial and clerical positions in the front office—are more likely to work nine-to-five and not be as absent from home.
2. Sharon Hargrove, *Safe at Home* (College Station, Tex.: Texas A&M Press, 1989).
3. This is a common theme in the memoirs of several baseball wives. See, for example, Bobbie Bouton and Nancy Marshall, *Home Games* (New York: St. Martin's Press, 1983); Danielle Gagnon Torrez, *High Inside* (New York: G. P. Putnam and Sons, 1993); and Hargrove, *Safe at Home.*
4. One positive change for baseball families in recent years has been the willingness of most major league organizations to allow players to take along their wives on some road trips. Some clubs even pay all the expenses for the wives for one trip each season.
5. Hargrove, *Safe at Home,* 85.
6. C. Wright and T. House, *The Diamond Appraised* (New York: Simon and Schuster, 1989), 299.
7. Although major league baseball has expanded to all regions of the country, most teams are still located in the northern cities, where professional baseball began in the 1880s.

Bibliography

Alexander, Charles C. *Our Game*. New York: Henry Holt and Company, New York, 1991.

Angell, Roger. *The Summer Game*. New York: Viking, 1972.

Blake, Mike. *The Minor Leagues*. Ada, Mich.: Gleneida Publishing Group and Winwood Press, 1991.

Bouton, Bobbie, and Nancy Marshall. *Home Games*. New York: St. Martin's Press, 1983.

Bouton, Jim. *Ball Four: My Life and Hard Times Throwing the Knuckleball in the Big Leagues*. Edited by Leonard Snecter. New York: World Publishing Company, 1970.

Brinkman, Joe, and Charlie Euchner. *The Umpire's Handbook*. Lexington, Mass.: S. Green Press, 1985.

Coakley, John J. *Sports in Society: Issues and Controversies*. St. Louis: Mosby, 1978.

Eitzen, D. Stanley, and George H. Sage. *Sociology of American Sport*. Dubuque, Iowa: W. C. Brown, 1978.

Gaston, Paul L. "Resurgence of Minor League Baseball." In *Cooperstown Symposium on Baseball and the American Culture*. Edited by Alvin L. Hall. New York: Meckler Publishing in association with the State University of New York College at Oneonta, 1991.

Gordon, Alison. *Foul Ball: Five Years in the American League*. New York: Dodd Mead, 1985.

Hall, Alvin L., ed. *Cooperstown Symposium on Baseball and the American Culture*. New York: Meckler Publishing in association with the State University of New York at Oneonta, 1991.

Hargrove, Sharon. *Safe at Home*. College Station, Tex.: Texas A&M Press, 1989.

Huizinga, Johan. *Homo Ludens: A Study of the Play-Element in Culture*. Boston: Beacon, 1950.

Lowry, Philip J. *Green Cathedrals: The Ultimate Celebration of All 271 Major League and Negro League Ballparks, Past and Present*. Reading, Mass.: Addison-Wesley, 1992.

Rader, Ben. *Baseball: A History of America's Game*. Urbana: University of Illinois Press, 1992.

Seigel, Barry, ed. *The Sporting News Baseball Register*. St. Louis: Sporting News Publishing Company, 1991.

Seymour, Harold. *Baseball: The People's Game*. New York, Oxford University Press, 1990.

Shlain, Bruce. *Baseball Inside Out*. New York: Viking, 1992.

Sullivan, William M. *Work and Integrity: The Crisis and Promise of Professionalism in America*. New York: HarperCollins, 1995.

Thornton, Richard H. *An American Glossary: Being an Attempt to Illustrate Certain Americanisms upon Historical Principles*. New York: F. Unger Publishing Company, 1962.

Torrez, Danielle Gagnon. *High Inside: Memoirs of a Baseball Wife*. New York: G. P. Putnam's Sons, 1983.

Trift, Sid (with Barry Shapiro). *The Game According to Sid* New York: Simon and Schuster, 1990.

Trujillo, Nick. "Working at the Ballpark: An Ethnographic Study." In *Cooperstown Symposium on Baseball and the American Culture*. Edited by Alvin L. Hall. New York: Meckler Publishing in association with the State University of New York at Oneonta, 1991.

Warshay, Leon H. "Baseball in Its Social Context." In *Social Approaches to Sport*. Edited by Robert Pankin. Rutherford, N.J.: Fairleigh Dickinson University Press, 1982.

Williams, Peter. "You Can Blame the Media: The Role of the Press in Creating Baseball Villains." In *Cooperstown Symposium on Baseball and the American Culture*. Edited by Alvin L. Hall. New York: Meckler Publishing in association with the State University of New York at Oneonta, 1991.

Will, George. *Men at Work: The Craft of Baseball*. New York: MacMillan, 1990.

Index